WITH SCOTT
IN THE
ANTARCTIC

WITH SCOTT IN THE ANTARCTIC

EDWARD WILSON
EXPLORER, NATURALIST, ARTIST

ISOBEL WILLIAMS

The History Press

For D.J.

First published 2008

The History Press Ltd
The Mill, Brimscombe Port
Stroud, Gloucestershire, GL5 2QG
www.thehistorypress.co.uk

© Isobel Williams, 2008
Introduction © Michael Stroud, 2008

The right of Isobel Williams to be identified as the Author
of this work has been asserted in accordance with the
Copyrights, Designs and Patents Act 1988.

British Library Cataloguing in Publication Data.
A catalogue record for this book is available from the British Library.

ISBN 978 0 7509 4879 1

Printed in Great Britain

Contents

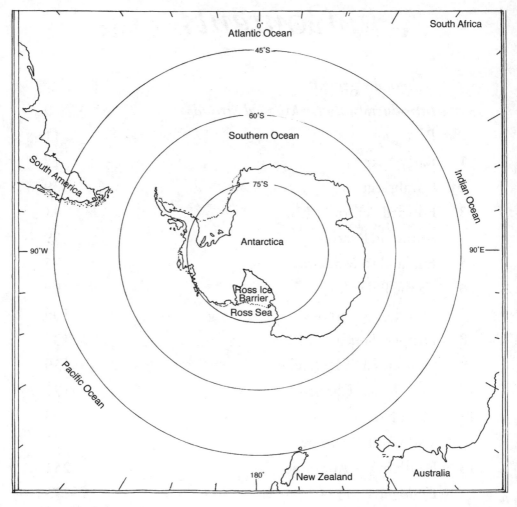

Antarctica

Acknowledgements

Whilst working on this book over the past five years I have discussed the subject with a number of people. All have been unfailingly helpful and enthusiastic and this has made the work a pleasure to undertake. Progress would not have been possible without the kind support of Dr David Wilson, Edward Wilson's great nephew, who allowed me access to the Wilson Family Archive at Cheltenham and who has made helpful suggestions on the work throughout.

Staff at the Scott Polar Institute have offered efficient and ready help. I should like to mention particularly: Robert Headland, Shirley Sawtell and Mark Gilbert and more recent help from archivist Naomi Boneham, Lucy Martin, manager of the picture library and Heather Lane, the institute librarian.

Anne-Rachael Harwood and Stephen Blake in the Cheltenham Museum offered unfailingly cheerful and knowledgeable assistance. Several colleagues read sections, or indeed all of the work and I must thank particularly, Doctors: John Henderson, John Millard, Athena Leousi, Robert Bratman and Noelle Stallard. Mrs Jacqui McDowell and Nigel Oram have also commented.

Many colleagues have offered specific comments on detailed sections, in particular: Professor Sir John Crofton, Lady Eileen Crofton and Dr Max Caplin on tuberculosis; Professor Hugh Pennington on infection in the Antarctic; Professor C.A.C. Pickering on 'allergy' at low temperatures; Professor Stuart Malin on the mysteries of magnetism; Professor Jeffrey Wood, of the Food and Animal Science Department at Bristol, on vitamin C in animals; Professor Christopher Bates, Honorary Senior Scientist in Cambridge, on the difficult subject of bone and tissue breakdown in scurvy. I visited Dr Robert Thomas of Edinburgh Zoo on several occasions to view and talk about penguins. The late Dr Mark Harries discussed hypothermia. I am greatly indebted to these colleagues. I accept responsibility for any misunderstandings or omissions.

In the library at St George's, Wilson's and my medical school, Nalini Thevakarrunai gave every help possible, as did Anne Blessley, the curator of Bushey Museum; Sarah Strong, Archives Officer at the Royal Geographical Society; Pauline Widdows of Cheltenham College and her assistant Jill Barlow. Jaqueline Cox of the Archive Department of the University of Cambridge and Gemma Bently, the (then) archivist at Gonville and Caius, were patient with my repeated questions concerning medical education in the late 1800s. James Cox, the current archivist, added further information. Professor Sir Alan Fersht gave me invaluable information concerning Gonville and Caius College for which I am grateful.

Many thanks also to Dr Michael Stroud for his introduction to this book.

Introduction

I have always had an interest in Polar history, perhaps wishing to put my own Polar endeavours into context, but before I read this book, Wilson remained an enigma. Clearly, I had come across many descriptions of him amongst the diaries and works of his fellow explorers. Scott, Cherry-Garrard and others had all sung his praises and he seemed admired by everyone, yet his spirit and character had eluded me. Indeed, when reading entries in Wilson's own Polar diaries, I had often found his descriptions of events almost curt and I had not really taken to the man. He seemed a strange puzzle. How could someone so clearly capable as a doctor, religious thinker, indeed real polymath, paint with such passion yet express himself so briefly, even coldly? I could not put these pieces together but Isobel Williams has let me do so.

This thoroughly and meticulously researched book brings Wilson to life. I now know that his many writings go way beyond Polar diaries and convey so very much more than I had realised. He had many strengths but he also had weaknesses, and this work provides a balanced portrayal. As such, it is in marked contrast to other modern accounts of the same expeditions which, although also carefully researched, have fallen foul of hopeless bias. Perhaps in an attempt to make the accounts more 'newsworthy', Roland Huntford for example lambasted Scott and all associated with him. He therefore failed to convey the wonderful qualities of these early explorers, essentially criticising them for acting like Edwardian Naval Officers, which is exactly what most of them were. Huntford also criticised Wilson and others for pursuing the cause of science beyond the simplistic goal of racing Amundsen to the South Pole, missing the point that Wilson was a scientist through and through. Isobel Williams has not made the same mistake. Instead, she has caught the man in context, conveying the time in which he lived and the environment in which he worked. The result, describing his development from childhood collector, through budding artist and doctor, to a mature and superbly capable Polar explorer, is a book that rates beside the best on this heroic age of exploration. A book that captures the soft, thoughtful, considerate heart of Wilson the man, as well as the horrors of man-hauling, hunger and the hardship of the Polar blizzard.

Dr Michael Stroud
July, 2008

Prologue

In March 1912, in a tent on the bitter Antarctic wasteland, three men lay dying slowly, overcome by malnutrition, dehydration and hypothermia. Outside the tent a blizzard howled. The temperature was minus 40°F. The men had had little food for days, no fluid to slake their thirst. One of the three was Edward Adrian Wilson, the Doctor, Chief of Scientific Staff and 'father-confessor' of an expedition that had aimed to win the race to the South Pole for King and Country. The two other men were Robert Falcon Scott, the leader of the expedition and 'Birdie' Bowers, a man renowned for his stamina and strength. All three had succumbed gradually to the appalling conditions of their return journey from the Pole.

Sixteen men had started on the final expedition in November 1911. They knew that they would be competing with a Norwegian team led by Roald Amundsen and each man hoped and dreamed of being chosen for the final push to 'bag the Pole'. Scott ultimately chose four companions: Wilson, Bowers, 'Titus' Oates and Edgar Evans from the group that had already endured nine weeks of energy-sapping travel. The five set off with high hopes, but when they eventually reached the Pole they found the Norwegian flag already there. There was nothing for it but to turn their backs 'on the goal of their ambition' and to face 800 miles of solid dragging to their base-camp on Ross Island. On this dreadful return two of the men, Oates and Edgar Evans, died earlier leaving Scott, Wilson and Bowers to battle on with their ill-fated effort to reach base-camp. The bodies of the three were found nearly eight months later, along with their personal and graphic accounts of the struggle to the Pole and their doomed attempted return. The terrible news of the death of the five explorers was blazoned around the world when the remaining expedition members eventually got back to New Zealand. In Britain hopes of welcoming the men back as the historic and courageous conquerors of the Pole gave way to a huge outpouring of grief. Over the weeks this sorrow was assuaged and partially replaced by pride in the men's achievements as accounts of their heroism and endurance were published in the national and international press. The country became inspired. Throughout Great Britain and the Empire men, women and children were excited and encouraged by the story. Scott's 'Message to the Public' that 'Englishmen can endure hardships, help one another and meet death with as great a fortitude as ever in the past'[1] caught the public imagination as an example of how to live and die when called to serve King and Country. The *Daily Mirror*, on 6 November 1913 wrote, 'these last letters should be a battle cry to the youth and manhood of England. They should inspire and give heart and courage'.[2] People of all ages soaked up details of the heroic adventurers and learnt what the human frame can make itself withstand. This made a lasting impression at an important time, just before the carnage of the First World War when the youth of the country was to be bombarded with sacrificial propaganda.

This book tells the story of Edward Adrian Wilson, a determined, self-contained, solid and deeply religious man who was the only officer to go with Scott on both his Antarctic expeditions of 1901 and 1910. After his death Wilson became a hero of Antarctic exploration, but he became an explorer by default. Whilst other Arctic and Antarctic travellers planned and dreamed of exploration and fame, Wilson's interests as a young man were primarily directed towards natural sciences and painting. From childhood he had a passion for recording wildlife and he was precocious in his scientific objectivity; he would never accept theories without testing them. Though these attributes were to be of benefit to the expeditions, they were not developed for this purpose – he trained as a doctor and passed his medical examinations in 1900. By 1901 he had little medical experience and he was asked to go on the first Antarctic expedition, as Junior Surgeon and Zoologist, as much because of his artistic ability as his medical abilities; neither had he trained for exploration. In spite of these apparent disadvantages, his contributions towards the expeditions became legendary. His personality powerfully affected those in contact with him; he became a close friend and important influence on Captain Scott, who wrote of Wilson, 'his kindness, loyalty, good temper and fine feelings have endeared him to us all. How truly grateful I am to have such a man with me and how much it lightens my responsibilities for the general well-being it would be difficult to express'.[3] Others agreed, 'if you knew him you could not like him: you simply had to love him'.[4]

Of his many interests exploration was only one. He was a naturalist, lifetime artist, doctor and researcher, involved family member and devoted husband. Above all throughout his life, even as a student, he was committed to a religious ideal and became by degrees a practical ascetic. His belief was that life is simply a journey towards eternity; this means that a successful life is judged by the effort put into it, not the outcome. Forgetfulness of self and actions to help others were his creed; he thought these more important than the bubble of worldly glory. He thought that life is measured by motives rather than by results, a belief that would have sustained and upheld him in the attempt at the Pole.

Some twenty years after his death, his wife Oriana collaborated with George Seaver to write his biography. The biography contains extracts of many of Wilson's letters to her. Sadly she destroyed much of the remainder of this correspondence before she died, although many of Wilson's letters to friends and his father's memoirs remain. Seaver's biography was obviously strongly influenced by Oriana and published many years after Wilson's father (who had a very strong relationship with his son) had died. Now, nearly a hundred years after his death, it is time for a reappraisal of his life.

I first became interested in Wilson when, as a junior doctor at St George's Hospital London, I sat in the common room surrounded by Wilson's iconic paintings. St George's was proud of their association with Wilson and Wilson enjoyed and appreciated his time there. He thought that the teaching was good and the range of clinical material excellent. He kept up his association with the hospital and after the first expedition returned on several occasions. Ill health meant that he did not practise as a conventional doctor in England but his medical training was an important part of his contributions in the Antarctic.

When Wilson first sailed to the Antarctic little was known about it and the interior remained a mystery. He would have known about the Arctic, which although dangerous and hazardous, had been opened up to a degree by successive naval expeditions, and explorations that were driven primarily by commercial and nationalistic impulses. The Northwest Passage (the sea connection north of Canada joining the Atlantic and the Pacific and thought to be a quicker passage to the Indies) was of strategic importance as a barrier to USA and Russian territorial claims and the Arctic seas yielded a valuable trade in whale-blubber for lighting and in seal fur. Scientific discoveries were a by-product of this trading, though many had potential commercial applications. By contrast the Antarctic was thought to offer few commercial opportunities and remained the world's last vast unexplored space. Wilson would know that a Royal Naval expedition, under the command of Captain James Cook, had crossed the Antarctic Circle in the 1770s reaching 71° S, 300 miles inside the Circle. Cook described the seal colonies on the South Georgia Islands but gave up attempts to find 'Terra Australis Incognita' although he always suspected that there was a landmass in the south. More than fifty years later, another naval officer, Captain James Clark Ross, had been sent to the Antarctic to gather information about the location of the magnetic pole, the position of which was of importance for navigation. Ross's expeditions reached the Antarctic and followed the mountainous coastline southwards until progress was halted by a wall of ice that he called the Great Ice Barrier.

He was not able to explore the interior of the landmass. The seas surrounding the Antarctic, however, gradually became familiar to whaling captains who headed south to kill whales and seals, when demands exceeded supplies in the Arctic. An appetite for Antarctic exploration and scientific development was whetted when zoological and meteorological data started to reach Europe. The continued importance of Antarctic research, particularly in relation to magnetism, was understood and in 1901 expeditions left Germany, England and Sweden for the Antarctic. The English expedition (under Captain Scott and with Wilson as Junior Surgeon and Zoologist) spent two years in the south of Victoria Land. The thrust of the expeditions was scientific and included a magnetic survey of the area and a collection of botanical and geographical specimens as well as exploration towards the South Pole. This emphasis was to have a powerful influence on the second British expedition in 1910 whose mission was not only to reach the Pole but also to investigate meteorological, zoological and magnetic phenomena.

Wilson thought Scott a man worth working for: 'I believe in him so firmly that I am often sorry when he lays himself open to misunderstanding. I am sure that you will come to know him and believe in him as I do.'[5] He considered there was important work to do in the Antarctic. He was prepared to lose his life in the Antarctic as long as he had fulfilled his duties to the utmost. He was a tough, loyal and brave man who wholeheartedly took part in the expedition that led to his death but for which he recorded few regrets.

I

Early Years

Men of Edward Wilson's family were explorers, entrepreneurs, businessmen, naturalists and soldiers; the family had a strong religious framework. For Victorians the family was both a refuge and the hub of their social life and Edward Adrian (Ted to his family) was part of a large and interconnected family. He was born on 23 July 1872, the fifth child and second son of Edward Thomas Wilson (1832–1918) and his wife Mary Agnes (1841–1930). His father was a doctor, a medical practitioner, in Cheltenham, Gloucestershire and Wilson was eventually to be followed by five younger siblings. He was born at a time when Great Britain was the hegemonic power of the world. Its citizens, in a way difficult to recognise in our multicultural age, were (in the main) proud that Englishmen were the undisputed rulers of millions. They did not question, and certainly felt no reason to apologise for, Britannia's right to rule the waves, believing that God had ordained the Empire for the benefit of the world. Every schoolroom would have a map that showed that approximately 30 per cent of the world was coloured pink, the extent of 'The Empire'. Children of the Empire, such as the Wilsons, born into middle-class households, were taught the importance of serving God, Queen and Country. They were proud to be British, and excited by the idea of serving the Empire.

Wilson was born in No.6 Montpellier Terrace. The house is still lived in, though the number changed. It is a good-sized house of four storeys and has sizeable rooms on the ground and first floor. When Wilson was born there was a nursery on the top floor, space for five live-in servants and a large kitchen in the basement. Nevertheless the household must have been fairly chaotic. Birth control was known but rarely practised and Wilson's mother already had children of three, two, one and 'under two months' at the time of the 1871 census.[1] The duty of married Victorian women, however educated, was to produce children and Mary Agnes did her bit. By the time of the next census in 1881 Mrs Wilson had eight children: thirteen, twelve, eleven, ten, eight (Wilson), five, two and a baby aged 'less than two months'. Already one daughter had died.[2]

Wilson had had the conventional upbringing typical of thousands of children in England in the 1870s with one very important exception. At a time when children were often over disciplined, over controlled and physically punished, his parents were caring and supportive, intelligently committed to promoting their children's health and happiness. They had the vision to allow their son unlimited freedom to explore the local countryside, to draw and to paint. Life was not boring. He had a happy childhood.

Cheltenham is an ancient town. It is recorded in the Domesday Book of 1086.[3] Medicinal spring waters, which brought prosperity to the town, were discovered in the early 1700s. Visitors paid to take the waters (and visit the small assembly room nearby for billiards and cards), which were claimed as something of a 'cure all' particularly for digestive problems. They certainly acted as a laxative.[4] The Wilson children would have thrilled to the names of the famous who had visited their town: Handel, Samuel Johnson and even King George III.[5] They would have been proud that the Duke of Wellington, victor of Waterloo, had tried the cure, as had members of the exiled French Royal Family.[6] These important visitors would have seen gentlemen's clubs, tea dances, hunt balls, garden parties and concerts. They would not have seen the backdrop of poverty, the struggle for survival, the appalling living conditions endured by the poor of a town that, like many others, had a huge divide between rich and poor.[7] But Dr. Wilson, the children's father, would have seen it all. In his work as a general practitioner, he visited and helped patients in all walks of life.

Wilson's parents had interesting ancestors. Dr Edward Thomas Wilson was descended from a family of rich Quaker industrialists. Wilson's great grandfather (1772–1843), another Edward Wilson, of Philadelphia and Liverpool, was a hugely successful businessman who made fortunes from both American real estate and railway development and was a friend of George Stephenson who built 'The Rocket', the prototype for steam engines. The War of Independence resulted in Americans claiming much property owned by the English, so this Wilson was remarkable in that he successfully recovered his estates. He returned to England with his wife, Elizabeth Bellerby, and lived in Liverpool until his death. His children inherited fortunes and wrote 'Gentleman' as their occupation after their names.[8] This was an important distinction that showed that they did not need to work for a living. His second son was Wilson's grandfather who, in 1861, was appointed High Sheriff of Pembrokeshire by Queen Victoria.[9] He was a keen and knowledgeable ornithologist; part of his collection became assimilated into the British Museum's collection.[10] Unfortunately, a series of poor investments meant that his children, although well-off, were not as privileged as their father and did have to earn their living. This they did to some effect. Wilson's father, Edward Thomas, the eldest son, studied medicine at Oxford, St George's Hospital London and Paris. He qualified in 1858 and was elected as a Fellow of the Royal College of Physicians of London in 1870.[11] One of Edward Thomas' brothers was the soldier and explorer Major General Sir Charles Wilson, who in 1865 conducted the first survey of Palestine and in 1884 commanded an expedition on the Nile in an unsuccessful attempt to relieve General Charles Gordon (Chinese Gordon), trapped in Khartoum by murderous Sudanese rebels. This expedition, when Wilson was eleven, brought Sir Charles national fame and must have thrilled the family. The *Illustrated London News* of March 1885 graphically fed readers' appetite for military matters by a series of specially-commissioned illustrations of his expedition.[12]

Doctor Edward Thomas settled in Cheltenham instead of opting for a more lucrative and prestigious practice in London. He worked in Cheltenham General Hospital for over thirty years, initially in the dispensary and then as Physician to the hospital.[13] He was a man of energy and courage and he was determined to help the poor and vulnerable in his hometown. The elegant neo-classical facades concealed many houses in a 'filthy and unwholesome state'; overcrowded (several families in one room) and without drains. Outdoor earth closets or pail closets would have been shared by many people. Drinking water was often infected and illness very common, particularly in summer when the shallow wells that supplied many of the cottages dried up completely.[14] Although busy with his large medical practice Dr Wilson gave time and energy to supporting public health measures to reduce disease. Such developments were often costly and therefore unpopular, but he persevered with innovations such as an Infectious Disease Hospital (to reduce person-to-person spread of infection), the training of district nurses and, most importantly, the provision of clean drinking water. He was a sophisticated and energetic man who passed on many of his interests to his son. He helped to found Cheltenham's Municipal Museum, and opened it in 1907, saying that the museum might be made one of the town's most valuable assets but in order to be this 'it must not stand still'. He was president of the Natural Science Society and, aged 81, spent his summer in the Cotswolds searching for neolithic implements. He was a founding member, with friends, of the local camera club, the sixth oldest in the country.[15]

Wilson's mother, Mary Agnes, too passed on to her son not only her deep religious beliefs, but also her enthusiasm for country matters and an artistic bent; one of her cousins was the Royal Academician, William Yeames,[16] an uncle designed the Tsar's garden. Mary Agnes' family came originally from Cheshire, but her forebears settled as businessmen amongst the expatriate English community in St Petersburg, Russia. It was there that both of Wilson's maternal grandparents lived and there that his mother was born. Her father, Bernhard Whishaw (1779–1868),

ran a successful Anglo-Russian trading company. He married
Elizabeth Yeames (1796–1879), also from a powerful expatriate English family, and the family was well enough thought
of to enjoy the Tsar's patronage. They spent their summers in
their *dachas* and their winters in the city. In 1848 they moved
to Cheltenham, probably for economic reasons, bringing their
younger daughter Mary Agnes with them. Here she lived for
the remainder of her life. Probably unusually for a Cheltenham
girl of the time, she travelled extensively to the Continent
before and after her marriage and was actually married in St
Petersburg in April 1866. Many of her family who stayed in
or returned to Russia, visited Cheltenham and the presence of
these Russian visitors must have added glamour to the family
and caused a frisson of excitement in the town.

This was a solid family, a family of 'doers' and enthusiasts,
members of the 'self-reliant and self-development' line of
thought. In Wilson's case at least, grafted to these characteristics was an overwhelming conviction of the importance of
faith. He and his mother shared a conviction in an all-powerful God at a time when the most entrenched precepts of the
Church were being questioned. In the nineteenth century the
concept of evolution shook and challenged the Church which
taught that the universe was created in six days as described
in Genesis. For years debates raged in the Geological Society
and the Royal Society of London as new evidence challenged
the Church's teaching, which implied that everything, mouse
to man and tree to mountain, was created at the same time.
Darwin published *Origin of Species* in 1859 after years of hesitation and anxious study,[17] tormented by the implications of
his ideas which claimed that man was not created separately
by an act of God but had evolved from lower forms of life
over millions of years. Darwin wrote that different species
including the human species evolved by random variation and
adaptation to their natural environment, a development he
called 'natural selection'.[18] For the supporters of the biblical
story of creation, the Creationists, this theory had profound
implications. Not only was it against the word of the Bible

but acceptance of the theory could shake the social and moral foundations of society and even threaten Victorian England's powerful class system, a system that mirrored the hierarchy of the natural world. It implied that men might have evolved from apes, that intelligence and morality were accidents of nature and that man and other new species arose from a series of random events and not from God's will. Darwin feared that he was 'the Devil's chaplain'.[19] Debates were fierce and passionate and have not been resolved to this day. Catholic academics still disagree as to whether or not random evolution is compatible with 'God the Creator'. In 2005 President George Bush said that he thought the theory of 'intelligent design', a version of creationism that disputes the idea that natural selection alone can explain the complexity of life, should be taught in American schools alongside the theory of evolution.[20] In the late 1800s, in a family as cultured, intelligent and interested in science as the Wilsons, arguments for and against would have undoubtedly been rehearsed but there is absolutely no suggestion that an appreciation that organisms can modify and adapt over time ever shook Wilson's belief in an all-powerful God. He incorporated Darwin's theories into his practical beliefs writing that God started life as a simple form, this form altered and developed into its designated role. God was present in everything: stones, trees, human beings and animals.[21]

Wilson's understanding that minor changes in species can be effected in a few generations may have been helped in a simple way by his mother's experiments with hens. Rather unusually for a Victorian housewife and mother, Mary Agnes was an authority on poultry breeding and published *The ABC Poultry Book*.[22] This book covers a wide range of subjects in alphabetical order. Topics include: 'Accidents, (including loss of birds by rail), Artificial incubation, Chilled eggs, Deformities, Rheumatism, Selling eggs and poultry'. Importantly, she grasped the concept that domestic animals could adapt to develop particular or new characteristics (for example, size or shape) by breeding with animals that already showed those characteristics; conversely, unwanted characteristics could be changed (although squirrel-tail deformity in hens is apparently difficult to breed out). Thus in a small way, in a Cheltenham chicken coop, she was able to demonstrate Darwin's premise to her own and probably her son's satisfaction.

Wilson's mother had hoped for a second son, she already had three daughters. When he was born she wrote, with some partiality, that he was 'the pride of the bunch' and 'the prettiest of her babies'. He had 'deep golden red hair, eyes rather small, a pretty mouth and a lovely colour'.[23] As a small child he was 'bright and jolly, clever and quick'. He achieved his childhood milestones early, by the age of one he could run and climb stairs and was beginning to speak. He was, and remained, deeply attached to his father, 'his love for him is most beautiful'.[24] When he was 2, because of the increasing size of the family and perhaps because of his father's growing reputation as a physician, the family moved to a larger house nearby: Westal on the Montpellier Parade. This was a large house of ten bedrooms, four reception rooms, a nursery, quarters for six house servants, a big garden and a private drive. The children had a (German) governess.[25] This size of establishment would be fairly typical for a successful man of the period.[26] The move was a success from little Ted's point of view. He spent his time in the garden digging, trundling stones around and helping his mother. Westal was to be the family home for the remainder of Wilson's life and he always remembered his years there with affection and happiness.

In his new home, Wilson's artistic ability became obvious at a very early age. He was always drawing, and 'never so happy as when lying full length on the floor and drawing figures of soldiers in every conceivable attitude'.[27] His pictures were full of action and from his imagination; he did not like to copy anything. Soldiers were a favourite subject. They were probably foremost in his mind because of his Uncle Charles' well-publicised explorations. Although his mother gave him drawing lessons, he was never to receive formal tuition. At three he was described as 'a broth of a boy, a regular pickle, open about his faults but tearful and ready to cry on very slight provocation'.[28]

At 5 he was drawing incessantly; drawing and painting were to become a daily activity, an addictive necessity to him. Other interests and hobbies of importance in his later life also developed early, particularly a mania for collecting: shells, butterflies and dried flowers and probably many other things. Though 'collecting' was a very general Victorian passion, his collections must have been trying, as one of so many children, but his remarkable parents seem to have encouraged rather than discouraged him and given him a special room for his collections. Other characteristics were more worrying. His childhood temper could be described as cyclical; affectionate and sunny moods could quickly change to violent temper tantrums and screaming fits. His father stopped one of these episodes with a few good slaps which had 'the most beneficial results, he became as good as gold and went to bed calling out, "Dood night, Dod bless you"'.[29] These mood swings were much more marked than in the other children. Perhaps they were provoked by the death of his sister, Jessica Frances, who died in February 1876, aged 16 months when Ted, who was devoted to her and next to her in age, was 3. The cause is recorded as 'Repeated attacks of convulsions'; these lasted for ten days.[30] Childhood convulsions may be due to many things including infection and high temperature. In 1876, Cheltenham had an outbreak of Scarlet Fever (which can cause a high temperature and convulsions).[31] The death certificate does not state the cause of Jessica's convulsion, but it is easy to imagine the effect that the imposed silence, the muffled whispers, the parents' dreadful anticipation and the final bitter outcome would have had on the household and on the psyche of a very young boy. Death was all too common in Victorian nurseries (infant mortality in Cheltenham from 1874 to 1884 was approximately ten times greater than adults)[32] but although he understood that Jessie was going to Heaven, her death nevertheless must have been confusing, incomprehensible and frightening to a child like Ted.

His interest in natural history developed at an early age. At 4 he had a passion for flowers. When he was 9, he decided that he wished to become a naturalist and aged 11 he took lessons in taxidermy from White, 'the bird stuffer'. His first attempt was a robin and he soon became nimble at this time-consuming and fiddly occupation. He always preferred country walks to games, and his collections of fossils, butterflies and feathers, and his aquarium, to lessons. His mother described him as 'a nice looking, curly headed boy, very affectionate but decidedly slack at school work'.[33] Early school was with his elder brother Bernard, and his teachers thought him clever, though his mother worried that he was 'untidy, often idle, with returned lessons of which he was not ashamed'.[34] It is easy to see why his attention strayed; the subjects taught were daunting, and by the age of 10 he was having lessons in Latin, arithmetic, English, reading, spelling and Greek. However, an ambition to do well was slowly asserting itself and he did work at school, so successfully that it was suggested that he might pass a public school scholarship (which would have helped his parents with the fees) if he was given extra tuition.[35] As happens today, his parents paid for this extra tuition and he was sent to a boarding school in Clifton, Bristol in 1884. The school was small, about twelve pupils, and here he met an imaginative, enthusiastic and tolerant tutor, Erasmus Wilkinson, who created an environment that suited Wilson well – he was taken seriously and high standards were set. This proved the right method for a fairly turbulent boy and he responded well. He became so anxious to learn that he sat with 'his back to his favourite beasties (the newts, frogs and mice which were allowed remarkably into the school room) which would distract him'.[36] Equally importantly he began to lay foundations for his future development, learning to value accurate and careful records, and beginning to develop the habit of critical assessment. These were skills that were to become important in his medical work and in his expeditions to the Antarctic. During his time at Clifton he developed and matured. His rages and furies became rarer. Aged 12, he began to think about the meaning of life and 'The Truth'; subjects that would absorb him and infiltrate his entire life. He started to try to relate his ideas for self-improvement into his day-to-day behaviour, wisely keeping these ideas and rules to himself.

In his reports the schoolmasters commented only on his good sportsmanship and excellent manners. He tried for a public school scholarship at Charterhouse and Marlborough schools, but failed, having, his father writes, 'been badly grounded in the classics',[37] but he valued the years spent at the preparatory school because he felt that he had been educated in the broadest sense of the word.

In 1885 his parents decided to rent a local farm, 'The Crippetts', near Cheltenham, where his mother continued to breed poultry and to practise 'scientific farming'. The children kept pets, Mrs Wilson bred Dexter Cattle and the farm teamed with wildlife. Wilson fell for the farm as soon as he saw it, an ideal home for a naturalist and collector. He spent his summers cramming all the information he could about the foxes, badgers, birds and butterflies, which were there in numbers. Remarkably he was allowed to spend nights and days on the farm by himself, sleeping on the bare ground in an effort to toughen his body. He was, by this time, a committed naturalist. He recorded animal habits. He made notes on birdsong, cloud formation, indeed anything that appealed to the naturalist and artist. He began to try to observe, memorise and reproduce the varied, often brilliant colours of the Cheltenham countryside. This was another skill of tremendous use in Antarctica, where sketches started on a march, were completed in the base-camp. Eventually he seems to have developed almost perfect colour recall and never appears to have needed to use a colour grid to help his memory.

Further school education was at Cheltenham College where he started in the winter term of 1886. The school was, and remains, the local public school. There were family connections: Dr Wilson was the Senior Medical Officer and a founder of the college boat club; military Uncle Charles was also an old boy. Wilson went as a day boy in September 1886, going home at night unlike the majority of the students who were boarders. This pleased him greatly because he could escape after lessons to 'The Crippetts' and record bird habits rather than playing organised games (which he disliked all his life). Cheltenham

College was founded in 1841 with the 'aim of educating the sons of gentlemen on Church of England principles to prepare them for careers in professions or the army'. The man who shaped English public-school education, Dr Thomas Arnold of Rugby School, stated that his objective in education was 'to introduce a religious principle' and pupils were told that what was looked for was 'first religious and moral principle, secondly, gentlemanly conduct, thirdly intellectual ability'.[38] These concepts seem to have been followed in Cheltenham and were well suited to a serious pupil like Wilson. He was not outstandingly brilliant but managed to juggle work and hobbies satisfactorily. Predictably he became a member of the natural history and ornithology societies and his accurate and patient observation won him many prizes for drawing. He had the scientist's love of knowledge for its own sake. For example, after starting to keep his own journal (having been inspired by Darwin's *Voyage of the Beagle*) he made notes on temperature, wind, birds, insects, zoology and 'miscellaneous', subjects of no obvious benefit to himself but recorded for his interest and learning. He also strengthened his 'scientific reserve', examining any precept thoroughly before coming to a conclusion; an independent review of the facts was essential. These naturalist and scientific enthusiasms are reflected in his school reports, which show that he had a talent in science, won prizes for drawing, had little aptitude for classics[39] and had an average mathematical ability ('works well but does not seem to grasp the subject').[40] In this he was given extra coaching and his difficulty with the subject was brought home to him later when he had to learn how to make observations in the Antarctic. Although to his teachers he seems to have been an intelligent but average schoolboy, he remained highly unusual by virtue of his religious convictions and inner 'voice' which remained strong. The Bishop of Gloucester confirmed him in March 1890.

He decided to follow his father into medicine. His schooling had prepared him for a professional career. Medicine attracted him because he had first-hand knowledge of the useful contributions his father had been able to make in Cheltenham. He would be aware also of the importance of his having a reliable income; he knew that his father still had six daughters and a young son at home. He had no bent to follow his elder brother Bernard and Uncle Charles into the army; his contemplative nature would have made him completely unsuited to the life. Medicine was a good choice. It offered a springboard for diverse opportunities: travel, specialisation in hospital, general practice, missionary work. In 1891 he took the Cambridge entry exams to study natural sciences and medicine. He did well and would have done better if he had not been ill at the time. He had hoped for a scholarship but he got a Certificate with Honours in science[41] and was later awarded an Exhibition of £20 (with £3 for the purchase of books) at Gonville and Caius College, Cambridge.[42] To satisfy the General Medical Council of his suitability to register as a medical student he had to pass a seriously daunting number of subjects including languages, mathematics, logic and botany,[43] but by now his intellectual ability had asserted itself. He had no difficulty with the examinations and like his father he managed to fit in innumerable interests in addition to his medical work.

2

Cambridge

Wilson entered Gonville and Caius College, Cambridge as an 'Exhibitioner', with his £20 a year grant, on 1 October 1891. He knew that Cambridge has been famous for its teaching for centuries. Alumni included: Isaac Newton, the mathematician who formulated the concept of gravity; William Harvey, who first discovered that blood circulates around the body; Charles Darwin, who shook the world with his theories of evolution; Lord Byron who shocked the world with his lifestyle and enthused it with his poetry and Thomas Lynch, one of the founding fathers of The United States. To a visitor Cambridge may impress with its grey stone buildings, grassy courts and chapels, but its reputation is firmly anchored to its huge intellectual and scientific contributions. When Wilson went to Cambridge the university had twenty-three Colleges. He arrived, holding the place in awe, but determined to play his full part in its life. His medical student registration certificate (number 20793) was signed on 9 October.[1] He was to read for a degree in natural sciences and for his pre-clinical medical degree.

The last decade of the nineteenth century was described as the 'golden era of the Cambridge medical school'.[2] This description was coined because although medical education had vastly improved, a classical overtone was still very much in evidence as it had been at Wilson's school. Students were still imbued with ideas of manliness and loyalty and the ability to govern was considered essential. The concept of 'a Christian gentleman' pertained and the undergraduates had to be familiar with

Latin, the classics and to be able to write well. The students would know that a medical degree from Cambridge would automatically open doors to the most prestigious and respected positions in the medical profession, opportunities not necessarily offered to students from other universities. In Cambridge, Wilson would have known that he was one of 'the chosen'.[3] To start with the instruction was general; the lack of specific scientific teaching was not a concern, indeed, too early an emphasis on specialisation in the sciences was discouraged.[4] However it would be inaccurate to think that medical studies were easier then than now. The requirements were certainly different, but they were daunting: medical students, to be registered by the General Medical Council, had to pass the Preliminary Examination with work done at school. Then they faced a long haul. Wilson went on to a series of further examinations with the aim of eventually achieving two degrees. The first was the natural science Tripos; this resulted in a Bachelor of Arts degree (B.A.) which, in spite of its name, was not in the arts, as most people understand them, but in chemistry, physics, mineralogy, comparative anatomy and much more. The second was the medical degree, Bachelor of Medicine (M.B.). Students did the first three years of the six-year medical course at Cambridge. Wilson faced regular examination hurdles. He passed Parts 1 and 2 of the first M.B. in the autumn of 1891.[5] In 1893 he passed Part 1 of the second M.B. in pharmacy. He passed the final pathology examination in December 1893.[6]

The following year he took the first part of the natural science Tripos, for his B.A.[7] Here he excelled and was awarded first class honours, having sat papers and done practical examinations in physiology, zoology and comparative anatomy, botany and human anatomy. He chose as his prize five volumes of the writings of John Ruskin, the art critic and social reformer, bound in blue calf, a valued treasure. This unenviable series of examinations were the norm for medical students, but by 1894, Wilson was very keen to get onto the clinical part of his course, which was to be done in London. His aim was to become a surgeon; he had had his fill of theoretical work and wanted to get down to the 'real' business. A painting shown at the Royal Academy of Arts in London in 1894 reflected his feelings. The picture showed a stylish-looking yacht surrounded by working steamboats and rowing boats. Wilson wrote to his father, 'Butterflies and Bees' is a picture in this year's Academy and it just gives my ideas of the six years' medical training. The first three are the butterflies up here, the three last are the bees in Hospital in Town and now the sooner I get there the better'.[8] Unusually, the Master of the College asked him to stay on for an extra year. The reason for this was said to be that he could take the second part of the Tripos and that he was 'a good influence'.[9] Whatever the reason, Wilson's parents, no doubt pleased that their son had been praised and singled out in this manner, persuaded him to stay on until 1895. He took two further examinations in this extra year: Part 2 of the second M.B. and the Part 2 of the Tripos. Although George Seaver says that Wilson failed both these examinations,[10] he in fact passed Part 2 of the second M.B. in the Michaelmas term 1895,[11] probably at a resit.

Although he had watched operations in Cambridge, by the time Wilson came face to face with a 'real' patient, he had already done four years of training and more loomed ahead. The final medical degree had to be taken after at least three years of clinical work in a teaching hospital. There was no clinical teaching in the Cambridge hospitals in the 1890s, so many students went to London for this training and returned to Cambridge to sit the final exam. Students had to pass exams in surgery, midwifery, general pathology, hygiene and medical jurisprudence. They had to produce certificates of 'diligent attendance' at the various courses.[12] No one reading these requirements could suppose that medicine in the 1890s was an easy option or that the titles B.A. and M.B. were not well earned. When Wilson got to London in October 1895 he would have assumed that a further three years would finally free him of the examination yoke, at least for a time. The fates decreed otherwise. He was eventually to be a student for over eight years, finally being awarded the M.B. on 7 June 1900.[13]

In relation to all the examinations he sat however, there is no doubt that he followed the route dictated by the authorities.

Gonville and Caius is one of the smaller colleges in Cambridge. It was established in 1348 by Edmund Gonville and was refounded and extended in the sixteenth century by a doctor of medicine, John Keyes. It flourishes still. The College is called Caius because Dr Keyes, who had practised in Italy, 'Latinised' the spelling of his name. The College buildings include a chapel, a hall (where a flag bearing the Gonville and Caius Arms that Wilson took to the Pole still has pride of place), a library and accommodation, all built around grassy courts reflecting the founders' aim of providing a communal place for study and prayer. Dr Keyes' legacies to Caius of three carved stone gates named 'Humility', 'Virtue' and 'Honour' are important landmarks. Wilson was billeted high above 'Virtue', in rooms that were later dedicated to his memory, with a memorial plaque on the door. The gates were built in Renaissance style and are generally admired by visitors, though probably hardly noticed by Wilson and his friends as they dashed underneath them in their day-to-day student life. Wilson, like the other students, had a 'gyp' – a servant to look after him – and his, by chance, was a man who served with his Uncle Charles on the Nile Expedition, a coincidence that must have made him feel proud. Caius has several connections with Scott's Antarctic explorations: the Canadian glaciologist Charles Wright who was on the second expedition, was an undergraduate at Gonville and Caius and the Australian geologist Frank Debenham was a Fellow of the College.

In Caius everyone would have known and been known by each other. Students studied a range of subjects, only a few were training for a medical degree. Disagreements and debates would have ranged and raged over the topics of the time: Darwin, art, literature, medicine. The students who joined in 1891 were said to be intelligent, also boisterous and rowdy.[14] In this group Wilson was hardly domineering, in fact he was relatively quiet, but beneath this exterior he was confident in his views and certainly not overwhelmed by young men trying to impress each other.

He was particularly unimpressed by the intellect of the students who had beaten him in the scholarship. Where he was unusual was that he was completely lacking in personal ambition in the sense of wanting to lead the group. Though in his early days at Cambridge he could still be aggressive, critical and argumentative and his temper could still break out alarmingly,[15] he never wanted to dominate. His saving grace was that he had a sense of humour and was tolerant of other people's opinions whether they coincided with his or not. He was easy to know, but difficult to know well. When he did give his confidence, however, he gave it completely and his companionship and considered thoughts on nature, religion, art and poetry were the reward; in discussions with his friends, he honed and tempered his thoughts on religion, life's meaning and life in general. These friendships were kept in good repair throughout his life and later, when he was on the expeditions, he regretted that there was no one to whom he could open up as completely as he did in Cambridge.[16] George Abercrombie, (1872–1961) was admitted to Caius on the same day as Wilson and trained with him also in London. Abercrombie went on to be a physician in the Orthopaedic Royal Hospital in Sheffield. John Roger Charles (1872–1962) was also in Wilson's year. Another solid citizen, he became a Fellow of the Royal College of Physicians in London and physician at the Royal Infirmary in Bristol. John Fraser (1873–1962) was also with Wilson throughout his student days. He went on to practise in Pietermartizburg and was the father of Wilson's godson. Incidentally none of these friends were awarded first class honours in the natural science Tripos as Wilson was; Fraser and Abercrombie were given third class honours and Charles second class. Wilson was exceptional.[17]

Wilson's weakness was his temper. He struggled to control it. Although probably uniquely for a medical student of his time his goal was to achieve perfect self-control, his resolutions were often blown away by an enraged outburst. But in his early twenties his temper gradually became calmer and he was obviously approachable and sympathetic because he became, unexpectedly, the mediator and peacemaker of his year; his peers obviously recognised his integrity and tolerance and could rely on his discretion. He would continue in this role for life. It was a responsibility he relished because it made him feel wanted and useful and that was enough for him. However he would never become a social animal, he lacked small talk. Concepts and ideas were his metier. In Caius he started to enjoy reading poetry, particularly Tennyson, who was to become a permanent love; he was reading Tennyson's *In Memoriam* and *Maud* on his fatal journey from the Pole.[18]

Students mostly relish their independence and freedom when they leave home, only too keen to try new experiences. However there is absolutely no hint of any impropriety in relation to Wilson's student days. Although as a 'fresher'[19] he took part in College activities actively and eagerly, there was another side to his character. Underpinning his surface enthusiasms he was a reflective young man, consumed with religious curiosity, unworried by personal or parental ambition and already thinking of himself as primarily answerable to his maker. By the 1890s, society was changing. Strict Victorian morality was soon to be lightened by Edwardian mores and many Cambridge students no doubt sampled the delights of the town. Wilson disapproved of any such activity, he was celibate; he tried to instil his ideals into his younger brother Jim, when he too went up to Cambridge a few years later. He advised Jim to have nothing to do with Cambridge town women:

> Our family is a bit above that sort of thing, even in fun it is not a sign of superiority or manliness – rather a sign of true manliness is to have the greatest respect for even the most degraded woman. Don't think there is anything you should learn about them practically because you will learn more than enough listening to your friends' conversation. Remember you are a gentleman more truly than most of them you meet who may cut a finer figure and live up to it. Don't ever underestimate your own power of example. You are responsible for the sins of others in so far as they are copying you – and you may save a soul alive and so cover a multitude of sins.[20]

His enthusiasms were all intellectual and he was avid for knowledge on any front: natural sciences, walks in the countryside to collect specimens (his room was always a jumble of animal skulls, bird's feet, claws and bones) and poetry. Fascinated by the arts, especially painting, and always keen to improve his technique, he drew incessantly. He read (particularly on painters), studied, joined societies, debated and talked. He had the knack (and advised Jim to cultivate it) of getting people to talk about themselves, a subject everyone finds endlessly fascinating and this must have helped with him being generally liked. But above all, his religious passion insinuated itself as one of the dominating and permanent obsessions of his life. It was at Cambridge that much of his questioning about life began to be clarified in his mind. In Cambridge he started to wrestle with the demands imposed by the New Testament on each individual. His concluded that truth is what is described in the Bible and exemplified by the life of Christ. He came to these conclusions after discussion and study but always formed independent opinions and was unconcerned about 'received' views. For example, after reading Thomas à Kempis he characteristically came to the conclusion that the lives monks led could be thought escapist, because they bypassed the everyday struggles of the common man and never advanced. He wrote that the self-abasement and self-restraint practised by ascetics should only be the first step towards a useful and productive higher life, and should be followed by higher social and humanitarian ideals. He wanted, when he had achieved self-control, to become so concerned about others' wellbeing that he could forget his own needs.[21] Through this questioning and self-examination he was laying the first steps towards the 'active mysticism' that dominated his later life. Many young people pass through a philanthropic and idealistic phase. Wilson was different: this was no passing phase and inner strength and aesthetic self-discipline were his ideal for life. He made an early start to live up to his ideals by adopting a frugal lifestyle and managing on less money than his father gave him, conscious that in comparison to the majority he was living a privileged life.

This undertow, which was undoubtedly the main passion of his life, was not forced on his peer group and many of them would have been astonished to learn of his 'inner life'. Sport was a counterbalance to too much introspection and rowing was his favourite sport. He loved its discipline and the stamina it demanded, his pleasure, as always, being in the effort to try his hardest: 'though everyone at one time or another wishes he were well out of it, there's a fascination about keeping oneself at the treadmill'.[22] He could not believe that some students went through their whole three years at Cambridge without rowing and he took part enthusiastically in the rowing races between the colleges. He did not represent the university but represented Caius regularly in both the second and the first boats. He took part in 'The Bumps', a hallowed Cambridge competition, flourishing still, when college boats line up one behind the other at marked intervals and in agreed order, and then row as hard as possible to catch and 'bump' the boat in front. The aim is to bump as many boats as possible whilst avoiding being bumped. Because of his rowing abilities, enthusiastic though uninformed comments followed his appointment to the first Antarctic expedition: 'He rowed bow in the Caius First Boat; may he succeed in bumping the South Pole'.[23]

Summer holidays offered travel opportunities. In 1892 Wilson went to Gottingen to attend the university there. He could speak enough German to get by, and had probably had a little teaching also from his sisters' governess, Fraulein Scharnhurst. As he travelled through Europe, he filled some twenty-three pages with notes on the artists he saw. Impressionists, or indeed Neo-Impressionists, were not his style but George Seaver states that the twenty-three pages of comments on the paintings and architecture of the cities he travelled (unfortunately now destroyed) showed considerable knowledge and discrimination.[24] He disagreed with his father that Rubens' women were hideous. He thought that the women in Rubens' *Descent from the Cross* were the most beautifully painted of any he saw in the Dutch and Flemish galleries.[25] Visits like this were a revelation to him because for the first time he understood that even the greatest artists received tuition. With some help, he thought he could improve. He did improve, but never managed to get drawing classes.

College rules in the 1890s remained inflexible. They were not seriously questioned – though Wilson was astonished to be disciplined for wearing a straw hat after dark only a few yards from the college gates.[26] But he took to the life well, managing not to be overwhelmed. He wrote to his father in January 1893 concerning a late return from home to university; 'No unpleasantness whatever arose between the tutor and myself, for I told him I had orders from a sister not to leave home before she returned'.[27] However, his inability to lie had one unexpected result – he was 'sent down' (expelled) for a short time after an incident that illustrates well the rigidity of the system. Anglers had tried and failed to catch a trout in a pond outside the town. Wilson came to the conclusion that the most likely time for success would be in the very early morning. The College gates were closed at 10p.m. (there was a Gate Fine Book), but he escaped into the countryside, caught the trout and got back into college possibly climbing over the 'Gate of Honour' from Senate House Passage. Without thinking of any consequences he sent the fish as a gift to the Master of the College, a Doctor Ferrers. Dr Ferrers was pleased with the gift but suspicious. He asked, in his curious high-pitched squeaky voice, for details of how the catch had been made. 'You were out of the College at three o'clock in the morning?'

'Yes.'

'You had leave no doubt?'

'No.'

Dr Ferrers sent him down in spite of appeals on his behalf.[28]

The Victorian era was a time of civilised but intense curiosity. It would be quite common for an educated man to speak Latin, Greek and a modern language, and also to be able to talk with knowledge on, for example, arts, science and history. Even so, it is difficult to escape the conclusion that Wilson took on too much; his enthusiasms and ranging curiosity covered many activities and topics, and prioritisation was not his forte.

Although not keen on organised sport he nevertheless was a member of the second rugby team, a member of the College diving team and above all, the Boat Club. He was also a member of a seemingly excessive and probably non-productive number of societies, which must have taken much of his energies away from his considerable medical load. He was secretary of the 'Fortnightly Society' and presented a paper on the 'Conquest of Mexico'. The discussion following was 'the best in the term' covering not only the morality of the conquest but also, somehow, the twelve tribes of Israel.[29] He was a committee member of the 'Caius Scientific and Art Society'. This society explored subjects in science, literature or art. Its rules were firm: members had to attend an agreed number of meetings and to be prepared to speak (he spoke on monasteries).[30] In addition he was flattered to be asked to become a member of 'The Shakespearean Society', an exclusive society not confined to students of drama, but reserved for the leading sportsmen in the University, which in reality he was not. He co-founded an 'Intellectual Sunday Evening' group which met to smoke, drink coffee and discuss music, art and poetry and which cemented his love of Tennyson. In addition he supported the Caius Mission, a philanthropic mission based in Battersea, a (then) poor area of London, which helped and supported children from deprived backgrounds. He was a member of a boxing and fencing club which met weekly when they 'cleared the furniture, put on masks and then fought each other with single sticks, getting whacked every two or three minutes and getting bruised for weeks'.[31] His days would have been spent moving at speed from his medical lectures to discussion groups, rugby, swimming and charity work. On top of all this he walked, drew and, importantly, meditated daily. This is a daunting number of activities, even for a Victorian. But somehow or other in between other activities, he managed to do enough work to satisfy his tutors, because his Exhibition, which could have been withdrawn, was continued throughout his time at Cambridge.

Drawing and painting remained integral. Wilson aimed to be able to draw so well that whatever the subject, it would look as if it might move, breathe or fly. Each subject had to be completely accurately drawn but it also had to show animation. On visits to London he visited all the places that he thought could stimulate or inform: the Zoo, The British Museum, The Natural History Museum, The National Gallery, Westminster Abbey. He also made copious drawings of the Cambridge wildlife. His method was to sketch in pencil and paint up later, a method he continued in the Antarctic. He worked and reworked his paintings and started to develop his method of colour notation, writing the colours that he saw on his pencil sketches and using this system as a colour shorthand and memory aid. This skill was to be gradually developed over the years to such an extent that he could reproduce his colour instructions months later, with astonishing accuracy. This ability almost became his 'signature' and was used with outstanding success in the Antarctic. But in Cambridge he was still learning. He was hard on himself: if he was not happy with a picture, it was thrown out, even if it looked attractive. The walls and floors of his rooms were littered with pencil and chalk drawings in addition to the skulls, bird's feet and flowers, and his room was a centre of activity. He amused his friends by doing quick portraits of them in pencil or watercolour or he could draw quick silhouettes.

While in Cambridge Wilson did not forget Cheltenham. He often returned. He was always conscious of the financial and emotional debt he owed, particularly to his father who in early 1894 paid for him to travel with a group of students to Belgium. Wilson made the most of this opportunity. He visited the cathedral at Antwerp, revelling in the wonderful golden light-effects and the beautiful music. He studied the paintings carefully and changed his mind about Rubens; Van Dyck, he now thought, 'had a far more refined style'.[32] Familial support was mutual. In August 1894, the family was devastated by the death of their youngest, petted and adored daughter, Gwladys, 'the gleam of sunshine' that had unexpectedly entered their lives in July 1889.[33] Gwladys died when she was 5 years old after an illness lasting only four days. She died of intestinal obstruction in her own little cot, her mother and her sister Mary with her.[34] The unfairness of the death, the lack of understanding as to why this should happen and the pain experienced by the family must have put Wilson's religious convictions of the transitory nature of life on earth as a preparation for a more important existence, to the test. But he behaved with an 'almost unnatural' calmness, making a pencil sketch of his dead sister. The sketch became his parents' most treasured possession.[35] The year of 1894 continued to be dreadful. Later a fire a damaged Westal with all the attendant disruption and anxiety.

By the end of the Easter term 1895 Wilson was definitely ready to leave Cambridge and face the world of the Big Smoke. Although the university has no record of him failing any examination, he obviously did fail Part 2 of the natural science Tripos and the second M.B. examination because his father writes that he had 'passed seven out of the nine parts triumphantly and could have managed one of the last if he had left the other alone'.[36] He almost certainly passed the second M.B. at a resit in the Autumn term of 1895.[37] The setback did not affect his medical career in the slightest. He ended his time in Cambridge with a flourish, winning the university prize for diving. He had been a clever, though not an outstanding student. The years at Cambridge had been a success. He developed as an adult but more particularly as a Christian, becoming not just pious but progressing in self-control and in the mode of Christian Aestheticism.

3

Edward Wilson, M.B.

In Wilson's time Cambridge students could virtually choose their medical school. Wilson went on a tour of inspection; he rejected St Bartholomew's Hospital because it was too big, St Mary's was too small. He eventually chose his father's medical school, St George's Hospital, Hyde Park Corner.[1] St George's was originally in the countryside, well outside London, but by Wilson's time urban sprawl had extended to Hyde Park and the hospital was part of the metropolis, near to the park and Kensington Gardens and opposite Apsley House (the erstwhile home of the Arthur Wellesley, first Duke of Wellington)[2] known as No.1 London, because it was the first house that travellers would see after the Tollgates as they arrived from the country.[3] In fact the hospital was in such a fashionable position that its entrepreneurial governors, who had to ensure a cash balance, were able to market the site for royal weddings, burials and coronations to some effect. In 1887 they collected £489 for 'letting' empty wards at five guineas each[4] and accommodating any loyal subjects who wished to watch a thanksgiving procession commemorating Queen Victoria's accession to the throne in 1837.[5] By 1897 they had increased this figure to £5000 by selling seats to watch Victoria's Diamond Jubilee Procession,[6] which Wilson watched from the hospital, sketching her in her processional carriage. Now the site has been developed as the Lanesborough Hotel, a hotel offering expensive and glamorous facilities that would have surprised and amazed its 1890 incumbents.

Wilson signed the pupil register on 28 September 1895 and entered the hospital as a third year medical student after having more than completed his preclinical requirements. His father would have had to pay the medical school a fee for the full duration of his training, £85 as a single amount or £90 in instalments of £40, £30 and £20 to be paid at the start of each year.[7] The hospital that he had joined offered excellent clinical teaching; its students had access to 350 beds. According to the hospital brochure of 1892–3, this 'advantageous arrangement' was 'due to the cordial relations between the general body of Governors and the Medical Staff and to the gentlemanly bearing of the Pupils which allow the Authorities to offer such extensive privileges without apprehension'.[8] Medical specialisation into, for example, surgery, obstetrics or clinical medicine, was already developed. No doctor could be expected to be an expert in everything and the hospital had ten Consulting Specialists in addition to Specialists and Assistant Specialists.[9] There were also resident junior staff (a relatively new development): four house physicians and four house surgeons. The medical students in Wilson's group would hope to progress to this exalted status. Their financial prospects were initially modest – the Resident Medical Officer, a doctor with perhaps two or three years' experience would earn £150 each year.[10] The importance of 'gentlemanly behaviour' was underpinned by the provision of a students' club where there was a reading room, daily papers and food, said to be at 'a moderate and fixed rate'.[11] However, Wilson usually managed to find cheaper venues.

Wilson did not live in the hospital. He lived in lodgings, first in Westbourne Grove in West London, moving later to cheaper accommodation in Delamere Crescent, Paddington. His move to London did not dent his determination to lead a frugal and simple life. In a letter to his father in 1895, he said that he had pleasure in living on as little as possible and having as little money in hand as possible. His lodgings cost eight shillings weekly, a tiny amount even then (the modern equivalent is less than fifty pence, approximately twenty pounds per year).

Breakfast was just tea and toast with watercress. For the rest of the day he either ate in cheap restaurants, presumably costing less than the students' club, where he would make friends with the waitress who would tell him when the meat was 'off', or exist on hot potatoes and coffee.[12] He walked to and from the hospital. He would be conscious that apart from his keep, his father might have to pay separately for instruction over and above the basic fees in, for example, anatomical dissection, practical pharmacy, practical surgery, practical medicine and histology. The price for an individual course averaged £3 and the total cost could be considerable. Students had to attend lectures in medicine and surgery for at least six months as well as midwifery, pharmacy and pharmacology, and the life of a medical student was a continuous round of lectures, outpatients and ward work with patients, delivering babies or assisting in the operating theatre. It was also a life that demanded mental toughness; a student could not survive if he became too involved with his patients. He had to be able to look after, and at the end of the day walk away from, all types of diseases, dreadful infections (no antibiotics), cancer, blood disorders, post-operative complications and deaths. An overactive imagination was bad for the student's sanity and could do him irreparable damage. However, Wilson seems to have thrived on clinical work, at least initially: 'It is just ripping . . . the teaching is perfect and in time I shall have a good shot at the F.R.C.S. [the higher surgical examination]'.[13] At this time he was determined to be a surgeon and he said he had learnt more useful anatomy in one week at St George's than he did in all his years in Cambridge.[14]

Excitement with work was not enough. Wilson was determined to improve in his artistic ability and to this end he read Ruskin. John Ruskin (1819–1900), born in the same year as Queen Victoria, was, by the late 1890s, England's greatest art critic and social reformer. As a young man Ruskin had travelled widely with his parents and became absorbed by the beauties of the natural world. Ruskin championed the painter, J.W.M. Turner (1775–1851), being very familiar with his work since his wealthy father had purchased many of

Turner's watercolours, and his most important critical work was probably *Modern Painters*, which he began in defence of Turner. Ruskin held the view that Turner represented nature with an accuracy that made him unique and he believed that the world could and should be interpreted and reproduced through art.[15] Ruskin's precepts on art, written in *The Stones of Venice* in 1853, would influence Wilson for life. Essentially, Ruskin wrote that nature should be represented truthfully. This meant that accurate, factual representation should be the basis of artwork. To this, interpretative thought, although integral and important, was secondary. A picture must always be faithful to, and knowledgeable about, its subject.[16] The 'truth' in drawing is essential.[17] These precepts were clarion calls to Wilson who became a committed follower. He aimed particularly at the first rule of careful, accurate and informed representation of his subjects. Later in his artistic life he too became a passionate admirer of Turner and when he was in the Antarctic he produced evocative and beautiful paintings of the land and sky, but his forte remained accurate and informed works. In his art, as in everything in his life, his core belief was that effort, rather than outcome (successful or otherwise), was of the greatest importance and this belief led him to cram each day with activity. His uncle, Sir Charles, facilitated introductions that allowed him to draw in the London Zoo (and indirectly led to him being included in the Antarctic party of 1901) and he managed to go there most days to study and draw animals and birds. He also haunted the London parks and the Natural History Museum. He spent days on Wimbledon Common, 'one of God's ditches', with his friend John Fraser.[18] Here they could draw and continue with their debates and arguments on anything from medicine and art to theology and politics.

In his early twenties Wilson had ginger hair, bright blue eyes and a freckled face. He had slender freckled hands, long fingers and a ready smile. He walked with a long, slightly stooping stride.[19] His only interest in clothes was that he kept reasonably tidy. He would give away any money he had to anyone he thought deserved it more than him. His one financial weakness was smoking.

Initially he worked at the hospital from ten until four. With other students he was good-humoured and friendly and his popularity increased when he began making quick sketches of the staff as well as his friends in lectures. He was always willing to lend out his excellent notes. He liked the clinical work and wrote, probably correctly, that his eyes were quicker to spot things than other students.[20] But his 'inner life' continued and expanded. To an observer he seemed a relatively quiet, but otherwise typical medical student: he played rugby and continued to row, he argued concepts and he sketched. But behind this routine day-to-day existence he started to try to put the religious and aesthetic ideals that he had worked out in Cambridge, into practice. His father wrote that here he really worked out his ideas on how he should live his life and honed them to an extent that he became strong enough not to be thrown by criticism. Each morning before going to lectures or the wards he annotated and paraphrased the New Testament, completing most of the Testament when he was in London. The practice of annotating spiritual readings was to become a routine that he continued throughout his life. He was not interested in originality; he was passionately interested in truth. He never altered the beliefs that he worked out at this time; they were part of his nature. He wrote, years later, 'Once foundations are laid they should be built on, and the more they are built on the more they disappear from view'.[21]

He was far from perfect and could still be arrogant. On one of his visits to Cheltenham, quite soon after he had started at St George's, his mother accused him of being so absorbed by the art of medicine that he was losing sight of its basic precept, namely sympathy with his patients. She urged him to be more intuitive. Already Wilson had come to the conclusion that much of the illness that he was seeing in the hospital was self-inflicted (particularly by drink) and he had difficulty in showing compassion towards patients he considered hypocritical or self-pitying. Wilson and his mother also discussed and explored the concept of the 'teaching power of sickness'. This suggestion – that some medical conditions can promote mental and spiritual fortitude, and conversely the lack of any experience of illness can result in a lack of fortitude – was to have a long-term influence on Wilson's thinking. On his final journey in the Antarctic, when he was looking after his dying companion, Evans, he thought that Evans would have shown greater resistance if he had been ill before. Mary Agnes had been brought up at the height of evangelical preaching in Cheltenham and was deeply religious. She would not have understood any lack of compassion. Indeed, impatience with patients is unexpected in Wilson, though doctors nowadays dealing with repeat drink- and drug-related emergency admissions may identify with his feelings, but he was very young to clinical medicine and his aims for perfect control and humility were still an ideal. He wrote to his mother in November 1895, 'I was glad to see you though I expect you found me unsympathetic as usual. . . . I expect my want of sympathy comes from my never having had an illness, which was not my own fault. . . . I shall get more openly compassionate as I see more illness, which isn't brought about by obvious folly or sin . . .'[22] Always the practical man, he acted on this resolve, making a deliberate visit to the local isolation hospital in Cheltenham in May 1896 when smallpox was raging. Here he observed every stage of the disease; digesting, reflecting and learning from what he had seen.[23]

Long hours, poor food, hard physical exercise, midwifery duties in the slums (long hours and little sleep) and time put in at the Battersea mission must have taken their toll. In October 1896, only a year after he had started at St George's, Dr Rolleston, one of the Assistant Physicians supervising Wilson's training, told him to go home for a week.[24] An unusual suggestion, but Wilson had tonsillitis and was obviously run down. The illness may well have been psychological as well as medical. He had cause for stress: another of his sisters, his older sister Nellie (Helen Edith, 1869–96), a nurse at Leicester Infirmary, had died of typhoid in March after looking after one of her colleagues.[25] After his enthusiastic start in London he was beginning to hate the life. He could not escape to the countryside often enough, he was shy and increasingly nervous of social gatherings (where he must have been a bit of a social disaster), he was under great pressure and was getting little sleep, and at twenty-four, he was beginning to wonder where life was taking him. His spiritual life could not sustain him completely. He reported episodes of 'abject misery, almost suicidal, alternating with feelings of extraordinary freedom and happiness' and he began to take sedatives.[26] A break in Cheltenham and at the farm, away from the smog and pea soup pollution of industrial London, helped to recharge his batteries temporarily. Then back to London, where, like the Impressionist painter Monet, he revelled again in the startling colours of the amazing London sunsets caused by that same thick smog; back to the daily over-filled routine of hospital, debating societies, rowing, drawing and visiting art galleries. His father writes that he was 'smitten to distraction' by Turner but disappointed by Tissot.[27] He moved lodgings again to the Caius Mission, near the River Thames, in the (then) slum area of Battersea. The building is still there. Although Battersea was as run down as Paddington, the move was sensible. The Mission was run by a couple, Mr and Mrs Leighton-Hopkins, who not only did their best to improve the lives of the slum-dwellers of Battersea but also tried to improve the life of their independent lodger by integrating him into their family. He wrote in November 1896, 'Living here in Battersea is a really good healthy change for me, as I hate Society, and here I will have to learn to put up with a certain amount every day'.[28] He also commented, 'The Warden and his wife were real parents to me in their kindness'.[29] This enlightened couple tried to look after him and to make sure he ate properly, but Wilson's particular gremlin was out again. For the next two years he skipped meals to attend lectures or visit galleries. He heard Nansen (the famous Norwegian Arctic explorer) lecture at the Albert Hall in London: 'a tall powerful fair-haired man with a good sense of humour and a good sense of pathos'.[30] He became increasingly involved in mission work and ran an evening club for children two nights a week. On

Sundays too, he was occupied with church work, writing that 'croup, adenoids, eczema, fleas and lice were the commonest variations to the universal smell which was worse in the fine weather and worst with the girls'.[31] Babies were brought along, to add to the general confusion. They had to be taken outside when they cried. Eye infections were so common that children who came to a lantern show with both eyes bandaged had to peep out from under the bandages for a few seconds, every time the picture changed.[32] He became an ex-officio member of the Church Council.[33] He walked miles on Sunday evenings to Marlborough Street to listen to his favourite priest, the Reverend Thomas Henry Passmore (1865–1941), who 'never said a commonplace sentiment' and was a forceful and original preacher who included a strain of mysticism in his sermons.[34] 'The little, fluent, hook-nosed, don't-care-a-damn man – as sound a Christian as I have ever heard'.[35]

At St George's Wilson inevitably joined societies. He sketched continuously. The specialists in the hospital recognised his talent and commissioned him to make drawings of their pathology specimens. He had to be quick and efficient, having to draw with whatever was available because of the rapid deterioration of the specimens. When he had to draw a diseased brain, he made do with an old paint-box, some throat brushes and shiny foolscap.[36] Dr Rolleston, his supervisor, asked him to illustrate his book on liver diseases and a friend asked him to illustrate a book on fishing. More distractions, but at least these new ventures had the advantage of payment and allowed him to repossess some of the things that he had taken to the pawnbroker. But these further activities were excessive, since his medical work continued unrelenting. He was part of a 'firm', a number of students assigned to a particular consultant, doing surgery as well as midwifery. He wrote, 'In the Hospital from 9a.m. till midnight, One accident after another'.[37] Somehow or other he had to fit in dentistry as well. He wrote home that he had 'nearly drawn three teeth (by mistake) in one go. A lower molar came out so suddenly that the impetus nearly brought two teeth out of the upper jaw; but I assured him he would have no more trouble with the lower one'.[38] In 1897 he had to take two more exams that counted towards the final M.B.: Part 1 in the Easter term (eyes, women, operative and theoretical surgery and surgical pathology),[39] Part 2 in the autumn.[40] On top of all this he seriously considered the possibility of working in Zanzibar under the auspices of the Universities Mission. He told his sister that he wanted to work as a doctor rather than a medical missionary 'which is more than one man can be'.[41] Fortunately parental objections resulted in an agreement to postpone this idea, at least until after qualification. Such unrelenting pressure must have had an effect on the physique as well as the psyche, but 1897 produced one unexpected bonus; in the Caius Mission he met his wife-to-be, Oriana Souper, who was staying with the warden, Mrs Leighton-Hopkins.[42] With Oriana, he instantly felt a rapport; here, he sensed was a woman to whom he could speak with freedom and confidence. For a few weeks after meeting Oriana he did not pretend to work but sat in Abercrombie's (a fellow student) room, smoking endless cigarettes. After this period of dumbstruck idleness he wrote to his mother, 'I have quite made up my mind to be a bachelor for life. I have thought about it a good deal recently and maybe I will write a paper on marriage sometime with all the symptoms and signs of acute love. They are very interesting when you come to think of them'.[43] He was clearly hooked.

It was a happy meeting. Oriana Fanny Souper (1873–1945) was a good-looking young woman with clear skin, brown hair, a straight nose and lovely blue eyes. She immediately showed a sympathetic and intelligent interest in Wilson that was a balm to him. She could listen to his ideas and return them to him, enriched by her contributions. For his part Wilson introduced her to the concept of mysticism and intensified her love of nature. Oriana was the eldest of five children; she had lost her mother when she was twelve and, with a younger sister and three younger brothers, she was well schooled in responsibility and self-discipline. The relationship soon became a wondrous necessity for both of them but there must have been many times when they despaired of the outcome. They were to marry four years after their first meeting but during that time they had to put up with separation and anxiety: Wilson became so ill that Oriana must have assumed that he would die. He was to spend twelve months away from England hoping for a cure for his illness.

The beginning of 1898 was a spiritually happy time for Wilson since he read the Life of St Francis of Assisi for the first time. He was never a man of theory. He had to wrestle with the Church's doctrine in the light of his own experience before he could accept it. Thoughts had to be translated into deeds to be of use to him. St Francis was a man who had rejected his wealthy and privileged background to become a poor and humble workman, who had started the Order on St Francis and who carried the stigmata of Christ's suffering on his body. The saint's life illustrated perfectly what Wilson, albeit in a very modest way, was striving for. By working for others St Francis epitomised all the truths Wilson had painstakingly worked out for himself. He wrote some time later to Oriana, 'I admire the man more than anyone else I ever heard of, and that's a thing no one can do without trying to follow him. I despair sometimes of ever seeing my way to it, yet I always feel that the method and the opportunity will turn up when it's time'.[44]

Although the start of 1898 was spiritually happy, Wilson was now obviously ill. His father noted shivering, bouts of temperature, dry cough, aches and pains and headaches. When Wilson returned to London from Cheltenham after a short Christmas break he stoically ignored his symptoms and restarted his usual hectic round: church services, working at the hospital, doing double duties at the mission, going to art galleries. But his temperature and cough persisted. Bravely, he avoided mentioning his problems when he wrote to his parents to introduce Oriana who was taking the post of Matron at a school near Cheltenham, 'There is a girl I have met at Battersea, a Miss Souper who is going to be 'Matron', she says, Useful Help I say, to the James' School. You must be kind to her because she is a connection of Mrs Warden. But you will like her I think'.[45] He seems to have deferred seeking medical advice (perhaps fearful of the diagnosis) until March, when he consulted his mentor,

Dr Rolleston. He was sent home again. His father recorded in his memoirs the dreaded news that tuberculosis had been diagnosed by the physicians in London. His sputum had been examined microscopically and a Mycobacterium, an organism that can be associated with tuberculosis, had been seen.[46] Immediate treatment was advised. His parents must have made the awful assumption that they were going to lose the fourth of their children. Tuberculosis was then a terrible disease caused by a pathogenic bacterium first identified by Robert Koch in 1882. It was 'the perpetual spectre in the background carrying off the young the beautiful and the talented'.[47] Half of the sufferers died.

With hindsight, it is unclear whether Wilson actually had tuberculosis or another serious respiratory disease. The evidence is inconclusive. What is certain is that he had a debilitating febrile illness with loss of weight, chest symptoms and subsequent scarring in his lungs. There are many types of mycobacterium; some cause illness, others do not.[48] Precise details of the mycobacterium type found during Wilson's illness are not available.[49] An alternative explanation to tuberculosis is a chronic pneumonia, with the mycobacteria seen under the microscope being non-pathogenic contaminants.[50] He certainly made an excellent recovery eventually; he lost his symptoms, regained his weight and, in the Antarctic, was one of the strongest man-haulers.

At the time, no one, certainly not Wilson, questioned the diagnosis. Tuberculosis had no cure and ideas as to the cause varied from divine retribution to vitamin D deficiency. Treatment, such as it was, depended on the patient's, or his relatives', income. Experience showed that high altitude and expensive spas or sanatoria might help cure patients, who were also given frequent high-calorie meals and obliged to rest for hours on verandas outside their rooms in the fresh, cold air. Exercise was forbidden in the early stages of 'the cure'. These measures were thought to allow the tuberculous lesion to heal.[51] So for many patients the diagnosis meant separation from family and friends, often for years, with death far from home a common outcome. Wilson would have known all this. He must have felt that his fate was to live a short life only. He could not think of a future with Oriana. Perhaps he was resigned to this. In the event he does not seem to have panicked or sunk into a deep depression, or become a hedonist like so many other sufferers, 'I have got me a bit soot-sodden' and he went home in apparent good spirits.[52]

In the 1890s spas accommodated not only patients but also any of their relatives and friends who could afford to visit.[53] Patients and visitors ate together at communal tables, no doubt giving ample opportunity for uninfected visitors or lightly-infected patients to develop full-blown disease. If he did not actually have tuberculosis when he went, Wilson was lucky not to catch it there.

Back then, the diagnosis was made predominantly on clinical signs and microscopic examination; no specialised X-rays or DNA probes were available in the 1890s. X-rays were only discovered in 1895 and it was some time before chest radiography became generally accepted; physicians were suspicious of the new-fangled technique and the apparatus was low powered and the films difficult to interpret. Wilson does not appear to have had an X-ray, although the consultants at St George's were aware of the development. Almost as soon as X-rays were available a 'Mr Bennett desired to bring to the notice of the Board the desirability of occasionally having photographs taken under the new system for the discovery of certain injuries'. The hospital purchased the equipment, plus an officer who hopefully could use it, in 1898.[54]

Arrangements were made for Wilson to go to a spa in Davos, Switzerland. However he sidestepped this treatment and, with the agreement of his physician, accepted an invitation to visit friends in Norway. Here he would benefit from the advised cold air, sunshine and heights, as a member of a house party rather than 'a patient' in a spa. He spent the summer of 1898 as a houseguest in Norway with his presumably uninfected hosts and other guests. He got on very well with his hosts, Mr and Mrs Rice, and called the place 'Liberty Hall'. Although obviously ill, suffering from chest pain and very thin, he was still physically strong enough to walk, climb, fish, observe birds, sketch and paint as he pleased.[55] He sketched, wrapping himself to the eyes in scarves and puffing on tobacco smoke to try and ward off mosquitoes and clegs, but his fingers and legs were so swollen with bites 'that they looked like German sausages'.[56] However he managed to capture the beauty and the vibrant colours of Norway, writing to his parents in 1898:

> Sunsets which get all the mountain flaming in yellow and red and gold, with contrasting greys and purples in their shadows, the red trunks of the Scotch firs blaze out like rods of fire, and the greens of the Spruces in the light all become orange and red. Then the snow patches become rose and blue in the shadow and the tones up from a yellow into a very light green and blue and then in a few minutes when you wonder what is coming next it all goes out. And you are left with sober greys and greens and mosquitoes. It takes a lot of yellow paint, a cast iron resolution and a power of tobacco to sit and sketch.[57]

He sketched and painted in the northern light from dinner to early morning and slept in the afternoon. He reported to his father that he was well and in August 1898 he returned home to spend the remainder of the summer at The Crippetts. However, secretly he still thought that he was going to die 'and that alone brings extraordinary peace of mind'.[58] He read the New Testament and this encouraged him. He said he was intensely happy. His intuition that he was still not well was confirmed by a medical examination, presumably clinical, which found ongoing signs in his chest. Arrangements were reinstated for Davos.

Davos was gloomy, overcast, cold, white and deadly dull, full of pensions and hotels. He was in a hotel initially. The regimen imposed on patients was strict but somehow Wilson managed, at least at first, to keep his sense of humour. He wrote that 'all the conversation at meals is all on bacilli (the cause of Tuberculosis) and hearts and weights and Huggard, (the doctor), and expectoration, even among decent looking people so that one hardly dares clear one's throat without feeling one

has said something tuberculosis'.[59] The treatment depended
to a large extent on the patients' temperature. A raised temperature meant active disease and this meant that physical
activity and smoking, (which was surprisingly allowed in the
sanatorium although patients were told not to inhale), were
forbidden. No temperature meant that a gradual resumption
of activities and smoking was allowed. Wilson was one of the
patients with a temperature and he was therefore trapped, an
unwilling prisoner, without the comfort of tobacco, the craving
for which made him want to 'bite everyone and run away'.[60]
Although, as his beliefs dictated, he tried to gain spiritually
from the experience of suffering and to cling to his belief that
this life is only part of a bigger picture, he became anxiously
uncertain. It is easy to understand why. He felt that he was
probably beyond cure, or at any rate without a useful future,
and he knew that he could die in Davos, aged 26, separated
from everyone he cared for, as happened all too frequently to
other patients. His family did not visit and the wearisome days
were spent lying for hours outside in the fresh air, attempting
huge meals and listening to other patients' problems, 'becoming a cabbage'.[61] He read, he sketched, he wrote letters – the
ink freezing in the bottle – and his confidential, understanding
correspondence with Oriana gained pace at this time as his
reserves gradually melted away. He read and meditated, particularly on the life of St Francis anticipating death and trying
to prepare himself for it.

But unexpectedly and miraculously, or so it must have
seemed to him, his temperature settled to normal, exercise
was allowed. He was allowed to smoke again. As his physical
condition improved so did his confidence and his mood. He
managed to climb to 800 feet, where he saw bear tracks in the
snow and although the climb caused breathlessness, chest pains
and dizziness, the attempt would have been completely impossible if his infection had remained severe. He went walking in
snowstorms and returned exhilarated. By early 1899 he was
definitely better physically. He started to skate, he made friends
and, as he wrote triumphantly, he smoked all day. In spite of

his definite clinical improvement he continued to look gaunt and ill and must have remained a concern to the doctors for a fellow-patient said, years later, that the greatest miracle he had ever heard of was that Wilson should have reached the South Pole.[62] But best, from his point of view, was the fact that other patients started to ask him for advice. He continued to feel that this role was a blessing and he thanked God for the assurance that he was wanted. He wrote to his father, 'I have come to feel that these last five months are an equaliser. I did too much during the last two years and now I have to sit back awhile. But I know there are one or two here who are happier for that very reason and that makes me as happy as anyone can wish'.[63] Overall he looked on the months in Davos as an experience that he had benefited from. With better health and spirits he wrote to Oriana, 'Take life as it comes and do what lies straight in front of you. Its only real carelessness about one's own will and absolute hope and confidence in God's that can teach one to believe that whatever is, is best. Don't you think this is the key to happiness in this apparently spoilt and disappointing life'?[64] By February 1899 he was out and about all day, filling a sketchbook with sketches of scenery, birds and local flowers. He found he could walk eight miles after a day spent climbing. Whether tuberculosis was the correct diagnosis or not, his respiratory illness had definitely resolved. He was allowed to 'regain his freedom' and go home in May 1899 'looking and feeling much better'.[65] He had been in the Spa for the best part of seven months.

A quiet life was advised. This was routine advice for anyone who had been sent to a spa, but advice that Wilson would ignore. He was again determined to live each day to the full. He wrote to Oriana that to 'save' his health and strength until he was sixty was not an option. How did he know he would live that long? He thought it was much better to 'wear a thing when its good and new, patching the odd corners as they wear out, instead of putting it away carefully year after year till at last the moths get in and its no good when at last you want to wear it'.[66] But his experiences had changed him; his family found him more reserved and moody than previously. He spoke little of his plans and his mother, a trifle unrealistically, was sad that he would not confide in her. He was clearly hoping against hope for a future with Oriana. But long-term planning remained difficult: he was still occasionally coughing up blood, he had no occupation or income and he needed to complete his studies but was not well enough to return immediately to the hospital. He probably hoped that the situation might clarify itself one way or another in a further few months, so he accepted another invitation to Norway. Here his physical improvement continued. He was in the countryside continuously. He painted and recorded the sunsets with awe. How difficult it was to capture and retain the memory of such beauty. How he wished he had Turner's mastery.

Later in 1899, when back in London, his temperature and cough returned. But by now his thoughts, hopes and intentions had crystallised. His and Oriana's commitment to each other had been tested enough. Procrastination was abandoned and on 19 October 1899, they became engaged. Fears about death, concerns about his career and the future were swept aside in a blaze of happiness.

Before he became ill, Wilson had studied for nearly two and a half years at St George's. He had covered most of the syllabus therefore, but he had been away for eighteen months and must have been very concerned about his ability not only to complete the course but also to revise all his previous work. He needed to study exceptionally hard to cover both these gaps and he had only two months to do it in. But better health and energy and his personal happiness gave him the determination to 'go for it'. With Oriana's help he moved to Stanmore, in the country and away from the smogs of London, and worked determinedly. In December 1899 he went to Cambridge for his examinations and was both delighted and surprised to pass.[67]

As a monomaniac on Physic and the allied sciences I have been found not wanting. I am admitted into the comparatively select circle of amateur and other druggists. The prospect of immediate admission to the degree of M.B. is the Christmas present which I propose to proffer for your acceptance. . . Therefore let all now at home take me at my own valuation and realise that for a cheap and easy solution of the difficult problems of life they have a near relative and a dear friend in a ginger-headed copper-knob named Ted, M.B.[68]

4

Antarctic Recruit

Although Wilson passed his Cambridge examinations in December 1899, it was some months before he was awarded the M.B. In addition to the clinical examinations, he had to complete his dissertation on 'Yellow Atrophy of The Liver', which included some cases supplied by his proud father. In Stanmore village he could roam on the common and draw, but he found the discipline of writing the dissertation hard. Also he missed being with Oriana. When it was finally completed, the dissertation had to be submitted to the examiners and agreed by them. His M.B. degree was formally conferred on 7 June 1900.[1]

In these months, Wilson needed to earn money. He was conscious that at twenty-seven he was still dependent on his father for his day-to-day existence. He was never to be a man who 'grew out' of his family and his love and admiration of his father was lifelong. His father was, as Wilson well knew, still supporting three of his sisters and his young brother James at Westal[2] and, as was common in Victorian households, helping other female relatives. So he was delighted when he was offered opportunities to earn money by drawing. He was asked to do illustrations for a publication, *Land and Water*,[3] edited by a friend from Cambridge, the author C.E. Walker, and further welcome income was made certain when Dr Rolleston from St George's arranged for him to do illustrations for *The Lancet*.[4] Dr Phillip L. Sclater (1829–1913), the secretary of the Zoological Society, an old friend of his father's and a man who would later have a pivotal influence on Wilson's career, allowed him free access to the society library and zoological gardens where he could draw and paint.

Wilson was a man who found it impossible to separate his artwork from its spiritual framework. For him the two were intimately intertwined. His drawings were an expression of his love for God. He explained this fusion to his father in a letter of 1899: 'My little bird-pictures are just visible proofs of my love for them and attempts to praise God and bring others to love Him through his works and that's why I love to give them away and hate to sell them. I can't believe God has given me such an intense absorbing love for drawing unless it was to be used in some way'.[5] He hated the business of actually selling the paintings. He would have preferred to give them away 'so that people would know God through his works'.[6] He wrote to Oriana in 1900:

> I tried a shop in Regent Street. A young man with well-pomaded[7] curly hair and a very smart frock coat came to me. I asked if I might show some drawings; he said he would *look* at them, and turned over the leaves as you might a *Whitaker's Almanac*,[8] and said, 'No use whatsoever for that sort of thing' and walked away. I am not disappointed because it's exactly what I expected, but I think it's useless to repeat it.

In the same letter he expanded again on his feelings towards his drawings:

> My pictures are the realisation of little things that have been treasured up in my mind, little traits of character picked up crumb by crumb in the fields and by hedgerows, at last pieced together and put into the form of something living. The realisation of every happy day I have spent in the hills is in the picture of a stoat I chanced to see; in the snake's, in that little head and one eye is all the fascinating quickness and supple gracefulness of all snakes I have known. The whole concentrated beauty of that glorious Norwegian forest at midnight is what I see in the picture of the sparrow-hawk's nest.[9]

Although, as expected, he did not sell many drawings on the fashionable market, support and appreciation did come, and from a welcome source. At the Annual Meeting and Dinner of the British Ornithological Union of 1900, Wilson's confidence was boosted by meeting two very distinguished artists, Archibald Thorburn (1860–1935) and George Edward Lodge (1850–1944). Both of these older men were already eminent in a world in which Wilson increasingly wanted to shine; Thorburn went on to publish *British Birds* and *British Mammals*, and Lodge illustrated the popular *Hudson's Birds*. Wilson was flattered by their kindness. They invited him to look at their work but more importantly, looked at his and gave valuable constructive criticism. Wilson's confidence was increased when, to his delight, he was proposed as a member of this prestigious society – a real accolade.[10] His self-assurance mounted when he was asked to look at plates of bird studies painted by an octogenarian, a Mr Hammond, who was known to be capriciously selective about who he allowed to see his work. An invitation to view was a compliment that Wilson appreciated. He wrote:

> Twenty volumes containing water-colour portraits of three hundred and sixty British Birds *in their surroundings*, the most perfect little pictures imaginable ... It is altogether one of the best things I have seen in my life; I enjoyed it immensely, but goodness me, I feel as though I should never want to touch a pencil or brush again.[11]

The pictures were his ideals of how birds should be represented and he felt he had much to improve, but although he was modest about his abilities, Wilson nevertheless had confidence that, as an acolyte of Ruskin, his strength lay not only in his technical abilities but also in his extensive background knowledge of his subjects. He certainly felt that his pictures were already worth more than the dreadful things he had seen exhibited, well reviewed and sold for eight and ten guineas. Paintings of animals had to be 'alive' and he was robustly critical of much exhibited work. As he wrote to Oriana in 1900:

> I spent an hour at the water-colour exhibition at Piccadilly . . . dreadful stuffed birds! There were plenty of flowers, nicely done but then they merely want a faithful copyist – anyone can do that but WHY don't they open their eyes to birds, which are so much more subtly beautiful than flowers? No one would think of painting preserved flowers – why on earth do they paint preserved birds?[12]

His parents offered to pay for art tuition, but he worried about adding to his father's financial burdens, and was no doubt conscious that he was not yet part of the structured career being undertaken by his fellow students from St George's, and did not take up this offer.

What should the next move be? Although Roland Huntford states in his book *Scott and Amundsen* that Wilson seemed uninterested in practising medicine[13] this is not precisely true. At this stage Wilson absolutely accepted that when he was well enough to work, his future lay in some branch of medicine, but which branch? His early ambitions towards surgery or missionary work were impractical because he was still coughing up blood occasionally, suggesting that there was still some inflammation present. General practice, his father's choice, did not appeal. The situation was complicated by the fact that he needed practical experience before entering any speciality. His friend from St George's, John Fraser, did three house jobs (approximately eighteen months more work) before specialising.[14] Wilson was all too aware of what was required. He wrote, to his father, in July 1900:

> I want, most sadly, say six months hospital work and say a month at Queen Charlotte's Hospital,[15] and until I have got that at least, I do not feel fit for 'the cure of bodies'. But this is also true that so long as I have to draw a living from you I am perfectly willing to do anything you want me to. I should hate

to think that I was trying to make things more easy for myself
while I was making them harder for you.[16]

As he pondered on his uncertain future and before he was
actually granted his thesis, Wilson was completely surprised
to hear from Dr Sclater, his friend in the Zoological Society,
asking if he would consider applying to join the planned
National Antarctic Expedition as doctor, naturalist and artist. The expedition was due to leave in July 1901 on the ship
Discovery. Wilson's father said the offer was 'a bolt out of
the blue'.[17] It was certainly a most wonderful tailor-made
opportunity; all Wilson's talents and interests were included
in the job description. He wrote in his diary that he accepted
at once, as he said, 'provisionally',[18] but in fact he appears to
have hesitated, writing back that he felt unqualified for the
post, probably frightened of hoping too much. On 1 June Dr
Sclater wrote to him again, expressing views that he would
scarcely be able to express as freely to a candidate today: 'I
am on the committee that makes the appointments and my
opinion is that you would be a suitable person for the post'.[19]
With this encouragement Wilson's courage hardened and he
went, as suggested, to see a leading member of the biologi-
cal sub-committee, Professor Edward Poulton (1856–1943),
professor of zoology at Oxford University. The interview was
successful. His uncle Sir Charles 'advertised' him in the Royal
Geographical Society and helped him by arranging meetings
with people who would be of help to him in his application. Sir
Charles wrote a letter of support to Sir Clements Markham,
the president of the Royal Geographical Society and 'father'
of the British Antarctic attempts, also. Sir Clements suggested
that Wilson should meet Robert Falcon Scott (1868–1912), the
then virtually unknown expedition commander. The interview
was arranged for 22 November.

Meanwhile Wilson, having obtained his degree, finally
started medical work proper. According to A.E. Shipley, a fellow Cambridge graduate and Wilson's future co-author of a
huge report on Grouse disease, Wilson was offered a two-year

appointment at St George's but was advised not to take it up. Certainly if he had taken up a hospital appointment he would not have been able to consider Antarctic exploration.[20] Instead he went to the local hospital at Cheltenham in September 1900, first as a locum and then as Junior House Surgeon. He gave anaesthetics and performed minor surgery. This experience was to be of good use to him in the Antarctic but he found the work hard and stressful. Not only did he work for days and nights at a stretch without much backup, but he was also single-handed with responsibilities for seriously ill patients. However he was clearly not destined for hospital medicine. Only three weeks after starting as House Surgeon, he pricked his finger whilst working in the post-mortem room. The finger became infected and swollen, the infection quickly spreading to glands in the upper arm, which filled with pus and made the arm too painful to use. He wrote that:

> I found my temperature to be 103°F while I was hunting for the head of a tapeworm in a small boy's excreta. Having found it and identified it under the microscope I went to bed, and then came the worst week of illness and pain it has ever been granted to me to experience.[21]

Antibiotics were unknown in 1900 and he needed regular morphine to control the pain. The glands in the armpit had to be lanced under ether anaesthetic. A drain was left in his armpit to release the infection. Wilson had to resign from the post. This was his sole hospital experience.

Whilst awaiting developments over the Antarctic project, Wilson's spiritual and moral development did not falter. 1900 was a year full of incident for Britain. The Boer War (1899–1902) between Dutch settlers in South Africa and the British was not going as anticipated. The British, far from crushing those impudent Boer insurgents as anticipated, had suffered a series of defeats and 3,000 had died by the time Ladysmith[22] was relieved. Field Marshal Lord Roberts, who had already lost his only son in the war, became Supreme Commander of the British forces and in March, Wilson's older brother Bernard sailed off to South Africa to fight.[23] Bernard's descriptions of life at the front are horribly vivid. He wrote to his family about being caught in bombardments of bullets flying from every direction and the difficulties of running across open ground in a hail of those bullets carrying his rifle, 100 rounds of ammunition, his haversack, bayonet, revolver, field glasses and water-bottle; the awfulness of the infections, sickness and wounds that decimated his unit[24] in which typhoid probably wreaked as much havoc as the bullets. By 1900 many young men had enlisted as a patriotic duty. But others had simply seen the war as an opportunity to get away from the repetitive drudgery of lives spent working fifty-five hours a week and with no hope of a better future. Some of these men had hardly travelled from their villages and had never been on a train, let alone a ship to Europe. They went off excitedly with their friends looking for adventure and hoping to return as heroes. For many of these, as was to happen in the First World War, the casualties, realities and horrors of the battlefield quickly shattered their ideals. Some however, including Winston Spencer Churchill, never seemed to tire of the thrill of the campaign. Churchill, who had been determined to get to South Africa, managed to get appointed as principle war correspondent for the *Morning Post*. He wrote with undiminished enthusiasm about his experiences in *My Early Years*.[25] Reports such as Churchill's did much to keep up public support, but Wilson remained impervious to patriotic fervour. Wilson was a pacifist; a brave and unpopular position when the majority of citizens thought that support for the war was every British man's patriotic duty. He was upheld by his religious convictions and convinced of God's providence and God's purpose, 'only man is vile'. He was particularly moved by a widely-reported battle between the British forces (which included a Canadian regiment that suffered its worst losses of a single day for the entire war) and the Boers, commanded by General Piet Cronje. This battle, on the banks of the Modder River, was bloody and destructive and resulted in the surrender of nearly 10 per cent of the Boer army. Such military success appalled Wilson. No jingoistic, xenophobic rejoicing for him. He wrote:

> Now I know what the duties of a soldier are in war, I would rather shoot myself than anyone else by a long, long way. I simply could not do it. The very thought of it now is a ghastly nightmare to me, chiefly the result of a very realistic account of our sinful – though as things are, necessary – cruelty over that bombardment of Cronje in the Modder. It made me cry like a baby and I threw away the paper in perfect disgust. A nation should be judged on exactly the same grounds as an individual. As a nation we have the vilest of sins, which everyone extols as the glory of Imperialism. One day, all this part of our history will be looked upon in its proper light.[26]

He would never deviate from these views.

At home his egalitarian, uncompromising and socially-uncomfortable opinions included strong views on the class distinctions that supported the lifestyle of the upper classes in Victorian England. He believed that time, not money, is our most precious gift, a gift that must be cherished and he was very conscious of the monotonous drudgery of the lives led by most Victorian servants who spent their working days support-ing that privileged minority. He wrote that upper-class freedom was bought by the sacrifice of workers and accepted selfishly without consideration of the social structure separating the 'have' from the 'have-nots' by a wide and impassable divide. He wrote in 1900: 'One by one, we, the few will be brought face to face with them and asked what we have done with our lives and the time they gave us to make the world better'.[27] He tried to live as simply as possible and later he and Oriana did not employ servants but shared their domestic duties.

Like us all, but perhaps reaching different conclusions, he pon-dered on life's purposes and on the perfecting power of pain. He thought any illness or pain that he had suffered was a valuable check to self-confidence, worldly success and ambition. Through suffering, he could empty the soul and let God in. He wrote,

'This I know is God's own Truth, that pain and trouble and trials and sorrows and disappointments are either one thing or the other. To all that love God they are love tokens from Him. To all that do not love God they are merely a nuisance. Every single pain that we feel is known to God because it is the most loving and most pathetic touch of His hand'.[28] More and more his inclinations were towards a Franciscan way of life. In September 1900, he lovingly created a picture of the saint he venerated. He gave this painting to Oriana.

In November 1900, with his arm in a sling, Wilson met Commander Scott and other members of the Antarctic Committee. Scott, 'who knew a man when he saw one', was sufficiently impressed with this thoughtful man, four years his junior, to 'practically appoint' him, health permitting, although there were many other candidates.[29] At this stage, Scott was Commander of *Discovery*, but not in total command of the expedition, although the appointment was definite enough to encourage Wilson to begin preliminary work for the voyage. Scott wrote in his account of the expedition that although Wilson's health was not perfect when he joined *Discovery*, 'his fitness for the post in other respects was obvious'.[30] From Wilson's point of view, his only concern was separation from Oriana, now that they were finally engaged and had achieved happiness and emotional security. He had to weigh up the prospects offered by this unexpected opportunity against a prolonged departure and the definite possibility of a non-return. But no other career option had been offered and this was a time when men routinely left their families for years in the service of the Empire. Wilson would have been accustomed to long familial separations. His uncle Charles had regularly been on long campaigns and his brother Bernard was a serving soldier. Before proceeding, however, he cautiously made Oriana give her written consent to an adventure that affected her future as much as his.[31] Oriana bravely agreed and with her consent in his pocket, Wilson felt free to proceed.

The feared medical interview with the Admiralty Medical Board was on 4 January 1901 and Wilson presented himself, still with his arm in a sling, having had a second operation to drain pus from the axilla. His mother, apparently still preparing herself for the worst, wrote that his body was frail and delicate 'a noble soul and spiritual. . . He is half a Holy-Spirit now'.[32] The exact implication of this is unclear, but fortunately the doctors took a more robust view and passed him as provisionally fit, but took the precaution of arranging a final review for July.[33] He was put on the National Antarctic Expedition pay roll from January and paid £23 initially, and thereafter £18 14s 4p (plus expenses) each month, a great help to his finances.[34] He met his future shipmates at the Royal Geographical Society and had lunch with Ernest Shackleton, (1874–1922), appointed as Third Lieutenant on *Discovery*. The medical examination in July was expected to be a 'signing off' and the subject of chest problems would not have been considered if Wilson had not felt it only honest to reveal his pulmonary history. His physique must have improved considerably in the twenty-six months since he had left Davos, or the doctors surely would have been wary of his appearance. Re-examination resulted in them changing their conclusions about Wilson's fitness to go to the South Pole. They decided, probably correctly, that there were signs of lung scarring and Wilson's appointment was not therefore recommended.[35] However, Scott by this time had decided definitely on Wilson and said that he would take him on his (Wilson's) own risk. Dr Rolleston supported the application.[36] Wilson agreed and the appointment was signed and sealed. He was delighted. He wrote:

> I think I am intended to go. If I had tried to get it I should have had many doubts but it seems given to me to do. If the climate suits me I shall come back more fit for work than ever, whereas if it doesn't I think there is no fear of me coming back at all. I quite realise that it is kill or cure and have made up my mind it shall be cure.[37]

He wrote to his father that if his expensive M.B. landed him at the South Pole it would be well worth the expense. It was a golden opportunity.

The time before *Discovery's* departure was busy. Wilson had to climb a steep learning curve. He had to prepare medical and scientific lists. He took a 'refresher' course in taxidermy at the Natural History Museum; his childhood lessons with 'White the Birdcatcher' being insufficient for this assignment. This was a skill that stood him in good stead. Much, too much he thought, of his time on the expedition was taken up with this smelly, tiring, but essential occupation of skinning and preparing the animals. In the Natural History Museum he familiarised himself with Antarctic and southern wildlife. Always industrious, he wrote an illustrated paper on seals for the British Museum and designed, at Scott's request, a crest for *Discovery's* crockery and paper.[38] The expedition was to have many home comforts: commissioned crockery, photos, a piano and a library. Scott was not unusual or self-indulgent in this. Amundsen's mess on *Fram* in 1912 had a similar piano, framed photographs and pictures.

During the time before departure, a long list of social engagements had to be endured: the Royal Geographical Society annual dinner, the Royal Society's dinner at the Athenaeum[39] and the Geographical Club's dinner at The Ship in Greenwich, to name but a few.[40] However these events would not have been the usual trial. Here Wilson would be meeting like-minded people whom he could respect, and share interests and exchange opinions with. Also being settled, secure and happy in his personal life, he felt more confident socially.

The advantages and disadvantages of marriage before the expedition were anxiously discussed, but by now the couple had waited long enough; they wanted the relationship officially blessed. They knew that the days before *Discovery* sailed could be their only time together, the future was totally uncertain; Antarctica was unknown and Wilson could die on the expedition. As soon as his appointment was confirmed, Wilson and Oriana finalised the wedding plans for 16 July 1901, just three days after his interview with the Admiralty. On the day before the wedding, Wilson, Oriana, his mother and Ida, one of his sisters, attended a service held by the Bishop of London on *Discovery*. The couple were given a three-tier, silver dessert stand by his fellow officers and Sir Clements Markham, the instigator of the expedition. On the 16 July, that long-awaited day, Dr Edward Wilson and Miss Oriana Souper were married in the Church of St Mary Magdalene at Hilton in Cambridgeshire where Oriana's father, The Rev. F.A. Souper, was the vicar. Bernard Wilson was the best man. Oriana's father conducted the service and the rector of Woolwich gave the address. The wedding was reported on in the local newspapers: 'A fashionable wedding was solemnised at Hilton Parish Church . . . the bride looked charming in a dress of white satin, trimmed with chiffon and lace, she wore a tulle veil with a wreath of orange blossoms. She also carried a bunch of white trumpet lilies'.[41] The marriage was to be extremely happy. Oriana and Wilson were well suited. They shared an intense friendship and had a devoted loyalty to each other. Oriana was not a social, chatty person but she had an excellent brain and could help Wilson with his work. Friends described her as a man's woman.[42] She was certainly Wilson's woman. He wrote to John Fraser, his friend from St George's, that he was 'as happy as it is given to mortals ever to be on this earth'.[43] Two days after his wedding he took Oriana to see the ship before going on an all-too-short honeymoon. In three weeks he had departed. *Discovery* weighed anchor on 6 August 1901 bound for the Cape, New Zealand and the Antarctic. Wilson was not to see his Oriana for more than three years.

The fact that Wilson was offered this 'golden' opportunity was due indirectly to the exertions of one man, Sir Clements Robert Markham (1830–1916). Sir Clements had pursued his vision of sending an expedition to the Antarctic over many years with tenacity, determination and astuteness. He had become interested in polar exploration when, as a 9-year-old he read about Arctic expeditions.[44] His interest and enthusiasm increased when, as a young midshipman on board HMS *Assistance*, he was a member of one of the unsuccessful naval searches sent to find any remains of Sir John Franklin's fatal Arctic expedition of 1845. Sir John's two ships and 129 officers and men had disappeared without trace on an exploration to open up the Northwest Passage, potentially a quicker route to the Indies' lucrative trade market. Also on *Assistance* was Lieutenant Leopold McClintock (1819–1907), who devised a man-haul sledging technique that so impressed Sir Clements that he became convinced that, with fit and disciplined naval men, the method was a better and more reliable form of transport than dog transport in Arctic conditions.[45] McClintock went on to use dogs successfully on polar journeys, but Sir Clements did not change his views on the superiority of man-hauling, where men pitted themselves against the unforgiving climate, terrain and isolation of the frozen continent and his influence was to have an effect on British Antarctic exploration. Sir Clements waged a long campaign for the revival of polar exploration which had lapsed since Ross's voyages and gradually developed his vision of organising, financing and supporting a National Antarctic Expedition. *Discovery* was the culmination of his long campaign. Sir Clements was a remarkable man. He spoke half a dozen languages. Long before he became president of the Royal Geographical Society (1893–1905), he had made two extraordinary contributions to mankind. Whilst working in the India Office he smuggled seeds and saplings of the jealously-guarded cinchona, or quinine plant, out of Peru and established it in India,[46] where it became the vanguard of the fight against malaria. But he did more; sickened by the excessive discipline of the Navy he later initiated a campaign for the abolition of flogging.[47] However he could be scheming, critical, devious and acerbic in pushing through his plans. Clive Holland, the editor of Sir Clements' book *An Antarctic Obsession*, wrote that few had Sir Clements' skills for background organisation or background intrigue.[48]

In July 1895, The Sixth International Geographical Congress took place in London. Deputations from all major European countries were present. Sir Clements was the Chairman. A statement of intent was published at the end of the congress which read that 'Exploration of the Antarctic is the greatest piece of geographical exploration still to be undertaken. That in view of the addition to knowledge in almost every branch of science that would result from such a scientific exploration, the Committee recommended that scientific societies throughout the world should urge in whatever way seems most effective that this work should be undertaken before the end of the century'.[49] Sir Clements was determined to push through this lofty goal in Britain's name. The British expedition would carry out geographical research as well as exploration in the Antarctic and, importantly, add lustre to the prestige and influence of Great Britain.

Funding was his most persistent problem and Sir Clements spent years tenaciously addressing this problem. But by the end of 1897 only £12,000 had been raised, most of it from the Royal Geographical Society and the publisher, Alfred C. Harmsworth, who donated £5,000. However donations received a spectacular boost when Llewellyn W. Longstaff (1881–1918), a Fellow of the Royal Geographical Society and a businessman, gave £25,000 to the appeal, altruistically stating that he wished to contribute to the advancement of knowledge of our planet.[50] Finally, after a distinguished deputation waited on A.J. Balfour (1848–1930), then the First Lord of the Treasury and subsequent Prime Minister, the government, after years of refusing aid, finally offered £45,000 on condition that a similar sum was raised by private subscription. The Royal Geographical Society who had donated a total of £8,000 to the project agreed to a final top-up. Thus the expedition's future was assured.

Sir Clements was the registered owner of the ship. He wanted a naval man as leader. He had a list of possibilities in which Scott was included, though not as favourite. Scott was connected to Sir Clements by marriage: a niece of Sir Clements had married a cousin of Scott's[51] and Sir Clements had noted him in 1887 when Scott was a midshipman and had taken part in a race between two Navy cutters in the West Indies. Sir Clements claimed subsequently that he had been impressed by Scott's good judgement, prudence and determination. He met Scott again, in 1897, when Scott, now promoted to Torpedo Officer, was training off Spain. When, with Sir Clements' support, Lieutenant Robert Scott of *Majestic* was appointed in charge of *Discovery*, Sir Clements gave him his energetic and wholehearted help and sent Scott letter after letter of advice.[52] He canvassed support for Scott's promotion.

Scott and his fellow officers had only a year to prepare for the expedition and the administration required was formidable: the ship had to be completed and animals, equipment and the scientific instruments had to be organised. Scott also had to assist in the selection of the officers and crew. These appointments included Wilson. Sir Clements had a habit, begun as a boy at Westminster School, of writing short descriptions of all his contacts. Although many of these are outspoken and critical, his report on Wilson is not uncomplimentary. Wilson's appointment, he wrote, had been approved in December 1900. Wilson had been recommended by his uncle, who had sent specimens of drawings and paintings of birds and fishes. He said that Wilson had a masterly hand and delicate touch and would be invaluable as an artist; he understood Wilson to be an efficient medical man and that he would be an amiable messmate. He noted that Wilson was not strong 'and must be saved as much as possible from hard work and exposure'.[53]

Of the many appointees to *Discovery*, Wilson's proved to be amongst the most successful. Scott, encased in the strict hierarchy of the Royal Navy, was to find in Wilson a non-naval companion to whom he could talk on an equal footing, in a way that was impossible with fellow naval officers. They became loyal personal friends.

5

England to Madeira

Tuesday, 6 August 1901, was a brilliant, sunny day. The sun glistened on the water as *Discovery* sailed away from the south coast of England on her historic expedition. She left a busy, colourful scene. Thousands had come to wave goodbye to the little vessel, with its complement of officers, scientists and crew. The King himself, Edward VII, saluted from the royal yacht and other prestigious yachts hailed *Discovery*. Little craft bustled around in the water. *Discovery* was registered as a yacht and so flew a Blue Ensign; the Admiralty had refused permission for her to fly the Royal Naval White Ensign (which had more prestige) on the defendable grounds that she was not a man o'war.[1] *Discovery* responded to the salutations by raising and lowering the ensign 'again and again', before she finally departed British shores.

Sir Clements had commissioned *Discovery* specifically for the 1901 expedition. She was expensive, costing £51,000 including the engines, and built by The Dundee Shipbuilders Co. She left Dundee in early June to sail to the East India Dock in London for fitting and coaling and to take on provisions. Londoners welcomed *Discovery's* arrival with enthusiasm. They crowded the quayside and occasionally the decks (to the disapproval of the crew who had their work cut out to complete their preparations) displaying an avid interest in all the proceedings. The stowing of the equipment, provisions, scientific instruments, etc. was a hectic task and apart from the actual work, time had to be made to show dignitaries around the vessel, see relatives and attend the dental check-ups that had been organised by Scott. These dental checks proved a sensible precaution. Ninety-one teeth were removed and 170 holes filled at the cost of £62.45. Wilson is recorded as having a tooth stopped.[2] Gilbert Scott, a royal marine member of the crew, said that some of the men who had many teeth pulled out had sore gums for weeks.[3] *Discovery* sailed from the Thames and headed to the South Coast on the last day of July cheered on by enthusiastic crowds and hooting boats. On board were important visitors, friends and relatives and all along the coastline the interest continued, locals waved from the shore and craft saluted. Neither Wilson nor his parents were on board. Wilson, with Oriana's help, was completing some last-minute illustrations and only joined the ship on the south coast. He had said 'goodbye' to his parents at Westal where, probably fortuitously, his father was fully occupied being host to a local meeting of the British Medical Association with a house full of guests.[4] As Wilson's departure grew nearer, Oriana naturally clung to her husband for as long as possible. She and Wilson had had 'the very cream of this life's happiness' on their honeymoon: 'Goodness me, we were happy there!'[5] They had a few more precious days together on the South Coast before joining the boat for the final departure.

The visit to Cowes was specifically planned for the ship and its complement to be inspected by the new king. Queen Victoria had died in January and King Edward VII and his entourage were in Cowes for the annual regatta. The Edwardian era was to prove a time of luxurious and wealthy display and the royal yacht was accompanied by a flotilla of glittering sleek yachts, whose beautiful outlines were in marked contrast to the solid, heavily-rigged *Discovery*. The King, as patron of the Antarctic expedition, came on *Discovery* with his retinue to inspect the ship and to meet Captain Scott, his officers and men. This was a significant compliment to Sir Clements. Accompanying the King was Queen Alexandra, a woman of charm and beauty, who was notable not only in her own right but also because of her web of relatives. She was the aunt of the last Russian tsar, Nicholas II, and sister of three European kings. Accompanied by their daughter, Princess Victoria, and dignitaries, the King and Queen toured the ship with interest: 'The smartest pieces of apparatus, the prettiest solutions and the most interesting microscopic bits had been put out for their inspection'.[6] The King made a speech, 'short and to the point' according to the engineer, Reginald Skelton, who thought that on the whole it was 'rather a good show'.[7] The Marine, Gilbert Scott, was more explicit. He wrote that King Edward said that he had 'often bid farewell to men going on active service, but that he was glad to have the pleasure of saying goodbye to us who were going on an entirely peaceful expedition for the increase of science and natural knowledge'.[8] Then, with difficulty, as the King was a stout man and had problems getting his hand into his tail pocket to get at the medal, Edward presented Scott with the Victorian Order, Class IV.[9] A member of the crew, overcome by the presence of royalty, called the Queen 'Miss'. Alexandra passed this off with grace, she was a kind woman. Thomas Hodgson, the biologist of the expedition, confided in his diary that the Queen looked very young but she was lame and deaf.[10] (Alexandra suffered from a hereditary form of deafness known as otosclerosis). The officers, including Wilson, were asked to sign their names on the royal yacht's visitor book. With all formalities completed and the royal party finally departed, casks of special king's champagne and whisky which had been brought on board to lubricate the royal palate were found to have been mistakenly left behind; an excellent end to the day. These were sampled, very satisfactorily, a few days later, but Wilson, who was made the mess's wine-officer, spoiled the fun by impounding the cases for medical purposes.

Oriana stayed on board as long as possible. But as *Discovery* sailed slowly westwards along the coast, eventually and all too soon, she had to disembark. In spite of her leaden heart she was courageous about facing an uncertain separation, after only three weeks of marriage and with no certainty that her husband would return. There were only a few tears. The parting was 'painful but happy and she smiling to the last was just as brave as she could possibly be'.[11] She waved until *Discovery* was just a tiny speck on the horizon. Wilson looked back through field glasses (Oriana's present) until he could no longer distinguish her. He was proud of her and of her pluck and determination to be cheerful. 'May God keep us for one another and we shall be ever more happy then'.[12]

As the vessel made its way to Madeira, she was an organised chaos of carpenters' stores, rope, canvas, explosives, equipment for landing in the Antarctic, scientific equipment, engineers' stores, clothing and provisions (including the tinned meat that was to cause such problems on the voyage). The expedition's finances were tight, but many firms gave goods at reduced prices. Messrs Colman gave flour and mustard. Cadbury gave 3,500 lbs. of chocolate and cocoa. Bird and Sons gave eight hundredweight of baking and custard powder and Evans, Lescher and Webb, interestingly, in view of the development of scurvy on the expedition, gave lime juice.[13] Jaeger gave specially manufactured outer windproof garments. The hold contained soups, fish and meat, thirty gallons of brandy, eighty of port and 800 of rum, thirty-six gallons of sherry and twenty-eight of Champagne. Other essentials were 2,800 lbs of tea and coffee, tobacco and separate supplies of jams and marmalades for officers and crew.[14] Also on board were gas cylinders and balloons; Scott had been persuaded that a balloon ascent could provide important information about the unknown Antarctic interior. There were two cats and two dogs: Scott's pet terrier, Scamp, and second-in-command Armitage's Samoyed, Vinka.[15] The husky expedition dogs were not on board, they travelled separately and joined the vessel eventually in New Zealand.

Discovery was rigged as a barque (a three mast ship). She was solidly built of several types of wood[16] that would withstand the huge ice pressures and strains that she would be subjected to, and double skinned, with airspace between the wooden skins for insulation. She had a coal-fired engine from which water could be drained in freezing conditions. A new design feature was that both rudder and screw could be detached and brought up into the vessel, (as was in fact done in the Antarctic). Although most of the crew viewed her with affection, she was in fact squat and black, her profile lightened by a yellow funnel and masts and white boats painted with a 'D' in black and gold. Since an important aim of the expedition was to advance work on terrestrial magnetism, no iron was used within thirty feet of the observatory on deck, rolled brass was used when metal was needed within the proscribed area, hemp was used for the rigging instead of wire. The iron-free area included parts of the officers' wardroom, so some of the cabin beds had metal springs, others had wooden strips. In spite of these elaborate precautions, however, there were so many tins on board that it was impossible to keep them all out of the sacred ring (as Scott wrote, their contents could not be preserved in brass).[17] Reginald Skelton, the engineer, thought that though the work on the hull was satisfactory, 'the iron steel or metal work performed by the shipbuilders is perfectly disgraceful. . . . As it is I consider the ship in all main requirements to be well fitted, but this is by no means the fault of the shipbuilders'.[18]

Scott thought the discipline of a naval crew would be an 'immense acquisition'. He worried about his ability to deal with any other class of men.[19] On the vessel strict naval discipline pertained and although in fact *Discovery* was not in government service (and so not subject to the Naval Discipline Act but to Merchant Shipping Laws) she was run exactly as if all on board were under naval command. Each volunteer, whether sailor, officer or non-naval scientist, signed on under Scott as 'Master' and voluntarily accepted naval conditions. The scientists, including Wilson, were treated as officers and ate in the wardroom. Wilson was one of two doctors appointed. He was the junior to Dr Reginald Koettlitz. When he was appointed it was planned that he would be one of a landing party of seven to over-winter on the edge of the Antarctic, leaving Dr Koettlitz, the senior man, on the vessel. Scott wrote later that although this idea was abandoned 'there were few things for which we had greater cause to be thankful than it had originally existed, for the second doctor appointed to the expedition was Edward A. Wilson'.[20]

The main problems with the ship were firstly a persistent leak, a problem that came to be known as 'the Dundee leak' and which necessitated continuous bailing and repeated examination in dry dock. The leak became more troublesome as the boat approached the equator and the wood expanded and Wilson was one of the many who spent hours of his time bailing out the water. Secondly, in spite of the manufacturer's hopes, there was excessive fuel consumption and the boat was slow. To reduce coal consumption *Discovery* proceeded as much as possible by sail but soon fell behind the schedule that demanded that she reached New Zealand by late November and on to the Antarctic for the summer season of 1901–2. Scott abandoned the planned visit to Australia and decided to sail straight to New Zealand. This change meant that the expedition dogs and tons of equipment that had been shipped separately to Melbourne, had to be diverted. Such problems of course, were well out of Wilson's sphere of responsibility. When, after the expedition, he lectured to doctors in his medical school about the expedition, his main complaint in relation to the ship's construction related to water condensation, and drips. The skylights either let water drip straight into the cabins, or a frosty rime built up inside the skylights and dripped slowly onto the worktables. He said that he had to keep blotting paper to the ready to keep going, and 'to pretend not to notice'. A more aggravating problem was that metal bolts, driven through the skin of the hull, allowed moisture to condense inside the cabins, soaking and rotting the mattresses and bedclothes. Damp also extended under the bunks, either soaking clothes in the drawers or, in low temperatures, freezing them into solid lumps of ice. Wilson was concerned that dampness was the precursor of a chronic form of rheumatism and he himself suffered badly with aches and pains on the expedition.[21]

As *Discovery* proceeded on her way from England to Madeira, the officers and crew were able to get to know their new ship and each other. Officers and scientists had individual cabins, which opened onto the wardroom. As an officer Wilson ate in this wood-panelled room at a long central table, using monogrammed china, napkins and table linen. A calendar presented by Sir Clements hung on the wall, listing all the anniversaries (including Wilson's appointment), in Sir Clements' spidery handwriting. Naval stewards served at table and there was a piano at one end. Gilbert Scott, one of the mess stewards, found his hours of duty long. He worked in the wardroom from 5.30a.m. until 1.30p.m. and followed this up by work in the stores and further service in the officers' mess until 10p.m.[22] The wardroom quickly became the centre of activity: discussions, debates, chess and card games were played in a fug of tobacco smoke and more than a hint of coal dust that drifted up from the coal bunkers below. The wardroom and cabins were made of mahogany. Each cabin had a bed with lockers underneath, a chest of drawers, a cupboard, a writing table and a place for books. Wilson loved his; he loved 'its own particular smell, for they all smell, fuggy, but comfortable – a compound of boots, soap, toothpowder, damp clothes, towels and what not'.[23]

The separation from Oriana must have been seriously difficult for them both, but Wilson was not actually worried about her. 'My mind is absolutely at rest about Ory . . . I have a happy vision of the last that I saw of her and it will be with me until I come back again'.[24] He took to shipboard life and discipline well. He was busy throughout his waking hours both with medical and artistic duties. He made sketches and records of birds and other animals, he had to organise the drugs and surgical appliances in the ship's small hospital and he had to sort out the taxidermy equipment and the stationery. An important medical duty was to inspect and taste the food that was due to be eaten each day. This was to make sure that the tins were not 'tainted', a problem thought to be the cause of scurvy, the perpetual terror of long voyages. This disease caused fatigue, swollen spongy gums, bruises and sores in the skin, muscle and bone aches, blood loss, fainting and, in severe cases, death.[25] The doctors were obviously determined to do everything possible to avoid this appalling condition which is now known to be due to vitamin C deficiency. In the early 1900s this was not known; the vitamin was not to be isolated for another thirty years. Dr Koettlitz, Wilson's medical senior, was convinced that scurvy was due to tinned food fermenting and producing a poisonous substance, ptomaine.[26] To avoid ptomaine poisoning, and therefore scurvy, the tins had to be tested and tasted by Wilson each morning. This was one theory he did not question. He was inexperienced in clinical medicine and he accepted the views of his senior medical colleagues that putrefaction caused scurvy; certainly his opinion would not have been asked for or wanted. No suspicious tinned meat was ever eaten on the voyage due to Wilson's attention to this duty. For the rest he was 'in clover'. 'My mind wanders back through to three weeks of another and more beautiful life, those last three weeks in England, but I don't miss it in the least just for the simple reason that it seems to have nothing to do with this world'.[27] Though seasick, he kept going, visiting the bridge regularly and drawing birds and a passing Spanish fishing boat.

Who were his companions of the next three years? They were a relatively young group. The average age of the entire complement was 27 while the officers averaged 30. Robert Falcon Scott was 32 years old when he was appointed to *Discovery*. As an officer accustomed to the Navy's rigid discipline, he well understood the concepts of conformity and obedience. He had no previous polar experience; before his posting to *Discovery* he had been the torpedo lieutenant on *Majestic* and had previously served on *Rover*, *Amphion* and *Sharpshooter*. When appointed, he was supporting his mother and two sisters financially and the appointment was a unique opportunity for advancement, fame and excitement, although when he actually applied, his chances of selection as expedition leader seemed slim. His application was, according to Sir Clements, strongly supported by his captain on *Majestic,* Captain Egerton, but in fact there were considerable machinations on the appointments committees before the appointment was formally confirmed on 10 June 1900.[28] When Scott was appointed, Sir Clements sent him volumes of advice: about further promotion, about how to deal with problems and about the conditions in the Antarctic.[29]

Overall responsibility for the expedition was originally shared with Professor J.W. Gregory (1864–1932), who was appointed chief of scientific staff. Ongoing schisms between the Royal

Society and the Royal Geographic Society over the question of overall command eventually resulted in Gregory resigning and Scott being given complete authority and responsibility for the whole expedition. Sir Clements wrote:

> Before handing over charge to Scott it was absolutely necessary to get rid of the useless Joint Committee. . . . I had suffered almost intolerable worry and annoyance from them during the whole time I had been in charge of the executive work. It was certain that the expedition could never be ready to start unless Scott was given a free hand . . .[30]

The professor's name however became an integral part of the expedition. The hut designed by him in Australia and erected at base-camp in Antarctica was known as Gregory's bungalow. It was thirty-six feet square and had a veranda 'more suitable for a colonial shooting lodge than for a polar dwelling'.[31]

On 30 June 1900 Scott was promoted to commander. He began the enormous task of preparing for the expedition in August. His organisational skills were formidable, he was charming and – an unexpected bonus in the absence of a formal scientific leader and Scott's lack of scientific training – he had a sympathetic and intelligent interest in every branch of the scientific work being undertaken. This interest was a trait that Wilson appreciated. On the voyage each scientist was required to produce a notebook summarising his work, which was kept in Scott's cabin so that each could see developments in the others' departments. Wilson quickly grew to admire and like Scott greatly. He thought him a really good man. His initial impression was that Scott was very definite about everything and that there was no fear of the expedition lacking a sense of direction. He liked the fact that Scott joined in all the work rather than standing on his rank.

Second-in-command and navigator was Lieutenant Albert Borlase Armitage, (1864–1943). He was a merchant naval officer and one of only two officers on board with any previous experience of polar conditions. In 1894–87 he had been part of an expedition to Franz-Josef Land, a group of islands north of Russia discovered in 1873, as part of the Jackson-Harmsworth Arctic expedition, so Armitage's polar experience was considerable. On the 1901 expedition he was ice-master and took over the sledging organisation. Importantly, on the subject of Antarctic exploration, he favoured ponies over dogs for hauling sledges, arguing that Siberian ponies could withstand the worst conditions and could be eaten when they collapsed. He named his daughter, born when he was in the Antarctic, Cecily Markham, after Sir Clements.

Armitage was appointed to *Discovery* soon after First Lieutenant Charles Rawson Royds (1876–1931), Royal Navy. Royds volunteered to join the expedition. He was well connected and came with strong references. He was efficient and popular with everyone, responsible for the day-to-day running of the ship and managed the role of intermediary between Scott and the men with tact. Much of the relatively harmonious relations on *Discovery* were due to him. He took charge of meteorological observations and helped with magnetic observations. He was also, importantly for the *Discovery* crew, a talented musician. Sir Clements was happy with his appointment. He thought that Royds was a first-rate seaman and decided he should be 'one of the Antarctic heroes'.[32] He was also satisfied with the appointment of Second Lieutenant Michael Barne (1877–1961). Sir Clements wrote: 'a charming young fellow and so zealous that he would have thrown up his commission rather than not go and a relation of mine which is also in his favour'.[33] Wilson discovered also that he was a cousin of the Mrs Rice who had been so kind to him in Norway.[34] Barne assisted in magnetic studies and supervised the deep-sea temperature work and the deep-sea sounding apparatus. Reginald Skelton (1872–1952) was the engineer. Skelton's initial contribution in overseeing the construction of *Discovery* in Dundee helped greatly, it is agreed, to reduce the problems with the vessel. Skelton became the photographer of the expedition and helped Wilson to skin and preserve the catches.

The third lieutenant, Ernest Shackleton (1874–1922), was to become a famous British Antarctic explorer. He was 'an excellent and zealous officer, the son of a doctor at Northwoodbut from Ireland. His great grandfather was the Quaker Shackleton who was the instructor of Edmund Burke'.[35] Shackleton had a love of adventure and the gift of the gab. He was in the merchant navy and planning to marry his fiancée, Emily Dorman. He was keen to join the expedition to advance his career and to make a name for himself.[36] He was put in charge of the ship's holds, provisions and stores and his scientific contribution was deep-seawater analysis, for which work he received specific training. He was to leave the expedition in 1903, officially because of poor health, when he was replaced by Lieutenant George Mulock (1882–1963) who joined *Discovery* as cartographer and surveyor from *Morning* (the ship sent out to relieve the expedition). Wilson initially did not like Shackleton. He was probably a little overawed by Shackleton's gift of the gab, 'I don't care so much for him. He is so beastly scientific',[37] although as he got to know Shackleton better he grew to appreciate and like him. Sir Clements' assessment of Shackleton was altogether sanguine. He considered him steady, high-principled, full of zeal, strong, hard-working, good-tempered and well informed.[38]

Wilson's immediate superior, Dr Reginald Koettlitz (1861–1916), was a graduate of Guy's Hospital, London. Six feet tall, with a drooping moustache, and thirty-nine at the time of his appointment in 1900, he had also survived Arctic conditions in Franz-Josef Land. This experience had given him the wanderlust and before he joined *Discovery* he had travelled widely. Sir Clements wrote that he was zealous and painstaking, but that 'his mind perhaps works rather slowly and he has no sense of humour but, on the other hand he is thorough and perseveering'.[39] Koettlitz's previous experience allowed him to help with the sourcing of purchases at competitive prices, including tobacco (two shillings a pound) and boots.[40] As it was assumed that his medical duties would be light, he was also the ship's botanist. His views on scurvy were absolutely in line, however, with notable medical authorities of the time[41] and he wrote in the Guy's Hospital Gazette that scurvy 'would not be cured by seeking for substances that have ignorantly been called 'antiscorbutic' and that lime juice had 'no useful effect against scurvy'.[42] His opinion was not just based on theory. On the Franz-Josef expedition the crew had been given lime juice every day as well as eating tinned meat. In spite of the lime juice, all the crew developed scurvy and two died. We now know that this was not because lime juice is ineffective but due to problems with the preparation of the citrus fruits doled out on the expedition. Lime juice is less potent against scurvy than lemon juice and its properties were further diminshed during transportation from the West Indies to England. But Koettlitz could not know this and his experiences in Franz-Joseph Land focussed his attention forcibly on the erroneous 'tainted meat' theory. Although he was aware of the benefits of eating freshly-killed animals, his emphasis in the early part of the 1901–4 expedition was on avoiding bad tinned meat rather than insisting that fresh meat was eaten daily.

These were the officers who, along with three scientists (the physicist and magnetic observer Louis Bernacchi (1876–1942), who joined in New Zealand; the biologist Thomas Hodgson (1864–1926), 'Muggins' to the crew; and the geologist Hartley Ferrar (1879–1932)), sailed with high hopes, bound together in an expedition and adventure which they hoped would bring scientific, geographic and material gain.

Naval discipline, rules and regulations were immediately imposed. In-keeping with the class distinctions of the time, officers and scientists were housed separately from the warrant-officers and the sailors. Wilson would not have had much close contact with the crew members, although after the expedition he gave much help to Able Seaman James Dell, who suffered from an infection in his arm on the expedition and was unable to work for years. Dell eventually went on to serve in the First World War and outlived Wilson by more than fifty-five years. Pay was an obvious divide. Scott received an annual salary of £500 (£41 13s 4d per month),[43] plus his naval salary, which made his appointment financially attractive. Armitage received £450 annually, Koettlitz £400 and Wilson £200.[44] The seamen received £27 7s, plus their naval pay of just over £28.[45]

Within a few days afloat, routines were quickly established that remained much the same throughout the voyage. On week-days officers took watches, performed their naval duties and made scientific observations. Scientists used the tow net and performed water salinity testing and meteorology work. On Saturdays the ship was cleaned. On Sundays Scott inspected the ship and took the weekly Divine Service. Wilson worked hard from the start. He organised the stores and equipment in the sick bay. He sketched continuously despite the pitch and roll of the ship that made his work difficult. He wrote to his father:

> Painting a bird that is swinging through 30 degrees every few seconds is trying, things won't stay as you put them. Your water is hung on a hook, your paper is pinned on a board and you hold your paint box: you yourself are wedged into the bunk cupboard and kept there by a boot on the chest of drawers opposite. You put your paint-box down to settle a wing for the thirtieth time and down it rattles and the paint goes all over the cabin. You jump to save the paint box and the corner of the board tilts the water tin off the hook and it empties into a drawer full of clean draw-ing paper; while a running drip takes the opportunity of coming from the skylight on to your painting. . . . It's a strange life teem-ing with quiet fun and everyone thoroughly enjoys it all.[46]

Really he was in his element. As resident artist he was often called to record birds and specimens caught by the scientists. In painting he could capture an image that was too obscure or fleeting for the camera. He was 'precise and deft in all that he touched'.[47] He loved to spend time on the bridge with Royds, Barne or Shackleton, a welcome change from work below deck. Familiarity with Shackleton made him increasingly appreciate the Lieutenant's good qualities; Shackleton looked out for him and would call him whenever there were interesting specimens or a lovely sunrise to be seen. His particular charm for Wilson lay in his encyclopaedic knowledge of poetry, particularly Browning and Swinburn. 'He knows every bit of poetry that has ever been written and is always ready to quote it.'[48] Shackleton was to become one of Wilson's best friends, a friendship which lasted until Shackleton's own expedition in 1908 when, in Wilson's opinion, he did not behave well towards Scott and Wilson broke off the friendship.[49]

It took a week for *Discovery* to sail from England to Madeira. This gave the officers and crew time to know the vagaries of the ship and to start to forge themselves into a team. The scientists tested and used their oceanographic and other scientific equipment. Wilson was able to attempt to capture the beauties of the sea in his paintings. Other officers were busy with their duties; Skelton was fully occupied, in the engine room. When *Discovery* arrived in Madeira on 15 August coal replacements were needed because of the excessive consumption: a filthy backbreaking job and Skelton's temper was further strained because of pain from a tooth abscess. Presumably he had missed the dental check organised by Scott before the voyage.

Madeira entranced Wilson. He had never seen anything as exuberant and picturesque: the lush vegetation, the brilliant colours, the exotic birds. He explored the island and set to work with his paints. His was reassured by Oriana's unselfish letters, which freed him to take full advantage of all the expedition had to offer. 'Dear Ory, I knew you would turn out trumps and never give way to despair and sorrow at our parting'.[50] He was so anxious to capture everything that he was still busy sketching the harbour when the ship got under way.

6

To *the* Polar Ice

Discovery sailed from Madeira on 16 August. Since conservation of coal was such a concern, she progressed by sail as much as was possible. To use sail, Scott had to follow the Atlantic currents and winds south-westward to South Trinidad, relatively near to the coast of South America, and thereafter, south-east to Cape Town, New Zealand and the Antarctic. Progress was slower than planned and the engines often had to be fired up so as to try to keep to the schedule. Scott stuck to his plans to miss out Australia and to limit the oceanographic stops. The important date in his calendar was to be in New Zealand by mid-November so that *Discovery* would be on time to push through the Antarctic ice-pack in the Antarctic summer.

Now they were a few weeks into the expedition, the officers and crew were more accustomed to their routine and duties. Wilson remained in his element, his strength recharged by the life at sea. He reported to his family that he was well and that he had put on weight. He took part in everything that was going on. He made sketches of his fellow-officers; he worked. Apart from medical duties, his zoological expertise was needed. He trapped different species of birds and sketched the flying fish that rushed past, sometimes 'flying' onto the deck, and was soon very fully occupied with skinning and preserving. This smelly task took hours and hours and had to be done quickly on a ship that rolled and pitched tirelessly. At temperatures of 90°F, the carcasses could deteriorate so quickly that he sometimes had to put them straight into formalin because they 'were stinking by the evening'.[1] He taught his skills to Petty-Officer Jacob Cross who also became an expert at skinning. The days after leaving Madeira were taken up with medical duties, skinning and painting.

On board, the organised routine continued: naval and scientific work during the week, religious observance on Sunday. For recreation officers and scientists passed the hours with chess, discussions, deck games, listening to Royds (a talented player) on the piano and reading. Each officer in turns became mess president. His duties were to maintain acceptable standards of behaviour. Fines were levied (usually a round of drinks), if the president decided that there had been a lapse in etiquette. Regular slide lectures were started early in the voyage. Wilson's opinion of Shackleton grew steadily. He appreciated Shackleton's friendly help and admired the way that he worked so hard. Hard work was always a passport to Wilson's good opinion, so he was unenthusiastic about his immediate superior Koettlitz, who he thought did less work than anyone on the ship. His admiration for Scott continued. 'The Captain turns to with all of us and shirks nothing not even the dirtiest work'.[2] He wrote approvingly that Scott was very definite about everything he did, nothing was left vague or indeterminate, and that Scott had a really balanced head on his shoulders, was thoughtful, performed little kindnesses and was ready to listen.[3]

The early part of the voyage was important to Wilson for several reasons: he recorded what was thought to be a new species of a bird, a petrel, in South Trinidad. This bird was distinguished from the other (numerous) petrels, by being brown and nesting earlier and higher on the cliffs than pale-bellied petrels. It was named after him, *Aestralata wilsoni*, a real honour for the young naturalist (years later it was reclassified as a sub-species of the Trinidad or Herald Petrel). Secondly, he had to make use of the anaesthetic skills learned in the Cheltenham Hospital. Engineer Reginald Skelton's toothache became intolerable, the tooth needed to be removed. A makeshift operating table (a carpenter's bench) was rigged up, Wilson gave Skelton the ether anaesthetic and Koettlitz removed the rotten tooth plus a few bone splinters. The procedure was successful though the doctors must have reflected with relief on the ninety-plus teeth that had been removed before the voyage as well as the innumerable fillings. As he came round from the anaesthetic, Skelton's singing and swearing gave them all something to write home about.

The 'Dundee leak' soon affected the whole complement. Men and officers took turns to pump tons of water out of the ship at least once a day. The builders had hopefully predicted that because of the layers of planking used in her construction *Discovery* would not leak, so no flooring had been put in the holds to lift the crates off the bottom of the boat.[4] Water flooded into the hold, the crates were covered with slime and many of the tins were rusty. Shackleton was given the unenviable job of unloading, re-packing and restoring the crates, and Wilson and Barne were roped in to help. Work went on round the clock. All the stores had to be carried up to the top deck. Wilson said it was a 'slimy, stinking, filthy job' (Scott said he was conspicuous for his energy) made worse by the fact that the stevedores in the East India Dock had thrown half-eaten tins back into the store. The stench was so overwhelming that they had to make a ventilation hole. Although a floor was built for the crates and the situation in regard to the provisions improved, the leak continued to be a problem throughout the expedition, a problem made worse, conversely, by the layers of planking used in the ship's construction, which made it difficult to localise where the water was entering the ship and practically guaranteed that water seeped through the inner skin at quite a different place from its entry through the outer skin.

When any ship crossed 'the Line' (the equator), Neptune, dressed in seaweed, appeared by tradition to greet and initiate anyone crossing for the first time. The ceremony was officially fun but was also an excellent opportunity for the crew to enjoy the officers' and each other's humiliations. It could be a hazardous business. In 1901 on 31 August, crewmembers dressed as Father Neptune, his Queen and attendants (Tritons) held court on a platform twelve feet above a large canvas, seawater bath.

The initiates were Wilson, Ferrar, Hodgson and eight crewmen who were to be introduced to 'His Majesty' in turn, blindfolded, seated on the platform and shaved with a soot and tallow mixture by the 'barber'. The barber's assistant's role was to stuff soap pills into their mouths after examining their teeth with a screwdriver. After the 'doctor' had completed his examination, the victims were dropped down into the bath and 'half drowned' by sailors who sat on them. The ritual astonished Wilson. He thought it was barbarous and recorded it in detail in his diary.[5] He was lucky though; he was the first initiate and managed to fall backwards into the christening bath before the plastering began. Koettlitz managed to avoid the initiation for a week and was eventually let off. He was probably frightened for his dignity. After the officers, it was the sailors' turn. Eventually Neptune's Queen fell repeatedly into the salty bath and the ceremony ended with the men going to their mess with a couple of bottles of whisky to round off the evening. Scott said there was an orgy[6] which turned into a drunken diatribe against the officers and quartermasters.[7] Alcohol was a grumbling problem throughout the early part of the voyage. Wilson said that the crew sometimes played games with the daily rum ration; one man would drink the entire ration and so be 'comfortably fuddled' once a week. Sometimes they saved their rum tots until they had enough to get really drunk.[8]

After crossing the Line *Discovery* moved by sail but she sailed badly, pulling to the west. Scott writes that they got comparatively close to South America.[9] The engines had to be fired so that *Discovery* could travel southwards to South Trinidad Island (approximately 500 miles east of South America). She arrived at the island on 13 September. Wilson saw a small inhospitable volcanic island, of scientific interest but visited rarely. The land, covered with pale yellowish-grey craggy rock, rose steeply from the shoreline towards peaks topped with fern and scrub.[10] Huge numbers of crabs contributed to the surrealistic, nightmarish feel of the place: the shoreline was alive with crabs. There were large red and green ones with black staring eyes which glared bulbously at their visitors and which could run up and down a rock face and jump five or six inches; and land-crabs, anaemic looking and globular, like black-eyed apples on legs, quick to bite and hidden in every cranny and crack. Thousands of birds circled round and round as Scott, his officers and scientists landed to explore and collect specimens and climb to the fern line more than 1,000 feet above sea level. The visit was propitious. Scott had arranged the exploration with care: in all, sixteen types of birds were found, including Wilson's *Aestrelata wilsoni*. The birds were preserved and identified and the results, along with Wilson's illustrations, were presented later to the Royal Geographical Society.[11] Skelton, having recovered from his operation, began photographing in earnest. He also became increasingly interested in the scientific programme and learnt to help Wilson with the skinning.

Discovery moved on to South Africa by sail as much as possible. The days were busy with the scientists examining and preserving their new treasures. Wilson was hard at it, painting up his fish and bird sketches and endlessly skinning and preparing specimens, an occupation he thought very good practice for his temper and patience. His day began in the early morning and continued until 10p.m. on a ship that rolled so much that everything had to be tied down. Scott continued to be agreeably impressed with his new officer and wrote to Sir Clements that Wilson had the keenest intellect on board and a marvellous capacity for work. Scott said that one minute Wilson would be sketching the sunrise, the next a new bird and the next sketching something down the microscope.[12] But, in spite of all this activity, as at medical school, Wilson retained his 'inner voice'. Each Sunday he had a private Communion after the morning service and continued to trust in God's beneficial influence in his life. He did not forget Oriana's birthday on the nineteenth of September (she was twenty-seven) and he longed for her letters in Cape Town. When he got them they were numerous and long 'but then mine's a special sort of wife'.[13]

Discovery reached South Africa on 3 October. In spite of Scott's efforts to limit scientific stops and use sail whenever possible, she was nine days behind schedule and had only thirty tons of coal. Wilson wrote that the entry into Table Bay was memorable for the 'table cloth of cloud' dappling the peaks on Table Mountain.[14]

In South Africa, the Boer War continued and martial law was in place in Cape Town. Afrikaner guerrillas were close by but, in spite of this anxiety, the British community received *Discovery* with warm interest and enthusiasm; a visit of this nature was definitely a novel experience. Entertainment was provided separately for officers and men. Warrant Officer Ford, delegated to make a speech of thanks, said that 'whatever the future held, he dreaded more the half-hour before he made his speech'. He told his audience that all aboard were volunteers motivated by 'that love of adventure and carelessness about danger, which is the birthright of any Englishman'.[15] Wilson was entranced by the varieties of birds and made careful notes: gannets, cormorants, gulls and albatross. He climbed Table Mountain and fairly revelled in the flowers: irises, lilies and orchids – a new surprise every few yards. In Cape Town *Discovery* took on coal and then sailed to the other side of the cape to the naval base of Simonstown. Here full facilities were offered and seaman Gilbert Scott wrote that here he could finally get his clothes washed.[16] During the short journey between the two docks a heavy swell coming from the Atlantic demonstrated *Discovery's* remarkable ability to roll, frequently more than forty degrees.[17]

A patriotic welcome awaited *Discovery* in Simonstown also. In spite of the martial law, which meant that the crew had to have passes, the British Admiral made every effort to give assistance. The ship was extensively refitted, the engine overhauled and the rigging reset, all at no cost to the expedition, and a further inspection was made of the hull in the hope of tracing the cursed Dundee leak. The deck was scraped free of splinters and pitch, further provisions were supplied and hundreds of pounds of unaccounted goods and services were given. In fact the Admiral supplied Scott with virtually all his listed needs including, despite the war situation, three seamen. The men, employed for 1s 6d per day, brought the crew to full strength. One of them, George Vince, was to be the only man to die in the Antarctic on the expedition.

Importantly, since investigation of the South Magnetic Pole was an important part of *Discovery's* brief, comparisons of the ship's magnetic instruments with the South African land-based instruments were made. Navigators had known the importance of the magnetic compass as a means of finding north (and south) from as early as the twelfth century. These magnetic readings differ significantly from the true north and south and by different amounts in different parts of the world. Ocean charts that show the difference between the magnetic readings and the true north, the magnetic declination, were first produced by the famous astronomer Edmond Halley in 1700–1 and were based largely on his observations on board HMS *Paramore*. The charts did not, as Halley had hoped, solve the longitude problem, but they were still of practical help to sailors in correcting the compass. Even in the eighteenth century Halley knew that the direction of the magnetic field changes with time, so revisions of the chart were needed and were made regularly in his lifetime; indeed, these recordings are still made today, though from satellites and aircraft. In Scott's time it was known that observations made at sea were not as accurate as land recordings, so to get as precise a picture as possible multiple observations needed to be recorded from all around the oceans and the magnetic equipment on ships needed to be compared with accurate values on land. *Discovery's* magnetic equipment was compared with readings in South Africa and afterwards in New Zealand. These recordings were a routine part of the remit of all expeditions to far-off places, but *Discovery* could contribute most significantly because, as there is so little land in the south, sea-based observations were of considerable navigational value. In addition to the observations, Scott hoped to get far enough south to make useful additions to knowledge on the South Magnetic Pole's location.

The halts that gave Skelton much work in the engine room found Scott working also. In Cape Town he dismissed one member of the crew who he thought a troublemaker and docked pay and leave from two in the engineering section for drunkenness (Seaman Scott says they were flogged).[18] Skelton wrote that drink continued to cause a lot of problems.[19] But Wilson did not comment on this; every halt was a source of increasing pleasure. He relished the opportunities to explore and enjoy each country's flora and fauna, a heaven-sent opportunity for a naturalist. In South Africa he also made interesting contacts with new colleagues and was introduced to the local wine. He labelled and packed the Trinidad birds and eggs to be taken home. He wrote to his father that 'the callow chick was growing into a fat, burly, brown-faced man'; by now he had put on a stone in weight, in spite of all his physical exercise.[20] Fears of a recurrence of his chest problems were forgotten.

Social activities abounded. The Admiral hosted a dinner for the officers and a party for the whole crew. The Philosophical Society hosted a dinner, the Governor a picnic and dinner. When he left South Africa, Wilson wrote that they were all sorry to part with the wonderfully unselfish and thoughtful Admiral and his sister. Scott wrote that *Discovery* steamed out of the harbour, 'accompanied by the cheers of the warships and proud of this last tribute of their generous sympathy'.[21] He wrote, 'Thus ends an experience that makes one truly proud of a glorious profession – added to the practical benefits of our visit one is deeply touched by the real kindness and sympathy shown by all; men and officers have had a glimpse of the real efficiency and meaning of our navy.'[22]

Discovery left South Africa on 14 October 1901 en route for New Zealand, twelve days after her intended departure. She followed a direct route, out of the normal shipping lanes. There were no communications; the ship was on her own. All too soon it was evident that, despite the South African naval efforts, the leak had accompanied her. The crew had to work at the bilges each day, pumping out the seawater. But, by the end of the month they caught the westerlies and the 'roaring forties'[23] which meant that they could make very good daily runs, often clocking up more than 200 miles a day.[24] Scott explains that *Discovery's* high rounded stern gave extra buoyancy though made her more difficult to steer.[25] As the ship sped along the noise was deafening, the timbers creaked and groaned, doors banged and everything not fixed down skidded away merrily as towering waves crashed on the deck. Wilson described the rolling powers of the boat as 'tremendous', though this never upset him. Once, when there was a particularly mountainous wave, the ship swerved round, the quartermaster was thrown over the wheel and Scott himself was submerged and had to cling grimly to the rails to avoid disappearing over the sides, as the monstrous sea swept over the deck and the spray dashed as high as the upper topsails.[26] This particular rogue wave flooded into the wardroom smashing the crockery; the deck was awash with dog kennels, planks, ropes and life belts. Polar clothes, just brought out of the hold, were soaked.

Painting tested Wilson's patience. Any brush or tube of paint that was not fixed ended up on the floor which became a jumble of books, ink, candle grease, medicines, soapy slops and paints. But it was 'a happy little hovel' that Wilson did not want to change.[27] For painting on deck he used a sketching box hung round the neck. This kept the paper comparatively dry most of the time. Scott wrote to Oriana saying that not only would Wilson's intellect and abilities win him a great name but that his kindness, loyalty and good temper were possessions that had endeared him to all his companions. He goes on, 'How truly grateful I am to have such a man with me and how much it lightens my responsibilities'.[28] Clearly, Scott already felt a degree of confidence and ease with Wilson that he could never allow himself with naval personnel.

By early November the sea was calmer but the ship went on rolling. Wilson thought that if it suddenly became still, everyone would be sick. In spite of this, he wrote, the most accurate work continued every day, occasionally enlivened by a burst of nautical language. He wrote that the beauty of the wild ocean is indescribable. The colouring and lights and shadows, the heavy black snow squalls are all so in-keeping with the rush and roar of the wind that is driving us on and the heavy thud of the seas as they break against our sides or on our deck.[29]

He was delighted by the number and variety of birds, recording twenty to thirty albatrosses at one time, plus every type of pet-rel, a small whale (of twenty feet) and gold crested penguins. He rigged up his laboratory on deck, doing his work and writing at a big (immobilised) table. His family was always in his thoughts and he celebrated Guy Fawkes Night on 5 November with his father's gift of a bottle of cherry brandy.[30]

By mid-November, *Discovery* had arrived at a position of particular magnetic interest. Anomalies had been noted to the north of the magnetic pole, close to the position they were at. Scott took the ship south as far as he could to record these changes. To do this he moved even further away from normal shipping lanes,[31] so there was considerable concern when a fire broke out in the forecastle early on 14 November. Although it burnt the woodwork considerably, it was quickly extinguished, but was a salutary reminder of the terrible dangers of fire to wooden ships, especially in such lonely waters. Wilson hoped that it was 'a scare that will be the best guarantee against fire in the future'.[32] He was always fatalistic, writing later in a way that can scarcely have been enthusiastically read at home when the letter eventually arrived: 'I hope I shall come back to you all. I believe I shall, but one cannot tell what God has planned for one's immediate future'.[33]

They were so far south that they moved into ice, seeing the first piece on 16 November, only the size of soup plate, but causing great excitement and winning Barne a bottle of cham-pagne for spotting it from the bridge. This foretaste was soon to be followed by large white and green lumps, moulded by the sea into fantastic shapes. This was a completely new expe-rience, as was the ice pack, two or three feet thick. To break through the solid pack the ship rode two or three feet above

the ice, then crashed down on it, her weight cracking and splitting the floe which cast a ghostly glimmer by night but was
distinctly un-ghostlike as they scraped and banged against the
boat. Wilson was on deck for hours recording the white and
grey snowy splendour, full of movement and sounds, so different to the white stillness of Davos.

Discovery pushed her way through the ice with her engines
fired. She reached as far south as 62.5° S by 139° E, less than
200 miles from the Antarctic, but her coal reserves were low,
there were time constraints and the ship needed to get to
New Zealand to pick up more equipment, provisions and,
importantly, the husky dogs.[34] She was turned north-east again
reluctantly as soon as the magnetic readings were completed.
This run was notable again for the quantity and variety of
birds, which followed the ship, a novelty for most of the crew
who, taught by Wilson who had the knowledge to identify
and name the visitors, began to learn to recognise them. These
birds varied from albatrosses with their wingspan of several
feet down to little petrels that flitted under the foaming wave
crests. Wilson listed the southern fulmar, black and white
Antarctic petrels, snow petrels, sooty albatross, as well as
cape pigeons.[35] To accurately record a new bird, and following
Ruskin's precepts, he painted its head, profile, top view, feet
and legs and completed the record with two full views from
front and back and one recording the outstretched wings.[36]
This time-consuming business, reminiscent of Stubbs' careful
depiction of horses, showed how he learned to understand his
subjects' structures. He and the other scientists remained keen
to get further specimens and Scott occasionally stopped the
boat or used a variety of devices to capture the specimens 'on
the hoof'. Wilson never seems to have worried unduly about
killing animals for scientific purposes or for food in spite of his
devotion to St Francis.

On 22 November Wilson was delighted to engineer an
unscheduled stop at Macquire Island (he had to bribe Armitage
with a bottle of liqueur to get Scott's permission).[37] Macquire was
the only stop made on the way to New Zealand and is a small

island 600 miles south-west of their destination. Scott, Barne and Wilson explored it together. Here, Wilson saw thousands of penguins for the first time standing to attention like ranked armies of soldiers. Very little was known about penguins in the early 1900s. Penguins in general and emperor penguins in particular were to become his great scientific interest. In Macquire Island there were no emperor penguins but two other varieties, the brightly-coloured king penguins and smaller orange crested penguins. Both sexes busily guarded their single egg, which they balanced on their feet whilst they sat on their haunches, their toes in the air. The birds tried to save their eggs from the attentions of the visitors by pecking at the men or whacking their legs with their flippers. The noise was deafening, the smell of guano (excreta) overpowering, but the men managed to take two live king penguins with them to New Zealand.

On this island the trio found a hut left by sealers with a superb collection of bird skins, some of them rare, including an albino penguin with a gold crest. All the specimens were neatly preserved, labelled and wrapped in paper. No sign of the collector could be found; there was certainly no corpse. But after some hesitation they left the collection intact, shutting the door on probable future deterioration.[38] Koettlitz dashed about happily collecting botanical specimens, Ferrar gathered geological specimens. Skelton was busy with his camera. Two seals were sacrificed in the interest of science. The visit, of just a few hours, was an undoubted success. Not only did the collections increase, but also the larder was stocked with meat and about a hundred king penguin eggs. The doctors and Scott understood that fresh meat might be helpful in the war on scurvy although they continued to think that putrefaction of tinned meat was of the greatest importance. On the island, Wilson, as always, made watercolour illustrations of the birds. These and his skins were sent back to London from New Zealand. He became so enthused by all the new wildlife that he started planning a project close to his heart. He aimed to write and illustrate a book on the birds seen on the expedition.[39]

As they progressed to New Zealand the routine continued, as did the debates and talks. For men brought up in
Victorian England debates were a routine feature of life and
these continued throughout the outward journey. One subject
that was debated was 'the ethics of sport' and Wilson was
practically alone in arguing that sport was a relic of barbar-
ity. He prophesied that it would die out in time in civilised
nations and thought that only Scott had realised previously
that the question of sport had another side to it.[40] He kept up
his correspondence, to be posted when possible, and he made
regular diary entries. He continued to admire Scott, writing to
his parents:

> He is a most capable man in every way. . . . I admire him
> immensely, all but his temper. He is quick tempered and very
> impatient, but he is a really nice fellow, very generous and ready
> to help us all in every way and to do everything he can to ensure
> us the full merit of all we do.[41]

Three days after leaving Macquire Island, Auckland Island was
seen. *Discovery* arrived off Lyttleton Head at midnight on 28
November 1901. The ship was berthed the following day and
given the usual enthusiastic, helpful welcome, one that rivalled
Cape Town. Wilson had his first glimpses of a land that he and
Oriana grew to love and hoped to return to.

Discovery was put into dry dock and again every packing case was unloaded under Shackleton's supervision.
Exhaustive attempts to find the cause of the leak were so
unsuccessful that when she put to sea again the leak continued with such vengeance that the mortified local contractor
felt obliged to organise further investigations at his own
expense. Although more defects were made good and the
ship thoroughly examined, water continued to get in. 'The
Leak' was well advertised; the sight of water pouring from
the ship in dry dock was all too newsworthy. From London,
Sir Clements had to assure the press that such leaking was
normal in a wooden boat and that Scott never thought it a

serious threat.[42] In New Zealand new additions to the crew included the physicist Louis Bernacchi. He and Armitage were soon busy co-ordinating magnetic readings on the land and the ship to validate the ship's compass .[43]

This was a stop that found Wilson over-busy. He had to get all his specimens ready to be taken back to England and to do this he was given access to the taxidermy room in Christchurch Museum plus an assistant, but even so the work was numbing. The skins of fifty wet greasy king penguins, that had been dead for a week, had to have the fat scraped off. He also had to blow and clean all his Penguin eggs. After days of this round-the-clock activity he decided to leave the ship and move to a hotel. He wanted to have a last taste of baths, space and good food. In a letter to his mother who had sent him a book of prayers and two photographs, a picture of St Francis and the altar of the church where he was married, he wrote, 'You must be very grateful to Ory because she has made all this time so much happier and easier for me'.[44]

> When I look back upon the extraordinary way in which it was made possible I feel more certain than ever of the reality of a guiding hand that leads us through all sorts of strange and unexpected and at the time most disagreeable paths very often, always with the very best end in view, so long as our wills are entirely given up to the guide who knows so much better than us what is best for us.

Perhaps thinking of his illness, he went on, 'Thank God Ory and I have seen and marvelled at so much obvious guidance even against our wills in our lives that we neither of us have the least fear of the outcome in the future'.[45] His passive acceptance of fate and his religious beliefs may seem simplistic. His younger brother Jim, who went on to be a Church of England minister, seems to have had grave reservations about Wilson's religious writings being made public and destroyed them after his death.[46] But Wilson was not a weak man. He had no fear for his own mortality and he had the courage to face up to issues that demanded action. Comments such as these should be read in relation to his day-to-day life, in which he trained himself to accept the good and the bad, health and illness, happiness and unhappiness as part of his allocated lot. Injustice would always rouse him. But, as he wrote in Cambridge, ordinary day-to-day life should not need planning and worrying, but rather, grateful acceptance.

In New Zealand the officers and crew took part in the obligatory social engagements. The officers were on a charm offensive, answering questions and criticism with care. Scott lectured on the background and goals of the expedition. To the usual question 'Why?' the reply was that the question missed an important point: 'How could they expect to know anything of the mighty universe of which the world is but an atom, if they didn't explore to its uttermost recesses their own little globe'.[47] Thousands of curious people came to visit the ship. The crew were plied with drink. The mess was presented with a 'pianette', bought for £40 for use in the Sunday services. Railway journeys to Christchurch were provided free, as was the port docking. Donations of £1,000 were given towards expedition costs.[48]

A visit to see traditional Maori dancing was arranged. Wilson decided that the demonstration was hypocritical and artificial. These Maoris, who normally dressed in European-style clothes, whose children spoke English and who attended a very English church, were dressed in grass petticoats and feathers and sang and danced and did the Haka. He thought that this was 'a childish presentation and a piece of barbarous acting, reminiscent of a pantomime'.[49] But his love of New Zealand was permanent and Oriana kept contact with and visited her friends in New Zealand for the rest of her life.

There were crew changes. Scott dismissed some of the crew and crewman Clarence Hare, destined to be of considerable medical interest in Antarctic folklore, joined the complement as did a flock of forty-five terrified sheep[50] and twenty-three howling sledge dogs, their kennels, exploration equipment, huts for the magnetic work, an extra forty tons of coal and

1,500 gallons of paraffin. Well-wishers stood around to wish 'Godspeed' to the overloaded boat, and usefully, to pull the fighting dogs apart. The expedition issued four sets of postcards to be sent at various stages of the voyage and an issue was sent from New Zealand.[51] The Eastern Extension Telegraph Co. allowed final farewell messages to be sent home free of charge and the ship was repainted.

On 21 December, after a service led by the Bishop of Christchurch, *Discovery* left Lyttleton to sail to Port Chalmers for coaling. Wilson said goodbye to a Dr Jennings, a general practitioner, with whom he had become friendly and who invited Wilson to return to his home after the expedition and suggested that Oriana make her home with his family when she came to New Zealand. The departure from Christchurch was another media event. Crowded steamers sailing beside *Discovery* hooted. A marine band on board one of them played 'Say Au Revoir, but not Goodbye' and followed them out of the harbour.[52] Thousands cheered and roared, their shouting mingling with the bleating and barking of the animals. Gilbert Scott said he 'had never seen anything like it'.[53] Luckily *Discovery* was clear of the harbour when Charles Bonner, a very popular crewmember, fell off the mainmast, dying instantly as his brains splashed over the deck. Wilson wrote that some of the men wept like children. Although drink was not mentioned in the coroner's report, engineer Skelton saw the accident as an object lesson for those who had been drinking too much ashore.[54] Seaman Robert Sinclair, who had apparently given Bonner the whisky bottle he was waving when aloft, stole away at Port Chalmers.

Forty-seven officers and men left the wharf at Port Chalmers on 24 December 1901. A cable was wired to the crew's relatives. Wilson wrote that they were all fit and well and that the men were almost without exception, an exceedingly nice lot. *Discovery* left for an unknown future in the unexplored Antarctic. Although Scott hoped for success in the exploration and for new scientific developments, his private fears were that the expedition's successes could be handicapped by inexperience. As the ship departed, he wrote 'The last view of civilisation, the last sight of fields and trees and flowers, had come and gone on Christmas Eve 1901 and as the night fell, the blue outline of friendly New Zealand was lost to us in the northern twilight'.[55] Wilson wrote, 'Now, neck or nothing, we are fairly started, thank God, and by His grace we shall do something worth the doing before we sight New Zealand and civilisation again'.[56]

Discovery was now totally isolated. She headed, in thick fog, towards an uncharted region barely visited. She had no wireless communication (Marconi had only recently sent the first transatlantic communication from Cornwall to Newfoundland); the long silence had begun. As Wilson sailed south, his father gave a paper to the Cheltenham Natural Science Society outlining the plans, questions and conjectures of the current phase of Antarctic exploration. Although anxious on his son's behalf, Dr Wilson was extremely proud that he had been chosen to go. But Dr Wilson and all the family knew only too well that whatever happened, even in the most fortunate circumstances, they could not hope to hear from their explorer for many months.

Discovery's instructions were firstly to get further south than previous expeditions, to explore and chart the coastline and as much of the land as possible and to find a suitable base from which exploration and scientific work could take place. After leaving New Zealand the ship proceeded south under sail whenever possible, or by steam; rolling, rocking and creaking in the waves. After eight days, thirteen sheep had died. Skelton hoped that the remainder would last until they could be killed and frozen, so that mutton could be enjoyed in the Antarctic winter. The huskies, so untamed that Armitage's Samoyed dog Vinka would not go near them,[57] did better; each dog had a man assigned to look after it. For the human crew discipline remained strict: when two men complained about the food (seal meat was strong with an unpleasant dark mahogany colour after cooking and had to have every scrap of blubber removed to make it palatable),[58] Scott paraded the offenders before the ship's company and stopped their grog and tobacco indefinitely. Christmas celebrations, apart from a religious service, were postponed because of Bonner's death, although a few gifts were opened. New Year's Eve was celebrated, however, with a whisky punch that was laced with too much lemon essence, but well received. Officers and scientists joined hands, sang *Auld Lang Syne* and became comfortably merry. Wilson reflected on the year past, full of happiness, and the year that would now have to pass before he could have any news of what was dearest to him. He wrote that they 'must feed their happiness with hopes and recollections and trust God. I well know that three weeks with my Ory is food enough for three years' hope and three years' happiness. God Keep her'.[59]

For some days *Discovery* progressed in thick fog. This caused Scott a feeling of isolation. No birds were visible through the pall and he was fearful that some monster iceberg would loom up.[60] When the fog lifted, they did indeed see their first icebergs, tabular with flat tops and sides, about a hundred feet high and several hundred feet in length. The ones they saw at first seemed impressive but were to prove small compared with the vast ice blocks that they were to see later. These were several miles long and coloured white and turquoise. On the *Discovery* expedition the largest iceberg seen was approximately seven miles long and 200 feet high.

On 3 January *Discovery* crossed the Antarctic Circle. Captain James Cook first crossed this geographical landmark in 1773. It is approximately 66.33° S and is the northern limit of the region where the sun is visible for twenty-four hours in the summer solstice. On that day *Discovery* nosed into the loose ice pack, her engines rumbling as she advanced cautiously through alternate open strips of water and ice, vibrating as the ironclad prow forced an advance. She got through the ice pack in less than a week, occasionally stopping to catch seals for the specimen collection and for the larder. The scientists recorded their soundings; the water depth was recorded as 2,040 fathoms.[61] Dredging was not successful; the lines got tangled and

Skelton thought that the scientists might be good at looking down microscopes and making theories but that they were devilish poor at the practical work, or getting their specimens.[62] Wilson enjoyed escaping onto the ice on the halts. His artist's eye absorbed the huge variety of ice shapes and their colours, blue, green and orange, and he sketched as many records as he could, which he worked up later. Meanwhile each stop produced more dead animals. The deck became littered and gory with skinned seals and penguins, which hung with the Lyttleton sheep on the freezing rigging. By now Wilson could remove skin and blubber in one go and separate them afterwards to prevent rancid meat and a deteriorating skin. He was covered in blood from head to foot. The stench on board became progressively worse.

Christmas was celebrated on 5 Jan 1902. Interestingly in relation to the later development of scurvy, seal liver was eaten for breakfast and seal kidney for lunch. This offal contains vitamin C. Wilson provided the cake, the holly, the crackers and cards. To mark the day *Discovery* pulled against a berg and skiing was attempted for the first time. The skis were long wooden planks and the skiers used a single stick, Nordic style, grasping the stick with both hands. Wilson thought it great fun to see to see all the men staggering around in all directions. No great urgency was put into mastering the technique. Scott had received conflicting advice on the subject and was a novice himself. After this expedition Scott realised the importance of skis in the Antarctic and took an experienced skier on his next Antarctic expedition.

After the Christmas celebrations *Discovery* pushed on through the floe, stopping intermittently to water the ship. Snowstorms limited visibility,[63] while ice ground the ship's sides and crashed against her bows. Shackleton spied a Leopard seal – a rare prize – and he, Wilson, Skelton and others caught the huge animal. It was eleven foot long, with a mouth full of dangerous looking teeth, a head bigger than a Polar Bear and weighing nearly a ton. Inside its stomach was an emperor penguin, swallowed nearly whole.[64]

By 8 January they had pushed through the pack ice and into clear water. The crew had their first view of the blue outline of Victoria Land Mountains. Wilson felt that a more glorious sight than the midnight sun was impossible to imagine.[65] The high snow peaks were covered in golden clouds and flooded with sunlight, 'a sight to remember'. The next day they were at Cape Adare, the north-west extremity of the Ross Sea. For the crew, arrival at the Antarctic was an amazing event. Many on board must have wondered if they would ever get this far.

7

Entering Antarctica

To grasp Wilson's experiences in the next months it is important to have some understanding of Antarctica. It is the coldest, windiest and most remote place on earth, a vast continent, a tenth of the world's landmass, spanning fourteen million square kilometres. In Wilson's time this was unknown, the continent unexplored. Although we now know that it contains most of the world's ice and water, has very little rain (less than in the Sahara Desert) and is covered by an ice cap that (Scott's scientists later discovered) flows slowly towards the coastline, this was all challengingly mysterious in 1902. The *Discovery* crew were soon to experience the freezing blizzards, the winds that can reach up to 200 miles per hour which sweep down from the Pole to the coast and the piercingly low temperatures. They were to learn that Antarctica places huge physical demands on its explorers who battle against cold, wind, dehydration, physical fatigue and in the interior, altitude problems. Nutritional science was in its infancy in 1902.

Discovery reached the coast via the Ross Sea, named after Captain (later Admiral, Sir) James Clarke Ross (1800–62), the nineteenth-century English naval explorer. This approach from New Zealand is frequently taken today, although many cruise ships reach Antarctica by the shorter route from South America, arriving at the South Shetland Islands and the Weddell Sea. The Ross Sea is bounded by the Great Ice Barrier, which (as was deduced on the Discovery expedition) is a huge floating shelf of ice between continent and sea. Although by 1902 men had landed, the interior had not been explored and the land and coastline had only been charted to a limited extent.

His first sight of the mainland moved Wilson. It was a glorious sight. Bathed in midnight sun, the blue outline of the high mountain peaks of Victoria Land, to the south-east of the Ross Sea, stretched back for miles, tall peaks jumbled with golden clouds. He drew the perpendicular cliffs, the drifting ice packs and the icebergs 'in all stages of perfection and decay and demolition'.[1] He was to go on to make an important panoramic sketch of the coastline, later reproduced by the Royal Society.[2]

The ship anchored off the peninsula, Cape Adare. This was a familiar name to the crew; in 1896 *Discovery's* own physicist, Bernacchi, had wintered there on the *Southern Cross* expedition. The 9 January 1902 was a day that Wilson would always remember; he landed on Cape Adare with Bernacchi and others. They had instructions to lay the first of a series of canisters that would show their route and their plans to a relief ship. Nothing illustrates the isolation of the early explorers better than their arrangements for communication. On Cape Adare the men left two cylinders, one containing official letters, the other private correspondence. These cylinders, at their pre-arranged message points, were a sort of life-saving paperchase and remarkably, these first cylinders were actually found by the relief ship the following year.[3] Bernacchi and Wilson had to manoeuvre their whaler through long stretches of drifting ice pack to get to the coast and eventually they landed on a pebbly beach backed by dark hills that rose steeply to 1,000 feet. This was the beach where the *Southern Cross* expedition had been based and that expedition's hut, surrounded by its messy remains and supplies, was still there. Wilson was fascinated by the 'millions' of Adélie penguins and their rookery: 'Such a sight.' These energetic little birds, named after the wife of a French explorer, d'Urville, nested on the beach and high up onto the hillside. The shore was the colour of anchovy paste from their guano, the place 'stunk like hell' and the noise was deafening.[4] Light brown Skua gulls circled and swooped on any unfortunate chick that had strayed from its parent. The scenery was captivating to an artistic eye: the brilliant sun, the calm sea dotted with bright white pack ice, the sparkling summits of the Admiralty Range. The hut that the *Southern Cross* expedition had left behind was in good condition and Scott opined that it would last for years in the Antarctic climate.[5] The hut still contained items that were useful to them: coal, Bovril, lime juice and dynamite.

From Cape Adare the coastline winds southwards past numerous islands and bays into McMurdo Bay, which was to be their eventual base, and eastwards along the sheer front of the Great Ice Barrier. *Discovery's* instructions were to sail to the eastern end of the Barrier, claiming for Britain any landmasses found.

After depositing the mail, *Discovery* moved on from Cape Adare, sailing south towards McMurdo Sound. Plans to find a clear channel close to the coast and to identify likely harbours were thwarted as the sea conditions changed rapidly. For the first time the crew faced the dangers of the ice pack. A thrusting tide encircled the ship with ice before avoiding action could be taken. Although full steam was applied, *Discovery* was in real danger as the combined forces of tide and pack ice carried her, seemingly inevitably, towards a chain of icebergs. Eventually, as the tide slackened and gaps opened in the ice, she escaped into open seas. Armitage, the ice-master, showed 'admirable patience' throughout.[6] The experience was unforgettable. Once in the open sea, *Discovery* moved on slowly southwards, the crew recording a coastline that had been completely unknown.

A hundred miles south, *Discovery* weathered another battle with the elements. On 13 January a furious gale, which reached force eleven on the Beaufort scale, blew up. Wilson said that there was nothing they could do but shelter in the lee of a volcanic rock island, Coulman Island, with the engines going as hard as possible to prevent *Discovery* being wrenched from her mooring. The wind raged, the rigging was encrusted with ice, as the ship strained to keep her position.[7] Wilson seemed to feel no fear; everything had God in it and was part of God's plan. He saw the storm with artistic eyes as the wind sent sheets of spray in every direction and waves dashed themselves into white clouds over the bergs. 'A wonderful sight, this heavy wind with a clear sky, no snow, but sunshine'.[8] But though he was content to entrust his fate to his maker, he understood nevertheless the baptism that Scott and the naval officers were going through. When the storm finally burnt itself out, Scott and the geologist Ferrar managed to land on the island to leave the second of the canisters for the relief ship; this time a red container lashed to a post high above the sea, placed on a red-painted rock.

On this occasion Wilson did not include any messages; he thought it was likely that the containers would stay undiscovered, for years. His time was spent painting and preparing specimens. So little was known about the Antarctic that this was a unique opportunity for him to show to the waiting world, through his paintings, the awful, still beauty of the place: how the rocky cliffs, their heads bathed in a benediction of sunlight, dropped into the sea; how crevasses looked pale pure blue and green against the white surface snow; how the water looked green in the sunlight. But although he wanted to enthuse and stimulate, he wanted above all for his recordings to be accurate. He used his well-tested method of colour memorisation to record the scenes, noting the colours on his pencil sketches and painting them up later, a form of colour shorthand. This was an ideal technique for the challenging conditions. As well as drawing he collected new specimens of seals, albatrosses, penguins and whatever came to hand. He used an empty coalbunker for his skinning work, getting into the bunker by dropping down the coal shoot. He stored the skins in an old packing case; not a very successful arrangement because coal dust got into them.[9] He wrote of his 'beastly butchers work, a duty much against the grain',[10] but he never seems to have questioned this role. He seems to have had a consistently objective and scientific approach towards the necessity of animal slaughter for mans' benefit.

The early days had their excitements. He saw thousands of emperor penguins in big colonies. On 15 January, he, Ferrar and two seamen went to collect a number of these birds that they had already killed, but left on a floe that was drifting away from the ship. The men got to the birds by jumping across the water from floe to floe and hauled the catch back onto a bigger floe. When this broke away, the four found that they too were drifting away from the ship. Before help arrived they had to keep themselves alive in the low temperature by running about and chasing a few remaining live penguins. They were stuck for more than five hours; a near disaster that earned the watch officer a serious reprimand.[11]

Discovery advanced southwards along the coast of Ross Island. On 19 January in the 'most perfect weather on earth' Wilson set eyes on one of the domineering landmarks of the area, Mount Erebus, the world's most southern active volcano. Its smoking crater towered to 12,000 feet. It was an 'immense table mountain bigger than that of Cape Town . . . no such glorious sight could be seen anywhere in the world' and to cap it all he was seeing it on a Sunday.[12] He sketched on deck all day. *Discovery* reached McMurdo Bay on 21 January. Scott had hoped that the McMurdo was actually a strait that cut off Erebus and her sister mountain, Terror, on islands. If this had been the case *Discovery* could have sailed past them and claimed to have achieved the most southern sea journey. But McMurdo was a bay and, Wilson wrote, the dream was short-lived.[13] So *Discovery* turned north again and then east to reach the Barrier. On her way she passed Cape Crozier. This Cape was to become a famous landmark in Wilson's story, but now it was just another of the pre-arranged message points. Here he, with Royds and Scott, rowed between lethally teetering icebergs to make a landing, leaving their two red cylinders, full of letters in a conspicuous spot in the centre of a penguin rookery. As they rowed, the swell 'broke into the caves and arches and tunnels of the bergs with appalling force and thunderous noises'. Wilson wrote that the water was full of penguins, popping in and out like black rabbits and also dotted about the bergs. He and Scott climbed a nearby mountain and from this vantage point they had a view that had never been seen before: the open sea with its streams of pack ice and then the cliff of the Ice Barrier, stretching away as far as they could see with, behind it, miles and miles and miles of ice plain, smooth under a glorious setting sun, its long undulations stretching southwards into infinity.[14] He brought back an albino penguin, which he planned to present to the British Museum. The crew were by now interested in penguins. Gilbert Scott described this one as pinky-brown with a white throat.[15]

As *Discovery* sailed round Cape Crozier en route for the Barrier, Wilson wrote that the shoulders of Mount Terror towered above them; the rock showing through the snow was blood red, he thought due to iron oxides.[16] He was keen to see the Barrier at close quarters. It had been well described by Ross and part of *Discovery's* brief was to investigate it. The Barrier, later renamed the Ross Barrier, blocks the south side of the Ross Sea like a flat shelf of ice hinged onto the coast. Its undulating surface is intermittently thrown into disarray by high pressure ridges and crevasses. When he saw it at close quarters, Wilson was disappointed; it was 'not stupendous in any way' but 'an endless low cliff of ice, all white, varying from a hundred to a hundred and fifty feet'.[17] Skelton thought that previous observers had exaggerated the sight, though he did wonder if the *Discovery* crew found the Barrier less awesome than expected because it was so much smaller than the enormous mountain ranges they had sailed past.[18] *Discovery* progressed along the Barrier, never more than a mile away from it, taking soundings every four hours,[19] and dredging beautiful collections of starfish, sea urchins and other treasures. Wilson saw everything with an artist's eye. He and Scott complimented each other. Scott, a natural writer, described all their experiences expressively and Wilson drew everything evocatively: caves, fissures, bergs, inlets, and wind-blown snowdrifts.

By late January 1902 *Discovery* had reached Ross's furthest position. From here he had reported possible land in the southeast. The *Discovery* crew, searching 'from below and aloft' were unable to see any land and Scott wondered if Ross's report could have been biased by the strange optical illusions so common in Antarctica.[20] He was keen to get to the eastern end of the Barrier and wrote that *Discovery* was making rapid progress, so much so that not only the engineers but also the engines were eager to see what lay ahead.[21] But as they passed Ross's record they began to see upturned bergs with earth and rock embedded in them. This must mean land. Fog stopped further observations until late on 30 January when they saw ice sheets of more that 100 feet in height. Wilson wrote that these were obviously supported by land and that evidence of land under the ice was becoming increasingly obvious.[22] But no actual bare rock was seen until, as the bell rang for the evening meal, 'real live rock' was spied high up. This confirmed land and was the first Antarctic discovery of the twentieth century. The land was named King Edward's Land, after the monarch who had given them 'Godspeed'.[23] Then *Discovery* turned back for McMurdo Bay. Ice was forming rapidly; they needed to get back to the western bases before they closed off. From their base on McMurdo, sledging parties would set out to explore the continent.

On her return along the Barrier, *Discovery* anchored in one of the inlets. A magnetic party went south. Weddell seals were killed for food and skiing was attempted. Scott did not think it was as good a sport as he had expected. The wind had raised irregular waves in the snow, called sastrugi, and predictably everyone fell and fell again. On 4 February the two observation balloons that had been transported all the way from London were finally landed. The idea behind this (some thought foolhardy) ascent, was to get a panoramic view of the southern parts of the Barrier, an idea suggested by Sir Joseph Hooker (1817–1911) the eminent botanist, doctor and traveller. The balloons only had baskets big enough for one passenger and when the first had been filled with hydrogen Scott, knowing 'nothing whatever about the business' as Wilson wrote,[24] made the first ascent. He rose to 800 feet. He saw the Barrier surface far to the south and could pick out Armitage's sledge party returning to the ship some eight miles distant. Shackleton made the second ascent and took photographs. Wilson refused an offer to take part. He said it was an exceedingly dangerous amusement in the hands of inexperienced novices. He said that 'the one man who had had instruction did not go up and if some of these experts don't come to grief over it out here, it will only be because God has pity on the foolish'.[25] The attempt was not repeated. Whilst the sledging party were away Scott, conscious of the dangers of scurvy, ordered the 'murderous' killing of yet more seals. By now the team were relatively quick at killing and skinning, but hauling the carcasses back to the ship remained tremendously tiring.[26] Wilson got sick of skinning, an endless job.

On 8 February *Discovery*, her rigging crusted with ice, re-entered McMurdo Bay and anchored in her winter home. Arrival Bay was a sheltered harbour, safe from ice pressure and with a good shoreline. Wilson wrote that they were protected from the south-east winds by hills. He could see Erebus puffing smoke and Mount Terror, and a mountain range that caught and reflected the pink glow of the sun with its wonderful violets night and morning.[27] The crew named their new base 'Hut Point'. It was to be their base for the next two years. From the base they were to do magnetic surveys, collect botanical and geological speci-mens and make sledging expeditions. These sledging expeditions included a 960-mile round trip towards the South Pole of which Wilson was one of the three members. In addition he was to cre-ate his principle artistic legacy. He painted and sketched tirelessly to create a record of Antarctica, its animals and birds.

After *Discovery* anchored, the shore huts and the kennels were erected quickly and stocked with provisions. This was to ensure that any land party was self-sufficient; it was all too possible that sections of ice could break away carrying *Discovery* with it, or that the ship could be damaged or even sunk by icebergs or shifts in the pack ice. Now the crew faced their first Antarctic winter together. More than forty men, with no communication with the outside world, on a continent bigger than all of China and India. Discipline remained strict. Wilson wrote in his diary that the cook was put in irons for insubordination and there was a lively scene on deck as he fought and was very obstreperous, but that having been left outside during the day, 'Brett came to his senses when he thought of being out of his bunk and in the cold for the night too'.[28] Wilson's early days ashore were spent in local exploration, testing sledges, skis and crampons and gaining experience with the dogs. Scott had received somewhat conflict-ing advice about dogs and only three of the officers had had any useful previous experience. Scott's polar model was the famous Norwegian explorer Fridtjof Nansen (1861–1930) who had made expeditions with and without dogs, but who was uncertain whether dogs or skis would suit Antarctic conditions and who thought that a combination of dogs and horses might be best on the Ross Barrier.[29] None of the party had trained full-time with the dog teams, as is now known to be important. Only Armitage, Koettlitz and Bernacchi had used sledging equipment before and when Armitage and Bernacchi tried the dogs they could not control them. Wilson, with the others, had to learn sledge craft. He steeled himself to whip the dogs to get them going. He would also have to steel himself to kill them. He read, walked, climbed and tried to ski, a purposeless activity he thought.

To the physical dangers of the Antarctic must be added the discomfort of lying in a cramped three-man sleeping bag. Wilson soon experienced all these problems and described the privations, discomforts and dangers of exploration vividly. He was part of the first exploratory sledge journey ever made on the Antarctic. His trip was only for four days, but this was enough to highlight the men's inexperience. No dogs were taken. Wilson with Shackleton and Ferrar were instructed go to White Island, one of the rock-topped islands on the Barrier south of Hut Point, to find out what lay beyond the island. The three men set off pulling their sledge, decorated with the sledging flag designed by Sir Clements, and displaying the Cross of St George prominently to show that each man was first and foremost an Englishman.[30] They set out on 19 February. As they knew nothing about the terrain they took a skiff, in case they had to cross water. They expected to get to the island by nightfall but, 'Man proposes and God does the rest'.[31] They discovered the mirage effects, so problematic in Antarctica. The island never seemed to get closer. Clouds and snow seemed to merge on the horizon making it difficult to make out landmarks and impossible to judge distances; ten miles could look like a mile. During this short expedition the trio pulled at a mile per hour for twelve hours in snowdrift. They learnt how blizzards could reduce visibility to a few feet. They all got frostbitten. Shackleton's cheeks and ears were white, Ferrar's nose also. Wilson's toes hurt excruciatingly.[32] When frostbite happens it is important to try and restore the circulation and Wilson rubbed Shackleton's ear so hard with

gritty snow that he peeled off all the skin and so learnt the benefits of gentle massage.[33] The three found that their boots and
socks froze together because the sweat from their feet had lined
the boots with ice. Only when they camped and pulled on their
long fur boots, did their feet begin to thaw. They cooked supper
(cocoa, pemmican,[34] biscuits, butter and jam) and then began
to get into their furs, an exhausting business. He wrote that the
furs were simply awful; they got frozen stiff like boards.[35] He
was troubled by thigh cramps which attacked him whenever he
moved and when they got into the furs, 'the other two were
bricks to me.... They dressed me first and having dressed me,
they put me on the floor and sat on me while they dressed each
other. At last we were all in our wolf skins and pimmies and
settled off to sleep huddled together to keep warm. We lay on
our Jaeger blouses, but the cold of the ice floor crept through
and the points of contact got pretty chilly'.[36] All three slept in
one big bag. Wilson said he longed to turn over but could not,
because he would have upset the others. So he laid still, drops of
rime dripping on his face and with his nose being tickled by the
reindeer skin hairs of his sleeping bag.[37]

They would probably not have been aware of just how much
the cold affected them. Apart from its direct effect on their body
temperature the cold would have affected their movements.
Our normal body temperature is 37°C, (or 98'6°F as Wilson
would have recorded it), but as the central (core) temperature
drops, so our ability to co-ordinate diminishes. At 36°C, our
grip strength diminishes and it becomes difficult to put thumb
and fingers together or even move the fingers normally. In their
little tent even routine tasks would have become a challenge
and they would have become slower as they dressed, packed
up their equipment, or just moved about the tent. The effort
of erecting the tent or getting the cooker to work would have
become increasingly difficult. Wilson would not have known
the reasons behind this, but he must have been aware that they
fumbled slowly with accustomed tasks.

They knew the importance of layering. To combat daytime
temperature they wore Burberry tops and trousers, woollen

balaclavas plus windproof coverings and mufflers on their head and neck. Under the Burberries were thick, double-knit woollen vests, woollen shirts and woollen sweaters. On their lower halves they wore thick 'long-johns', two pairs of trousers, three or four pairs of socks and reindeer-skin fur 'finesco' – which became stiff and immobile in the cold and were topped by puttees to keep out the snow – or boots. Gloves were half mitts, which never came off; removable mitts, which covered the thumbs and fingers; and a third pair of fur mitts, hung around the neck. Wilson also wore a knitted cummerbund reaching from his chest to his hips, anchored by shoulder straps. At night they took their wind suits off and changed their socks for sleeping-socks. Wilson, like everyone else, discovered that perspiration froze quickly and his outer clothes trapped the sweat so that he walked in a sort of armour, rigid and difficult to move in. Nothing could be dried except the socks, which had to be changed night and morning to prevent frozen feet.[38] When the day boots were taken off they had to be shaped so that the men could squeeze into them the next morning.

Late on 20 February, they reached the summit of White Island at 2,700 feet. Here they could look over the goal of their future explorations. They saw a wonderful sight: as far as the eye could see was a level ice plain, the true Great Barrier surface, with a range of high snow-capped mountains, the sun setting behind them, to the west. Shackleton took bearings and angles, Wilson sketched. Then they picnicked on hot cocoa and bacon. They could feel justifiably proud of their achievement. This first exploration was successful in that it established that there was a safe route to get onto the Barrier and then south. This, they thought, would be an ideal first provision depot on the Barrier. The expedition also demonstrated graphically the problems of exploration and the need to get really familiar with their equipment.

At base-camp in the last days of the Arctic summer, the men began to improve their sledging and skiing techniques. Scott had also received conflicting advice about skiing and most of the officers and men had no experience whatsoever before their early attempts on the expedition. Scott's personal experience of snow was that of throwing snowballs at his sisters in Devon.[39] When Nansen advised him on skis, neither he nor the ski-makers advised on ski-skins, which would have helped the skis to grip on an ascending gradient.[40] The skis that the expedition used were wooden ones; seven feet long and weighing about 20 lbs a pair. Ranulph Fiennes says that Scott sensibly decided to assess skis by trial and error using realistic sledge loads and knowing that the extra weight on the sledges was 100 lbs for five men.[41] Scott was very conscious of the ratio of the weight to be pulled versus the pulling power. Skelton later complained of 'articles being weighed to a hundredth of a pound, instructions being given not to beeswax the thread or to go easy with the brass eyelets on account of the extra weight'.[42] Skelton thought Scott was right to be careful but thought that he was fussy and he could not understand why Scott listened to Shackleton so much because Shackleton was just an ordinary 'gas-bag'.[43] Wilson does not comment on this but he would have been aware of the weight implications. By dint of experience the teams found the benefits of skis: crossing crevasses was safer and skis distributed the men's weight more evenly on soft ground, stopping them sinking deeply into the snow. Scott arranged for the men to practise skiing and Chief Steward C.R. Ford broke his leg when he was several miles from the ship. Wilson and Koettlitz went to get him. They splinted the leg and then brought him back to the ship and set it. Skelton commented acerbically, 'Of course he is a very clumsy sort of person. I don't think anybody else would have succeeded in breaking a leg'.[44] But Ford was conscious of Wilson's sympathetic qualities as a doctor, 'the way he nursed and washed me and fed me when I was ill will never be forgotten'.[45]

On 4 March 1902, a party of twelve set out for Cape Crozier, the Cape at the entrance to McMurdo Bay. They were to update the information left in the canisters for the relief ship and to deposit new mail. This expedition proved how right Scott was when he worried about the crew's inexperience to cope with Antarctic conditions. He wrote later that the sledges had been badly packed and that their knowledge was inadequate about the food, how to set up the tents, how to use the cookers or even how to put on their clothes.[46] Wilson was not on this expedition though he took part in the eventual search party and looked after the injured. He wrote that the party took two twelve-foot and two eight-foot sledges, commenting that these would have to be hauled up snow slopes of 500 feet and then carried across a rocky plateau and then down to the sea ice.[47] Lieutenant Royds was leader. After four days he decided to split the group when conditions became atrocious. Himself, Koettlitz and Skelton went on. Nine men were sent back to base under Lieutenant Barne's inexperienced leadership. When this group became caught in a blizzard, Barne decided to try to make a break for the ship. Two men in the party, Steward Clarence Hare (who had joined in NewZealand) and Able Seaman George Vince, had fur finesco rather than boots on their feet. None of the party had crampons. As they slithered and slipped on the icy surface Hare and Vince got lost. Vince shot down a slope and disappeared forever. Hare, 'a thin youth of eighteen', also disappeared, it was feared, permanently. His arrival back at the ship after forty-eight hours, with no signs of frostbite or any other problem was a great relief. Scott 'looked as if he thought that the dead were really walking in'.[48] Hare had been unconscious for thirty-six hours. His last memory was of going towards a patch of rocks, which he hoped would provide some shelter, wearing his heavy woollen blouse and gabardine outer clothes over warm under-clothes. Perhaps he survived the sub-zero temperatures because he managed to position himself in the lee of a rock, pulling his arms inside his blouse and covering the opening in his hood, so saving his hands and face from freezing.[49] He must have been covered with enough snow to give insulation and warmth but allowing sufficient air for breathing, a sort of primitive snow hole and a technique since developed for survival in extreme conditions. At base, Hare had no signs of frostbite but was found to be hypothermic. Wilson, 'deciding to run no risks, put him in blankets in the magnetic observatory at an initial environmental temperature of 17°F, higher than the temperature recorded on the ship which was 0°F, and warmed him slowly to 34°F, when he moved Hare to the sickbay. Hare had no long-term effects.[50]

Wilson looked after the other survivors too. A seaman had an ear the size of a cricket ball. One man's fingers were so bad – enormous blebs full of fluid with the ends of the fingers like dark purple grapes – that Wilson thought they would drop off. But the ulcers gradually healed and the nails grew back, though the skin always remained ultra-sensitive.

This expedition as a whole was a failure, but the groups' experiences resulted in modifications being made to the equipment and their provisions. Royds reported that the soups took too long to dissolve, wasting fuel, and that butter (unsurprisingly) travelled badly. There were problems with whistles, knives, the top of the tent and the string on the food bags. He said that daily food bags were a good development.[51] These problems could be addressed, but nothing could be done about the extra weight caused by frozen perspiration. This was a problem throughout the expeditions and in this instance a three-man sleeping bag weighing 45 lbs at the start, weighed 76 lbs at the finish.

On 21 March they celebrated the anniversary of *Discovery's* launch at Dundee, appreciating Wilson's father's cherry brandy and cigarettes at dinner. This was followed by a discussion on the title for the winter magazine they were planning. They chose *The South Polar Times*. Wilson continued busily looking after his patients, drawing, reading and starting preparations for his last outing before the winter: an expedition to leave food depots for the following year's sledging expeditions. This was an expedition that was planned to last for three weeks; in the event, and in spite of warmer sleeping bags, snow shoes and each man being put charge of his own equipment, the outing was not a success. The dogs refused to pull, some even refused to stand, and had to be dragged. Excessive mirages made distances impossible to judge. On their first day out, 31 March, they only managed five miles in five hours. When they camped the temperature was so low that any piece of metal they touched, the cooker or even a spoon, stung the skin like a hot iron.[52] Wilson wrote:

> In the morning you put on frozen socks, frozen mitts and frozen boots stuffed with frozen damp grass and rime and you suffer a

good deal from painfully cold feet until everything is strapped on the sledges and you are off to warm up to the work of a beast of burden. There's a fascination about it but it can't be considered comfort.[53]

After four days they decided that it was too cold for sledging and turned back, depositing a provision cache on the ice. Once they were heading homeward the dogs pulled as fast as they could. They kept their sledge flags flying. Wilson thought that the flags would show the ship that they had not turned back because anything was wrong.

Soon *Discovery* was frozen in. The forty-seven men were to winter further south than any other human beings. They could not know what precisely to expect, but Scott emphasised the potential dangers. He reminded the men that blizzards could develop so rapidly and with such force that anyone could become completely disorientated and lost a short distance from boat or hut, as was to happen. Being caught in an Antarctic blizzard is like trying to see through the inside of a table-tennis ball; there is virtually no vision. Koettlitz lectured the men on the dangers of frostbite but he lectured monotonously and failed to capture their interest. General duties and mess companionship continued. In April, Wilson followed the tracks of emperor penguins going north. Although he was interested in all Antarctic wildlife, these were the birds – their broad yellow head patches merging with a golden wash on their upper breasts – on which he would become a particular authority. They caused great interest because so little was known about them. It was not even known where they spent the winter, though it was thought unlikely that they would have evolved specifically to breed on the polar ice. Skelton suggested that the birds spent the summer on water in the south, before migrating north. It is now known that against enormous odds, emperor penguins battle over a nine-month period to produce a single chick in the depths of the Antarctic winter.

On 23 April the sun disappeared, leaving the men to the polar winter and almost complete darkness for almost four months. Throughout the winter the doctors' duties were to keep the officers and sailors healthy in the long, dark, freezing days. Scurvy, the dread of all long expeditions, was their biggest fear and was in fact to erupt, though when he lectured on the *Discovery* expedition later, Wilson was sure that every possible precaution had been attended to.[54] The actual cause of the disorder was not known and ascorbic acid's effectiveness was not unequivocally shown until the 1930s, but Scott, Koettlitz and Wilson would have known that James Lind, an eighteenth-century naval surgeon, had conducted the first ever controlled trial on the problem using citrus fruits amongst a variety of other treatments. He achieved a complete cure in two sufferers with two lemons and an orange each day for a fortnight. Others with the illness, given different treatments, did badly.[55] Scott and his doctors would have been well versed in the fact that when James Cook took citrus juices on his long sea voyages, not a single man died from scurvy and that the Royal Navy had adopted this cure with initial success. But they would also know that by 1900 the lemon juice preventative treatment had lost support. They could not be expected to understand the subtleties of this 'sea change', or why lemon juice had apparently become ineffective. In fact, the juice's apparent inefficiency was an unlooked-for result of a series of political and economical decisions. During the European wars of the 1800s, Britain had started to buy limes from the West Indies instead of European lemons. Limes are less effective than lemons against scurvy.[56] To make matters worse, the juice was bottled under conditions which damaged the heat-sensitive vitamin, so it is hardly surprising that the citrus fruit given out in the later part of the 1800s was not effective.[57] Fresh meat was thought to give protection, but even if this had been so, the Navy issued much tinned meat. These decisions inadvertently set the scene for the return of scurvy. In 1900 the prevalent opinion and the advice accepted by Wilson and his superiors was that scurvy was due to micro-organisms in tinned food, the so-called 'taint', though a serious effort was always made to provide fresh meat. Killing parties were out whenever the weather permitted. Although the *Discovery* expedition had its fair share of scurvy, the accepted medical advice was followed.

In addition to scurvy there were other medical worries. 'Polar Anaemia' had been reported on previous expeditions and Wilson took specimens of blood throughout the expedition to check for anaemia. This problem was thought to be due to lack of light and to cause depression, aggression and sometimes psychoses. To get light into the ship, Scott provisioned 1,500 gallons of kerosene for lanterns, candles and a windmill generator for an electric circuit. The generator was a constant source of irritation to Skelton because it kept breaking down in the high winds and it was eventually demolished,[58] but the reason for the attempt was absolutely sound.

Men living closely together in a dark, monotonous environment with little outside activity, posed a potentially explosive situation, but throughout the long Antarctic winter there was no hint of mutiny, no serious violence and no communication breakdown, although there were obviously irritations and quarrels. The ship was run through a three-way hierarchy: officers, non-commissioned officers and ratings. Benacchi, who had been on the non-naval *Southern Cross* expedition, wrote later that the formalities at dinner helped to preserve an atmosphere of civilised tolerance such as had seldom been found in polar expeditions, and that the naval tradition was of infinite benefit.[59] Wilson had no criticism of the discipline. He probably thought that it was the natural way to run an expedition. He continued to admire Scott and appreciated the fact that he took on the role of scientific leader; Scott was endlessly planning new theories and new methods of observation and Wilson thought that he did it well. Wilson himself took part in the overnight rota for meteorological observations and had by now become so friendly with Shackleton that the two took daily walks to nearby Crater Hill to make the recordings from a spirit minimum thermometer and an aneroid barometer. He never tired of Antarctica's beauty but he despaired of recording its true colours: Mount Erebus with its roll of smoke, lit up by beautiful pink and lilac opal tints against a sky of pale yellow. The stars were brilliant and the sky a deep ultramarine blue.[60]

The 'activities' programme included moonlight football, amateur theatricals and animated weekly debates. The first edition of *The South Polar Times* was presented to the Captain after dinner on the first day of the winter. It was edited by Shackleton the first winter and Barnacchi on the second, and produced every month. The format was: an editorial, a summary of the events and meteorological conditions of the month, scientific articles, caricatures, acrostics[61] and puzzles. Everyone could contribute. Articles, poems, drawings, cartoons and quizzes (hotly contested) were submitted and editorship required tact, but Shackleton was successful and the magazine flourished. Wilson and Shackleton arranged an 'Editor's Office' in one of the holds, furnished with packing cases and lit by candles. Shackleton fixed a rope to the door to allow him control of who came in. Wilson was an important contributor. He made sketches, drawings and silhouettes and wrote articles. He wrote 'Notes on Penguins'[62] and drew no less than three penguins on the title page of the first issue. He thought that the first edition was 'thoroughly appreciated', even by those who had been caricatured.[63] It was hoped that publishing a volume of copies of *The South Polar Times* after *Discovery*'s return to England would help the expedition coffers. Eventually 1,000 copies were produced, costing seven guineas each initially,[64] later ten guineas. Smith Elder Limited produced these copies and reproductions now change hands for hundreds of pounds. The originals of *Discovery*'s Polar Record Journals are in the Royal Geographical Society in London. *Terra Nova*'s journals are in the British Library.

Scott wrote that although it was difficult to say who was the most diligent, he thought that it was Wilson who was always at work. He wrote that Wilson was always performing a hundred and one kindly duties for all on board.[65] Wilson certainly continued his demanding regimen. His day started with the milk and tinned food check. At 7.30a.m. Ford, the chief steward, woke him with, 'Dr Wilson sir, milk inspection sir'. Often he found that the condensed milk had gone off and he wrote of the joys of tasting mouthful after mouthful of sour milk as soon as he had got up. He also had to sniff the tins: meat, sardines, fish and soup.[66] Then he checked the ventilation in the living room, a task he did with such thoroughness that occasionally people appeared for breakfast in fur mitts as protest (Koettlitz preferred a cigar-laden fug and eventually Scott had to give orders about when the skylight should be opened). The next task was the 8a.m. meteorological observation, afterwards, supervision of bird skinning and working up sketches, preparing drawings for *The South Polar Times* and making zoological notes. He did a second meteorological observation with Shackleton, climbing to 950 feet, up Crater Hill. During these months he converted his rough sketches of the coastline of Victoria Land into an enlarged and detailed record. Although he worried that so much close work under acetylene gaslight would damage his eyesight, he does not seem to have had particular problems.[67] He wrote to Oriana:

> this work of Antarctic exploration is very different from the work I had planned for myself some years ago. And yet I do honestly believe that God's will is being worked out for us in what we are doing and though it may seem to some more 'worldly' and 'scientific' than 'spiritual' yet there is a spiritual work to be done here. And as for its main object, the acquisition of knowledge pure and simple, surely God means us to find out all we can of His works, and to work out our own salvation, realising that all things that have to do with our spiritual development 'are understood and clearly seen in things created' and if it is right to search out his works in one corner of his Creation, it is right for some of us to go to the ends of the earth to search out others.[68]

The winter routine started with breakfast from 9 to 10a.m., consisting of porridge, bread and jam, supplemented on two days a week with seal-liver. Afterwards the deck was cleared and daily prayers observed. The morning's work was followed by tea at 2p.m., an informal meal, perhaps the most enjoyable meal of the day; nearly everyone had toast smothered in butter. Dinner was a formal affair of soup, meat (tinned or fresh) and dessert. The weekly president enforced rules of etiquette: no betting, no contradicting the president and no consulting reference books. He often had to impose the fine of a round of wine and after the meal there was often a stampede to the library to check a fact or two, despite *Discovery* having sailed without an *Encyclopaedia Britannica*. Dinner began and ended with grace and after the meal there was a toast to the King's health. To while away the evening the officers played bridge, whist or chess; read or listened to the gramophone. Nearly all the wardroom smoked, though Wilson mostly did not, and by the end of the evening the mess was a fug, much to the annoyance of non-smokers. Mess bills were one of Wilson's duties; he did this duty carefully, but disliked doing it because he thought it a complete waste of his time.

The two hourly meteorological observations included night duties which all the officers did in turn, some more willingly than others. Armitage and Koettlitz eventually had little choice but to volunteer at the Captain's suggestion. Wilson and the other officers sometimes had to crawl to the observation hut in blizzard conditions. They clung onto a guide rope (often buried in snow) and got some flitting vision by carrying hurricane lamps. Wilson wrote that ten yards from the ship 'you could be as completely lost as ten miles'.[69] Thirteen different observations had to be made including cloud cover, temperature and weather conditions. It was the most exhaustive and detailed record and in bad conditions the whole procedure could take a long time. The officers took turns at the night readings, staying up all night to make the two-hourly recordings.

Throughout the winter from Monday to Friday routine duties took place. On Saturday there was a general clean up for the Sunday inspection when the men had to line up on deck in two rows in the freezing conditions. Following inspection there was the church service and then the much-anticipated mutton for dinner. Baths were organised once a week; Wilson, like other officers, had his in his cabin. The debates, scientific and non-scientific, showed the men's range of interests. Topics included: favourite poets, Tennyson or Robert Browning (on a vote Tennyson won); the nature of the Great Ice Barrier ('in which everyone had to speak for twelve minutes')[70]; women's rights ('we all have to speak, or rather we all do speak at these entertainments and those who don't feel equal to talking sense, talk nonsense')[71]; and conscription. Wilson's biggest contribution was to the debates on seals and penguins; 'seals' lasted for over four hours.[72] 'Penguins' was a lively little debate and he thought he had picked up some new ideas from other people. Throughout the winter the scientists and officers lectured, to the mess deck in 'Professor Gregory's' villa, on sledging, geology, wireless technology and other subjects of interest. Royds entertained them by playing the piano, sometimes for hours at a time. He also organised a slide show.[73]

Wilson often thought of home. He wrote to Oriana when it was Easter time in England that he thought of the freshness and green and colour of home. He thought of the feathery willows of Crippett Wood and the squirrels and the wood anemones. He wrote that there was no sadness in his thoughts but only a longing and hope and belief that he would enjoy them again with her.[74] He knew that joining the expedition had been the right decision. He only wished that he could show her the beautiful Antarctic mountains, the ice and the sky.

All holidays were celebrated to relieve the monotony. The 15 May was Lady Markham's birthday. Victoria Day was celebrated on the Queen's birthday, the 24 May, and Skelton's birthday, Scott's birthday and the anniversary of *Discovery's* arrival in London, were all reasons for a refill of the wine glasses. The biggest celebration was reserved for Midwinter Day on 23 June when the mess deck was gorgeously decorated with wreaths and garlands of coloured paper. This was an old naval custom. The men put out their pet photographs on the mess deck tables and the stoker's table produced a magnificent ice statue of a frost king with a crown.[75] The tables were decorated with artificial holly and lots of little union jacks. There were menus (one now in the British Library). Each man received a card from Oriana and a gift from Royd's mother.[76] Skelton took photos, which came out well. Christmas lunch was turtle soup, a 'generous helping' of mutton, mince pies and jellies, washed down with an 'excellent dry champagne'.[77] They sang solos, duets, part-songs and they finished off the evening with excellent port and Auld Lang Syne; a riotous success. Later in the week a play, starring Frank Wilde (who had been on the expedition to Cape Crozier, in which Vince had died) in 'Ticket of Leave', was another success. Gilbert Scott, who looked extremely pretty as a female,[78] and another seaman, supported Wilde as his ladies. Two of Wilson's anniversaries were celebrated in the winter – his wedding on 16 July and his birthday on 23 July; he was thirty and wrote in his diary that he was as childish as ever.[79]

For the first time, as the long monotonous Antarctic winter drew on, irritation and moodiness creeps into even Wilson's diary. Like others reliving their feelings in their diaries, he wrote that he had never realised, to such an extent, the truth that 'familiarity breeds contempt' and he wrote that

> it is just about as much as I can stand at times and there is absolutely no escape. I have never had my temper tried as it is every day now but I don't intend to give way. It's a hard school down here but I wouldn't have missed it for the world.[80]

What caused this is not known but the long weeks of darkness with no exercise would take their toll on any vigorous man. But the return of the sun on 22 August was an occasion for happiness. Wilson and Shackleton climbed Arrival Hill to see 'the sun, the whole sun and nothing but the sun' and pronounced the event a great joy.[81] Wilson described the faint red glow over the hills and said there was enough diffused daylight to read the observations out of doors without a lamp. *The South Polar Times* came out on 26 August. The crew's winter confinement was finally over.

Preparations for sledging were started. Modifications were made to the sledging equipment. Dog harnesses were designed and produced. Tents were altered. Roomier three-man sleeping bags were made. The sledge runners were sheathed with nickel-plated steel. Food supplies were weighed and divided into weekly or daily rations and put into little linen sacks ready for the expeditions.

Trials were begun at the end of August. Scott concentrated on dog trials. He had already decided that the main expedition of the Antarctic summer of 1902/03 would be a journey south to set a southern record and Wilson was his first choice as his companion. Wilson was surprised but delighted. He wrote to his mother, 'I believe I shall survive this trip all right and if I don't I shall still feel that I had no reason to refuse it and was meant to go; it lies straight in my path and I am not going to shirk it. To-morrow is my last night in bed for three months'.[82] Why Scott chose Wilson is uncertain; there were three officers with previous polar experience and a shipload of disciplined naval men who could have been chosen. Probably Scott, feeling the loneliness of command, felt at ease with Wilson in a way that would have been impossible in the naval hierarchy. In many ways Wilson's was a complimentary character to Scott's. Where Scott was agnostic, Wilson was deeply religious. Where Scott was ambitious, Wilson was content to be a facilitator and not a leader. Wilson was able to put his point of view in a way that Scott could accept. He was self-controlled and detached, whilst Scott could, and did, show his temper. Wilson's influence and advice was felt before they started out. Scott's original plan was that two people should make the journey, but he deferred to Wilson who favoured three on the grounds that a third person could seek help if one was injured. Shackleton became the third man. Scott's plan was to set out in mid-October with the dogs. Barnes would leave earlier to lay a depot, Bluff Depot, at 79.30° S.

They hoped to reach the Pole. Wilson wrote that they would go as far south in a straight line on the Barrier, reach the Pole if possible or find some new land. To get there would mean crossing 1,480 miles at sixteen miles per day for 100 travel days. He knew how demanding the expedition would be but he thought that he was prepared for all its trials. Also, although unconcerned with personal fame, he knew that success would bring huge prestige to the expedition. But he wrote: 'I am hoping to be back at the end of two years and to see what my wife is as a companion'.[83]

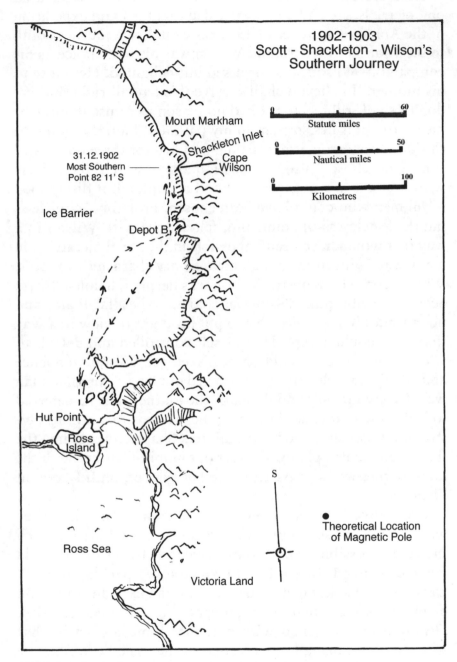

1902 Southern Journey

8

Furthest South

The arrival of spring in late August 1902 meant sledging sorties. Funding for the expedition was only guaranteed to the end of the Antarctic summer, i.e. early 1903. After this time, unless Sir Clements had raised further funds, *Discovery* would have to return to New Zealand. The activities during the summer would therefore be: scientific work, exploration and, most importantly, a new 'furthest south'. The aim was to push over the Great Ice Barrier as far as possible and even get to the Pole. Support parties would haul supplies onto the Barrier; the bulk of the hundred-day journey would be done by Wilson, Shackleton and Scott.

Their early experience on the Antarctic had highlighted British inexperience. The dogs' teams had modified harnesses that needed testing, as did the pros and cons of large or small dog teams. Scott planned a series of spring expeditions and Wilson was on one of these in early September, a survey of the coast to the north of their quarters and a trial for the dogs. The group included Scott, Shackleton, and Wilson in one tent and Skelton, Ferrar and a Bos'un, Feather, in the other. The group travelled northwards along the Ross Island coast taking four small sledges and fourteen dogs, each sledge pulled by three or four dogs depending on sledge weight. Shackleton and Wilson had a heavier sledge and four dogs, 'two pullers and two sooners as they are called. Why? because they would sooner do anything than pull'.[1] For this sortie Wilson and Shackleton shared a three-man reindeer-skin sleeping bag with Scott. Each night before pushing into the bag they took off their finesco fur boots, turned them inside out, then peeled off two pairs of socks, leaving the third pair on, to be covered by night socks. The two soaking pairs were put inside their shirts to dry in relative warmth.[2] Wilson discovered that he was a good sledge cook, an important attribute since fuel consumption was a critical part of any expedition. They used a Nansen cooker, designed by the Norwegian explorer and still used. The cooker sits on a primus stove and has two chambers, an outer one, in which snow and ice are melted and an inner one, in which the food is cooked. Wilson found that he could light the primus, melt snow in the outer section for tea and cocoa and cook the food in the inner part in about twenty minutes. He thought that anyone who doubted his abilities should try the experience for themselves in temperatures where just touching the metal burnt the skin. This first sortie only lasted for three days, so the group did not truly experience the physical privation, monotony, cold, hunger and sleeplessness so evident on the longer journeys. But the outing gave them a taster of this awfulness to come. Their achievement was that in three days they charted a new section of coastline and found new islets.[3] Ferrar investigated the geology of the rocks and found they were volcanic. They field-tested the sledge meter and the modified harnesses, which chafed and were not used afterwards. When they turned back, the dogs, knowing that they were pointed homewards, pulled well and made nothing of the weights.[4]

It was on an expedition led by Armitage that scurvy first made its dreaded appearance. Armitage's brief was to explore those formidable mountains west of their base on Ross Island. A magnetic pole journey was high on Sir Clements's list of priorities and Armitage's group set out on 11 September, intending to find a path through the mountain barrier. To general surprise, Armitage took skis on the expedition, the first sledging party to do so. (Armitage had a well-known dislike of skis, and Skelton thought that he had advised Scott against them). Both the conditions and physical problems plagued this group. Seven days out, high into the mountains in a blizzard and fog-bound, the physical worries surfaced. One man complained of a sprained ankle, another of sore gums and others of limb pains. Because of his concern about the men's health Armitage decided to limit his exploration to short journeys. Leaving his sicker companions, he led a small group to an area that he hoped would give access to the interior, and so discovered the important route stretching inland through the mountains,[5] one that was to be used later for inland exploration. He took half-plate photos.[6] Back at camp he became alarmed by the deteriorating condition of two men whom, he recognised, were now clearly suffering from scurvy. The dreaded development meant that after thirteen days, he decided to return to the ship as fast as he could. He arrived back on 26 September.

On *Discovery* Wilson was busy supervising meteorological observations, doing his medical work, tasting the milk, smelling the food and adding to his seal collection. When he examined the returnees he despondently confirmed the diagnosis. He said it was 'not pleasant to find that in one of the men, scurvy had fully declared itself, so that we know what to expect from the sledging work this summer. History is evidently going to repeat itself in the south notwithstanding the care that has been taken to avoid it throughout this expedition's history'.[7] Three men had badly swollen legs; Ferrar's were swollen up to his groin and one man's legs were badly discoloured. The remainder of the party seemed fairly well but 'not above suspicion'.[8] Wilson noted that the haemorrhages behind the front teeth preceded signs on the front of the teeth for days; he recorded the purple spots on the thighs, legs and arms; the haemorrhages under the nails and the thickening around the knees that could stop the knee bending.[9] He worried about sledging parties still out on the ice. Scott was away depositing supplies at Bluff Depot when Armitage got back to the ship with his invalids. He was therefore the senior officer and he acted decisively and well. After consultation with Wilson and Royds he threw away the tinned meat and ordered that fresh meat should be eaten daily. He tried to make the quarters as warm and comfortable as possible, and ordered a more liberal diet.[10] He increased the allowance of bottled fruits and put lime juice on the tables. Some thought his finest move was to give the cook, a lackadaisical and uninspired chef, a memorable dressing down, informing Brett that his bonus depended on the food becoming more palatable.[11] Scott thought that he had threatened to hang him at the yard-arm.[12] Whatever persuasive measures were used, the quality of the food improved dramatically. It is now known that it is the offal (liver and kidney) in animal food, rather than muscle, which contains ascorbic acid.[13] With Brett's improved efforts, the dishes of seal liver and kidney were pronounced delicious. 'Suddenly, Brett could cook, a possibility that had vaguely occurred to the men but now, thanks to Armitage's "encouragement" became a reality'.[14]

If the men had had adequate vitamin C reserves in their bodies they could have done without the vitamin for weeks.[15] Armitage's men were away for less than ten days when they developed signs of scurvy, so their diet on *Discovery* had inadequate amounts of the vitamin for their needs. Scott still believed that ptomaine poisoning in decayed tinned meat was the cause. 'As long as a man continues to assimilate this poison he is bound to get worse and when he ceases to add to the quantity taken, the system tends to throw it off and the patient recovers'.[16] Wilson and Koettlitz examined the entire ship's company; they found several men with congested gums, two with very unhealthy gums and two with leg problems. Wilson, always an inquiring thinker, was beginning to question the tainted meat theory, but having been persuaded against citrus fruits he had no plausible alternative explanation and was prepared to consider any theory. Infection, or even damp living conditions, were thought to exacerbate or even cause scurvy and Scott and his doctors organised a thorough clean up of the ship. Nothing serious was found. Wilson wrote that the linoleum covering was in good condition and had little damp or dirt below it; the bedding was dry and comfortable. But the scurvy proved slow to resolve and Wilson wrote despondently that 'It seems almost necessary to fall back on the tinned foods for an explanation and yet these have been regularly and systematically examined and plenty condemned'.[17] But on reflection he thought that fresh seal meat had solved the problem and he hoped that the regular serving of fresh meat could permanently avoid it. But the problem did recur famously, both on this expedition and on the expedition of 1910. This suggests that the men were simply not eating enough fresh offal (or adequate fresh citrus fruit). Although they wrote with confidence about seal meat, the confidence was misplaced. Koettlitz and Wilson simply did know the cause of scurvy.

Wilson was fascinated by emperor penguins. These birds are the largest of the seventeen penguin species and can grow to four feet in height and weigh six stone. They are characterised by broad yellow patches on each side of their heads, which merge with a golden wash on their breasts. In late September he followed a large group going south towards the Barrier away from the open water and food and towards, apparently, starvation. He wondered if warmer temperatures had confused the birds into going south rather than north to breed or if their instinct told them that the ice was going to break up.[18] Emperors were to become an overriding scientific interest, so he was fascinated to learn that an expedition that had gone to Cape Crozier to update dispatches for the relief ship, had found a large emperor rookery. The party under Royds brought back three young birds.[19] Skelton, a member of the group, photographed the birds. He wrote thoughtful comments on the bird's habits[20] and he was the first to suspect that the emperors never seemed to leave the sea ice. It is now known that emperor penguins are one of the few species that make their home permanently in the inhospitable Antarctic. The species has evolved fantastically to adapt to the conditions in their unlikely habitat. Their feathers are short and spade-like, densely packed on the outside for good waterproofing, but downy and soft on the inside for insulation. Under the feathers is a thick layer of blubber for further insulation. Emperors actually breed on the ice, up to fifty miles inland and in the height of the howling, dark Antarctic winter, when temperatures can average minus 45°F.

The birds walk and slide to the breeding sites in March. They engage in their long courtship ritual, standing belly to belly, touching each other's beaks and cheeks and warbling metallically, in April. They copulate in May and a few days later the female lays her single egg, transferring it almost immediately onto her mate's feet – both sexes have a protective flap of skin and feathers that drops right down to their toes – and the egg rests in its cocoon. The female then makes the long journey back to the sea to feed and reinvigorate herself. During her absence the male guards and incubates his precious burden in his brood-pouch for nine weeks. He survives in the darkness, without food and drink and at temperatures of minus 45 to 60°F, losing more than 40 per cent of his body weight over this time. He keeps warm in the caterwauling gloom by huddling and shuffling with the other males in a tightly-knit circle. Each bird's position varies in the group as he shuffles around; sometimes he gets to the relative warmth at the centre of the group, and sometimes he is on the outside. During this time the eggs remain at a steady 35°F. When the fattened female returns, just after the egg hatches, she finds her own mate by his vocal 'signature', which she has learned during their extended courtship, amongst the trumpeting hundreds in the colony. After a touching reunion, the chick is transferred to the female and the male leaves for the coast and food.[21] These facts, assimilated slowly over the years, were completely unknown in 1902 and Wilson's scientific curiosity was thoroughly aroused. He asked for permission to go to Cape Crozier himself. When this was refused, with a distinct diminution in enthusiasm about his southern expedition he wrote:

> I am afraid that this long summer journey is taking me right away from my proper sphere of work to monotonous hard pulling on an icy desert for three months, where we shall neither see beast nor bird nor life of any sort nor land and nothing whatsoever to sketch. Anyway it is *the* long journey and I cannot but be glad that I was chosen for it. *If* we come across anything but Barrier it will be exceedingly interesting.[22]

With daily seal meat now on the menu, more supplies were needed. Wilson went seal hunting again with Barne and three seamen. They brought back 1,000 lbs of meat, cutting up the seals where they were killed. This was an exhausting and revolting job. The skin and blubber could be removed without much difficulty but it was impossible to cut the meat off the bones and to get it onto the sledges without getting covered in blood and blubber and smelling for days.[23] But this expedition also had scientific merit. Wilson recorded that flags that had been stuck in the ice the previous season had moved forwards. This showed the first definite evidence of movement in Antarctic glaciers.[24]

Scott had led a group of three on a southern reconnaissance journey. Shackleton was a member of the party, which was only out 17–19 September. They had a difficult few days and returned having accomplished nothing 'except the acquisition of wisdom'.[25] But when the group returned Wilson recorded that Shackleton had blistered fingertips and was generally 'done up' having lost pounds in weight.[26] This was the first indication that Shackleton might not be as strong as he appeared and probably from this moment Wilson began to have doubts about his friend's fitness to face the extreme conditions ahead of them. In the event Shackleton was to be seriously unwell on the southern expedition; his symptoms may have been due to medical conditions in addition to scurvy. But Wilson does not seem to have mentioned his anxiety about Shackleton's health to Scott.

The scurvy outbreak had two important consequences. Firstly, Scott, Wilson and Shackleton would not start before the end of October in order to make sure that none of them showed signs of scurvy. Secondly, the southern expedition would have to carry seal meat. Since they needed to make their sledge loads as light as possible, they cooked the meat in margarine to reduce its weight. This was highly successful from the haulage point of view (140 lbs of meat was reduced to sixty lbs) but hopeless in relation to scurvy prevention; any vitamin C in the carcasses would have been destroyed. They could probably have preserved the carcass's vitamins by freeze-drying, but this would not have reduced weight and anyway, the method was unknown to the explorers.

The delay in setting out shortened the length of time that the men could be away from *Discovery*; they needed to be back in time for the relief ship. This meant that a polar attempt was unlikely, but allowed sufficient time to investigate the south. Scott planned for support parties to carry provisions as far south as possible to conserve the dogs' energy. He calculated that a twelve-man support party would allow the southern party to go a third further than would be possible if they carried all their own equipment and supplies.

Scott drafted instructions to cover his absence. At Wilson's request a paragraph was added, which has not survived, suggesting another journey to Cape Crozier to get an emperor's egg, and if possible, a freshly-hatched chick for the Natural History Museum.[27] Wilson wrote to Oriana:

> If anything happens to me so that you can't see me again in this life and you want to hear about me from those who do get home, will you please make a point of seeing the Captain and Royds in preference to anyone else. . . . Do not be cast down, *kind Lady mine*, Don't give way to despair. . . . There will be nothing for you to be ashamed of in me, my wife, and the thought of meeting you eventually will keep me cheerful and, I pray God, more unselfish to the end. . . . God keep you.[28]

This does not mean that he wished or hoped to die. It merely means that he was content to put his future in God's hands. After the southern party had set out, Royds fulfilled Wilson's request and returned to Cape Crozier. His party found a wonderful treasure, an emperor egg, which they carried back triumphantly. This find showed, definitely and without doubt, that emperors breed in the Antarctic. Wilson was denied this moment of scientific fulfilment because by the time Royds got back to the base, the southern party was far away. He would not see this cherished and historic find for weeks.

The party had planned to leave on 31 October. They had a pre-departure celebration dinner. But bad weather delayed them for a day so they were treated to Koettlitz' special offering: a full plate of fresh mustard and cress each,[29] the first green food for months. Even today, Antarctic workers say how they crave the crunchiness and flavour of fresh fruit and vegetables. Eventually the three men set out on 2 November, three days after their supporting parties. They had provisions for thirteen weeks and more dog food than they expected to need.[30] They were given an enthusiastic send-off. Photographs were taken of them, the nineteen dogs and the five sledges, each decorated with its sledging flag. They carried twelve pairs of skis for the supporting party who were on foot and who, it was considered, would do better with skis. The dogs had never been in such form; for the first few miles two men had to sit on the sledges to slow them down.[31] Many of the ship's company accompanied them noisily as they started off, but gradually dropped back and the three were alone.

Wilson had spent the days before departure carefully checking his equipment. He knew that his safety depended on little as well as big matters. He sewed on buttons with twine; he checked his skis, fur boots, burberries, headgear and hand gear; and everything on the sledges.[32] He wrote to Oriana and he wrote in his diary:

> Can anyone, I wonder, realise exactly what it is, leaving the ship and all one's companions except two, for three months in this desolate region to walk down into a completely unknown south, where as far as one can see nothing awaits one but an icy desert and one literally carries one's little all on a sledge.[33]

The men on this historic adventure were very different. Scott was a man used to responsibility. He was ambitious, purposeful, hard-working, temperamental and tended to impatience. Shackleton was also ambitious, but he was more impetuous: an adventurer, an excellent conversationalist, a good organiser and a very hard worker. Wilson's personality was different.

He remained without ambition for personal fame. He was taciturn, but determined, calm and discrete, supportive of the other two and enjoying their confidence. Roland Huntford in his comprehensive book, *Scott and Amundsen*, describes Wilson as 'bitter'.[34] Nothing could be further from the truth. Wilson was upheld and comforted by the conviction that he was doing God's will; he was married to a woman who had his entire confidence and who supported him completely. Also he was involved in an activity that was more exactly suited to his interests and qualifications than any alternative could have been. No writing about, or from, Wilson justifies the epithet 'bitter'. However Scott's description of the three pulling the sledges is revealing:

> It was my turn to drive to-day. Shackleton led and Wilson pulled at the side . . . Shackleton in front, with harness slung over his shoulder, was bent forward with his whole weight on the trace; in spite of his breathless work now and again he would raise and half turn his head in an effort to cheer on the team. . . Behind these, again, came myself with the whip, giving forth one long stream of threats and occasionally bringing down the lash on the snow or across the back of some laggard. . . On the opposite side of the leading sledge was Wilson, pulling away in grim silence.[35]

Like all explorers the three hoped to push at the frontiers of knowledge. Was Antarctica mostly an ice field or a massive continent? Was there land or water between them and the Pole, or did the ice sheet continue endlessly?

The first day suggested that dog pulling worked better than man-hauling and the three caught up with Barne's support teams by the afternoon of 3 November. The group was scarcely making a mile per hour and slipping and slithering in their finesco on the hard snow (their boots were too cold to walk in). When they were given the skis their 'efforts were absurd'.[36] They could not budge the weights on the sledges as the surface was irregular and very slippery; no one had advised about the need for underside skins.[37] Wilson and his two companions also continued on foot for the next few days. He often had to run to keep pace with the dogs and his legs and knee ached horribly. When he was able to use his skis again, with his single bamboo stick, the going was much easier. A few days into the journey Shackleton started the 'most persistent and annoying cough'.[38] This cough was to continue for days. On 7 November a blizzard kept them in their tent. They lay in their sleeping bags (separate reindeer bags on this expedition) reading Darwin's *Origin of Species*, sewing, talking and sleeping, and so the day passed. Snow Petrels circled around, the dogs whined and barked. Shackleton coughed.

The whole group – Scott, Wilson and Shackleton and their support groups – progressed slowly southwards, passing and re-passing each other. After a week, the three men had covered fifty geographical miles and reached Bluff Depot, which Scott had provisioned in October. Here they replenished their sledges and waited for the support party which caught up on the night of 9 November. Shackleton's cough was very troublesome.[39] To help the man-hauling support party to keep up, Scott transferred some of their loads to the dog sleighs. The men found that even with this extra load the dogs pulled so well that Scott decided to alter his plans and go on without the support party. He reasoned that the dogs would still be able to pull as fast as the men, even with loads of over 2,000 lbs.[40] David Yelverton, in his book *Antarctica Unveiled*, says that this decision would have a momentous effect on the party's fortunes for two reasons: it removed the support that would have allowed Scott to grasp the vast scale of the land that lay south along the route to the Pole and it removed any possibility of Scott, Wilson and Shackleton discovering the pass onto the Antarctic glacier, 'the gateway', that, in a later expedition, won such fame for Shackleton.[41] In any event the party of fifteen men could congratulate themselves that they were nearly at the seventy-ninth parallel, the 'farthest south ever reached by man'. Before the support party turned back, Wilson examined them all and found that they were all well and free from any trace of scurvy.[42] Photographs were taken, the sledge flags and the Union Jack flying bravely, and the support party turned homeward on 15 November. Now Scott, Wilson and Shackleton faced an empty white wilderness of more than 700 miles stretching to the Pole. Each footstep would be a new conquest of the great unknown. Scott sent his final instructions to Armitage at base saying that if he had not returned before a date when the ship could be frozen in, he should take the ship back to New Zealand, leaving a party at the hut to be picked up the following season. Wilson, brief as ever, said he was glad to have dropped the other parties 'so we can now shove along as fast as we can'.[43]

They had hoped that they could continue their good progress with the dogs but their confidence began to diminish almost as soon as the support party disappeared.[44] After only one day, on 16 November, the surface snow was so sticky and crystalline that the dogs could not pull and the men had to start relaying. This meant pulling part of a load for a certain distance, returning for the remainder and pulling that too, so covering three miles for each one advanced. They were to continue this back-breaking slog until the night of 15 December: twenty-nine days.[45] Even when the load was divided and dogs and men strained at the traces, it was back-breaking work. On the first day they covered only two and a half miles southwards before their lunchtime break and five by the evening, having actually covered fifteen geographical miles.[46] Geographical rather than statute miles were recorded, because it was easier to relate these measurements to degrees of latitude. There is a difference between the two measurements. Geographical miles are longer than statute miles; seven geographical miles are equal to just over eight statute miles.[47] Two more days on, they had only added eleven miles to their total southward pull. Wilson prayed for a wind to sweep the surface crystals away, 'The dogs are getting very tired and very slow'. Only five days after separating from the support team, Wilson's early optimism had given way to mindless endurance, 'I am afraid we shall disappoint the ship in their expectations of a far southern record'.[48] The men tried to encourage the listless dogs by pulling in the traces with them, one in the front, the other at the side, the third using the whip 'all too frequently'.[49]

At last, on 21 November, the men woke to sunshine and a cloudless sky that showed distant land in the south-west; new patches cropping up further and further in the distance. Scott and his companions changed their plans, deciding to travel south-south-west instead of due south, reach the land if possible and leave a depot containing much of the dog food, three weeks' provisions for themselves and anything else 'not absolutely necessary to our wants'.[50] Lighter loads would make it possible for them to cover longer daily distances and they could pick up the depot on the return.[51] Wilson thought that anything was more promising than the 'slow and tedious plod to the south on an ice plain, simply to beat a southern record'. Also he would have something to sketch and maybe they would find something that would explain the extraordinary Great Ice Barrier.[52]

The snow surface improved and the sledges rode over it, but the men sank still deeper into it with every step they took. The dogs were totally weary and driving them had become 'a perfectly beastly business'.[53] They were clearly weakening and the men gradually came to the conclusion that this was as much to do with their food as to the conditions. This was Norwegian torsk (dried stockfish) and had been recommended by Nansen. Scott took the fish instead of the Spratt's cod liver oil biscuits that he had originally planned to buy.[54] Scott thought that the food had deteriorated as *Discovery* went through the tropics. There was nothing the men could do about this[55] and they hoped that the effect was temporary. The only thing that they could do was to kill the dogs by rote, feeding one animal to another. Later, it was found that the food had rotted en route and was covered by a green fungus. The dogs were therefore getting pitifully little nutrition and no vitamins.

As they progressed new land kept on appearing south-west and south-south-west and they journeyed slowly towards it, sometimes helped by winds that allowed them to use sails on the sledges. There were long gaps between the land. They had no feeling that they had discovered anything approaching a continent. They thought that the landmasses ahead of them were islands.

At this stage the three were on full rations. They cooked three times a day. Breakfast was a mug full of fried bacon and pounded biscuit, washed down with two large cups of tea and a dry biscuit 'or two'. For lunch, biscuits and two cups of hot Bovril chocolate with sugar and somatose. For supper they had two large cups of pemmican, a thick soup of meat, juice and fat, to which was added red ration (a peameal bacon powder mixture), crushed biscuit and powdered cheese, all boiled up in water with salt and pepper and a soup square. To follow this they had hot sweet cocoa boiled with plasma, a hydrolysed protein additive, and dried biscuit.[56] Although hunger gnawed at them Wilson thought, wrongly, that they were actually eating enough. His knowledge of the calorie requirements for this type of exertion was, along with everyone else's, completely inadequate. Mike Stroud, the Antarctic explorer, physician and an expert in stress nutrition, showed that over a sixty-eight day man-haul in 1993, he and Ranulph Fiennes burned well over 7,000 calories per day.[57] Wilson, Scott and Shackleton were eating much less, a little over 4,000 calories per day. But even if they had eaten absolutely vast daily amounts, they could probably not have absorbed more than 7,000 calories. Absorption is limited by a metabolic ceiling.[58]

They tried different ways of marching. They marched by 'night' when the sun was lower and ate lunch in the evening and supper at 3a.m. They varied the relay routine, leaving one of the men to put the tent up and prepare the meal after the first relay whilst the other two went back to pick up the rest of the load.[59] When Wilson was by himself he made supper and sketched. This gave him his first attack of snow-blindness,[60] a problem that was to affect them all too frequently. He was also relieved to have a break from whipping the dogs. But although beating animals was against the grain for all of them, as for other explorers, Wilson always accepted this necessity though he called it 'a perfectly beastly business'.[61]

On 25 November, steering by compass and dial, Wilson recorded that they had crossed the eightieth parallel.[62] Scott wrote delightedly, 'All our charts of the Antarctic Regions show a plain white circle beyond the eightieth parallel; the most imaginative cartographer has not dared to cross this limit and even the meridional lines end at this circle'.[63] The next day they gave the dogs a day's rest and as wind swirled around, they rested in their tent and Wilson occupied himself with the surprisingly domestic tasks of darning, mending, cooking and reading Darwin. Then they went on south-south-west towards the land, now only about fifty miles away. They aimed at a gap in the line of apparent islands. Wilson was re-enthused. He thought the snow-covered peaks, bold cliffs and headlands looked beautiful. He wrote that they were all fit and well though their appetites were immense, '*how* we enjoy the food'.[64] They added slices of dried seal meat to their lunch to try and satisfy their huge appetites.[65]

They hoped and thought that they could still achieve something worthwhile. Their ability to keep going obviously depended greatly on their food supply. By 29 November they estimated that at four miles per night it would still take ten more nights of monotonous exhausting grind to reach the land. David Yelverton in *Antarctic Unveiled* explains that when the three left their support party they had food for eighty-four days. At this stage they had enough for a further eighteen days exploration southwards before they needed to turn back. With reduced rations they could extend this time by three days,[66] suggesting the 20 December for beginning the retreat. With no relaying and ten miles per day they could possibly reach 84° S. This would be a significant achievement; they would be well into the area that, as Scott wrote, was blank on everyone's map. They would be able to record whether land continued that far and if so, whether the land was continuous or split into islands.[67] But fate did not favour them. On 2 December Scott, left to prepare the meal, managed to set the tent on fire; 'luckily', Wilson wrote, he 'was able to grab the thing the moment the flame came through to the outside and put it out'.[68] They were left with a head-sized hole, which Shackleton had to mend before the next blizzard. On 4 December, Wilson recorded that they had run through the first can of oil too soon.[69] This was equivalent to being fifteen days short on the round trip and meant that they stopped heating their midday meal and ate frozen chunks of seal liver, sugar and biscuit instead. Since all the water had to be melted on the stove, their liquid intake would have been reduced. Dehydration is a significant problem with heavy exercise. Overbreathing loses fluid. Their basic fluid intake was already reduced so dehydration must have added significantly to their fatigue.

On 9 December the first dog died. Wilson opened him up and found signs of acute peritonitis. In spite of this the dog was fed to the others and their performance improved immediately. Within a few days they were feeding the eight or nine best dogs with dog flesh as well as fish. Wilson killed them by stabbing each one in the heart. He did not think the dogs had overt scurvy, but he did think that they could have suffered from ptomaine poisoning caused by their fish food.[70] This did not stop him feeding the dogs with their dead companions.

> Dog don't eat dog certainly doesn't hold down here, any more than does Ruskin's aphorism in *Modern Painters* that 'A fool always wants to shorten space and time; a wise man wants to lengthen both'. We must look awful fools at that rate for our one desire is to shorten the space between the land and us. Perhaps Ruskin would agree that we are awful fools to be here at all though I think if he saw these new mountain ranges he might think perhaps it was worth it.[71]

Progress towards the land continued to be appallingly difficult. On 12 December, relaying, they made three miles. Wilson wrote, '*Some* day we hope to get there and drop some of our load, making a depot that we can pick up on the way home. Then we push south, I hope at a faster rate with lighter loads.'[72] Shackleton too wrote that they must plant the depot soon, because they could not continue much longer. But Wilson's courage did not desert him even though it took them thirteen, rather than ten, days to reach the final depot position and yet another trying to get onto the land over the chaos of ice ridges, crevasses and valleys. But, he thought, it was 'a wonderful sight'.[73]

If the dogs were ravenous, so were they. Food was an obsession. They never got into their bags without feeling that they could have managed at least two more suppers. They dreamt of food constantly and 'food-dreams' became a regular breakfast conversation. They were either sitting at a table with their arms tied, or grasping at a dish as it slipped out of their hands.[74] Sirloins of beef and cauldrons of steaming vegetables also swirled through their dreams. Wilson dreamt that he was shouting unsuccessfully to get a waiter's attention and that the beef turned to ashes when served up, that a pot of honey that had been poured turned into sawdust. He longed for fresh milk and a big cake.[75] Such was the obsession with every last morsel that when they divided everything into three portions, although the man who made the divisions felt obliged to take the smallest share, arguments and disagreements followed. Shackleton solved this problem with 'the noble game of shut-eye'. He got one of them to turn his head away when the food was divided and this man decided who would eat which portion.[76] Murderous feelings subsided. It is now known that there are hormones that are important in the control of appetite,[77] but the relationship of hormones to hunger dreams is not clear.

Having finally secured the depot (Depot B) on land they pressed on to the south on the night of 15 December. At last, after twenty-nine days, they found that they could advance without relaying, an inexpressible relief, but the conditions remained bad. Wilson recorded good and bad in his diary. That day, the sight of a beautiful double rainbow around the sun, and a good supper, lifted his spirits; but he had to kill another dog. Their only hot meal was supper; their midday meal was a hurried, cold snack. By now they were in a significant negative food-to-energy balance. As their fat reserves burnt up, they would also be losing the muscles essential for strength and stamina. Wilson suffered from pains in his feet, sunburn, chapped skin, cracked, sore, ulcerated lips, skin ulcers, diarrhoea, broken teeth, frostbite and eyes that felt as if they were full of hot sand in spite of cocaine eye drops. He often marched blindfolded because of snow-blindness. He wore leather goggles with slits cut in to see through, or glass and wire goggles with slit leather patches on each side of the glass (plain glass goggles frosted over).[78] Wilson's goggles were bound with velvet and were probably not strong enough to prevent snow-blindness, but they must often have allowed insufficient vision for his artist's eye and he undoubtedly made the situation worse by taking them off to sketch. Scott wrote that Wilson would sit outside the tent and sketch for a few hours after an exhausting day and was intrigued as to how accurate the sketches were. When he tested them with actual angular measurements he found that they were astonishingly precise.[79]

Wilson's opportunities for useful medical intervention were limited. He carried a meagre medical pack: a sort of first-aid kit containing drugs that are puzzling to the twenty-first century physician but immediately recognisable to his peer group in 1902. It contained chalk-powder, a soothing application for burns;[80] morphine for pain relief; bismuth, probably for digestive problems;[81] a lead compound, probably for sprains and bruises;[82] a strychnine tonic to stimulate the appetite;[83] and sodium lactate for its sedative properties and to 'limit nitrogenous waste'.[84] The pack also included quinine for 'rheumatics' and fever;[85] cascara, a laxative;[86] calomel, also a laxative;[87] chloral hydrate for its claimed powerful antiseptic properties;[88] and liquid cocaine. To these he added sticking plaster, tweezers and scalpels. He could deal with cuts, bruises, burns, constipation and snow-blindness; he could advise on cold feet and hands, give first aid in the event of fractures or other injuries, and little else.

On 20 December one of the dogs dropped dead in harness and several others 'looked as though they would like to'.[89] They would not pull, they seemed as weak as kittens. Wilson was butcher every night now, and any hope of getting any dogs back to the ship had been given up.[90]

At some date around 21 December Wilson told Scott that the group had developed signs of scurvy. Scott noted on 24 December that Wilson had informed him some days previously, but Wilson's diary makes no mention of it until 24 December when he wrote that his examination that day had shown that both Scott and Shackleton had suspicious gums.[91] Wilson suspected the bacon, a possible source of ptomaine poisoning and 'taint', and this was cut out of their allowance.[92] The timing is of interest. In a clinical study on scurvy, a volunteer, previously on a full diet, bravely took a diet with no vitamin C whatsoever for months. He did not develop any clinical signs for three months.[93] The development of scurvy in the explorers after only forty-eight days suggests that the men suffered from vitamin C lack, (a prescorbutic phase), before starting out on their trip and further supports the premise that the diet on *Discovery* was significantly low in vitamin C. The possibility of one invalid bringing disaster to the whole party was obvious. But still they decided not to turn back, continuing south grimly. Wilson wrote that they had again cut back on their lunch seal meat and biscuit to eek it out so that they could go on as long as possible. He still said that he felt well and that they were all in good spirits.

As they progressed, the mountain range unrolling on their right gave way to a further group of high hills. Wilson sketched the whole panorama. Throughout the expedition, his work constantly and accurately reflected the stillness, beauty and grandeur of the Antarctic. Pictures of purple-blue ice, lime-green midnight sky and the sun on the mountain tops were seen and appreciated by thousands after the expedition. They remain superb, lasting and original records.

By 24 December they were beyond 81.33° S. They abandoned one sledge, with all the dog's fish, but still managed only eight miles. By Christmas Day they were abreast a mountain of about 7,000 feet. Its solitary position made for a conspicuous landmark and they named it 'Christmas Height'.[94] Showing a triumph of the human spirit, they celebrated. Wilson thought of his family. He read Holy Communion. He also thought about his food, which had been increased magnificently for the celebration. Having been hungry for weeks and visibly thinner,[95] he lingered over the description. Breakfast was strong sweet tea (they had had no milk since they had left the ship), biscuit and a pannikin (container) full of biscuit crumbs and seal liver fried in pemmican, followed by a spoonful of blackberry jam, brought especially for the celebration. After breakfast they took photos of themselves, grouped in front of the camp and flying their flags and the Union Jack, setting off the camera with a string. At midday they had double helpings of hot chocolate and plasmon (fortified milk), biscuit and more blackberry jam. When they camped for the night they had pulled the sledges for ten miles, leaving the dogs loose to lope along – it was a relief to the men to know that they could manage this. They celebrated with triple rations: biscuits and a tomato soup square, followed by a small plum pudding heated in cocoa and decorated with a sprig of artificial holly. Shackleton had hidden these in one of his socks, a defiant gesture to fate. They could not light the pudding as the brandy had turned black in its tin,[96] but for once they enjoyed a sense of replete wellbeing, 'the reddest of all red letter days', and divided the food without 'shut-eye'.[97] Their content was only marred by the realisation that they would probably have to turn back in three days because of their low food reserves. Also lurking in the background was the sword of Damocles, scurvy, already affecting two of them.

All three suffered with their eyes and often only kept going with cocaine eye drops. They blindfolded the affected eye and sometimes kept going with only two functioning eyes between the three of them. But on 26 December Wilson had a particularly bad attack of snow-blindness. His left eye stabbed and was so painful and bloodshot that for once, he could not go on. He lay in his sleeping bag, groaning in agony. The drops were no help – the lid was too swollen to be rolled back – and the pain was only contained by morphine. The next day he skiied blindfolded and Scott described the new landmasses unfolding on their right to him. These were a range of gleaming black and deep-red mountains rising to over 10,000 feet with a long cape headland beyond. They camped early on 28 December so that they could photograph the scene, the biggest mountains and the furthest south they would get. Wilson, slightly improved, managed to record the panorama with his one functioning eye, so that they would still have an accurate record if the photograph did not turn out well. He was now pleased with their progress, writing in his journal that they were beyond 82° S and

> though we shall not have done a good record towards the South Pole, we have the unlooked-for, hardly expected, interest of a long new coast line with very gigantic mountain ranges to survey and sketch, a thing that to my mind has made a far more interesting journey of this than if we had travelled due south on a snow plain for so many hundred miles and back again.[98]

The sketches that he made match the photographs well. Modern maps show that they must have been about 82°05½S 165E.[99] Although they could see right along the range to a cape beyond, they could not tell whether this was an inlet, with the land continuing, or the end of the range. If they could have gone on only for a few more miles they could have solved the problem, but another dog had collapsed and progress was so slow that it would be late before they could reach the end of the cape and visibility might be bad. Scott decided on a brief dash on skis the next day.[100]

But on 29 December they were thwarted by a blizzard and could not go on until the following foggy day when Wilson and Scott went south on skis. They knew that if the weather lifted they should be able to see beyond the tip of the cape and to find whether there was an inlet with land running south, suggesting a continent, or a strait, showing that the land ended there. The weather did not lift. The light grew worse. They had to turn back.[101] With less than two weeks' food to get them to Depot B, they started the long trek northwards on the 31 December. They hoped against hope that the weather would clear enough for them to see the far side of the cape. But visibility continued to be poor and denied them their prize. They could not say whether the land they had discovered continued on a scale sufficient to justify the term 'continent'. If they had been able to make a valid claim to this knowledge it would have compensated them for the disappointment at not getting near the pole, and heaped more fame on the *Discovery* expedition. As it was, this information would not be revealed for years. However the three could claim the furthest south record. They had pushed man's knowledge beyond 82.17° S.[102] They had discovered the mountain range that flanked the Ross Ice Barrier. Wilson said that the peaks ranged from 10,000–13,000 feet and were probably granite. The highest mountain was to be named Mount Markham.[103] In addition they had mapped nearly 300 miles of coastline. Wilson's name lives on in the region; the cape they so wished to see around was later named Cape Wilson.

The return to the ship was to take thirty-four arduous days. They were tortured by hunger and by the dreadful fear that they would not locate their food depot. They were eating so much less than they needed that they were in a severe negative balance. They knew that any delay due to injury, or a storm, could be fatal. They all suffered from scurvy, and Shackleton's health deteriorated significantly.

During their first four days northwards they travelled for thirty-four miles, crossing huge pressure ridges carved up by wide crevasses, filled in and bridged over by compacted snow.[104] Three of the remaining eleven dogs died. One dropped down too weak to walk; they pulled him on the sledge to the camp where his hungry neighbour immediately killed and ate him.[105] Scott decided that it was useless to keep food for the dogs on the sledges and decided to distribute it. Clearly not all of it was rotten because two dogs became obviously stronger.[106] But in spite of this, the men were doing virtually all the man-hauling themselves. As each dog died or was killed he was fed to the other dogs. Should the men have eaten the dogs to supplement their diet? If Wilson thought, as he said later, that the dogs were suffering from ptomaine poisoning, there would have been no question of man eating dog.[107]

By 13 January they knew that they were near the depot they had left in December (Depot B). But they woke to a thick blank whiteness and could see nothing. As they ate their reduced rations their fear of missing the depot was very real, so when the pall lifted and they saw the depot flag through Scott's theodolite telescope the relief was immense. 'We were not a demonstrative party, but I think we excused ourselves for the wild cheer that greeted this announcement';[108] they knew that they would be having a fat hoosh that night. At the depot they removed the silver strips from the sledge runners which they thought made the sledges run slower and repacked the sledges, getting rid of any unnecessary items, leaving themselves with one pair of skis for emergencies, which Shackleton used, and deciding what to do with the two remaining useless dogs (Wilson killed them). He wrote that Shackleton was now definitely ill and was coughing, very short of breath and wheezing. Shackleton's gums were dark and swollen; he was deteriorating rapidly. Any attempt to help with the work made him worse. Scott also had signs of scurvy. Wilson just had a plum-coloured lump on his gums.[109] Shackleton's symptoms were potentially disastrous. They were still 160 miles from the ship and had sledges loaded with a total of 525 lbs to pull.[110] Shackleton wrote later to his mother that he had collapsed completely on 14 January due to overstrain and haemorrhage, but he said that the other two had been awfully good to him, only allowing him to do small jobs around the camp. Wilson and Scott did all the pulling; if Shackleton had broken down completely they would have had to pull him too in relay, though Scott doubted if he or Wilson had the strength for this.[111] In the event Shackleton could not get out of the tent on one day but otherwise he was able to just walk or ski.

Human endurance and courage can persist through awful circumstances. On 15 January, Wilson wrote that Shackleton had had a very bad night and was very breathless during the day, also that they had fallen into a crevasse together, holding themselves up on their elbows and harnesses, but when they camped Wilson made a sundial and learnt about rope splicing.[112] It is said that the only thing to fear is fear itself; that too good an imagination is a disadvantage. There is no suggestion that Wilson's courage ever failed him or that his imagination played destructive tricks on him; his faith kept him serene. But Shackleton's health did become a sort of barometer for the mood of the party. Wilson and Scott were improving on more seal meat (and, they thought, because they had excluded bacon from their diet), but Shackleton alternated between good and bad. Progress was variable: Saturday 17 January, nine miles; Sunday, very little; Monday, nine miles. By the 21 January Shackleton was well enough to temporarily take his place in the traces but soon had to give up, so Wilson and Scott pulled grimly (Wilson says gaily) on.[113] Wilson hoped to get back to their first depot in seven days. They were desperately hungry. The surface snow was heavy. Wilson's eyes were weak and he gave up any attempt at reading. He slept as soon as he got into his bag.[114]

Shackleton improved very gradually. By late January he was able to ski. Scott wrote that in spite of his disbelief in skis, if they got back then Shackleton would owe much to the pair that he was using.[115] On a glorious sunny 25 January, though they were still over twenty miles from their next depot (and ninety-five from the ship), the sight of smoke puffing from their old friend Mount Erebus gave them encouragement, though Wilson's eyes were too bad for him to sketch, his fingers were painful, his knee hurt and his lips were raw. They all wore sun hats; the cold areas that formed under their moustaches and whiskers became frozen and encrusted in ice.

They finally arrived at the depot they had left in November on 28 January. Here they found letters, chocolate, sardines, port, raisins, prunes, pemmican and other luxuries, more than enough to reach the ship.[116] They ate a substantial meal. Scott suffered badly afterwards. The pemmican had probably swollen in his stomach and he could not sit, stand or lie down comfortably. He received scant sympathy, so he was delighted when, the next morning, Wilson left the tent rapidly with his face pea green in colour.[117] But in spite of the extra calories, Shackleton got worse again; he was more breathless, restless and unfit to move.[118] For the first time he seemed to lose his courage and become despondent.[119] It is unclear what precisely the problem was. He clearly had scurvy: Wilson had said that he was coughing and breathless, but that there were more serious symptoms which he did not detail.[120] But even if he could have made a confident diagnosis there was absolutely nothing that he could do. His medicine bag did not contain anything to treat heart or chest problems. His only thought was to get Shackleton back to the ship before another blizzard caught them. He and Scott eased Shackleton out of the tent and into his skis and he kept going, just.

February opened with a successful march. They were buoyed up by the knowledge that there was only twenty miles to go. On 3 February they were delighted and relieved to see Skelton and Bernacchi hurrying towards them. 'Clean tidy looking people they were'.[121] Skelton and Bernacchi filled them in on their missing three months. The main point of interest was that the relief ship *Morning* had arrived with food, letters, parcels and some new personnel. The provision of a relief ship to resupply *Discovery*, and if necessary rescue the crew, was an integral part of Sir Clements Markham's plans and *Morning* was the result of his further prolonged negotiations. With lightened hearts the three men trudged the final part of their expedition. Skelton and Bernacchi pulled the sledge, their flags flying gaily, towards a *Discovery* decorated from top to toe with flags and with the whole company thronged on the rigging and gangways. On the way back they met Sub-Lieutenant Mulock who was to join *Discovery* from *Morning*. Mulock must have been startled at the explorers' appearance: frostbitten noses and lips, skin like leather, long sooty greasy hair and beards and, as they warmed up, strongly smelling; they had not taken their clothes off for over thirteen weeks.

The *Morning* crew had brought news from England and the world: Edward VII had been crowned in August 1902. Balfour, who had been loath to support the Antarctic project, had become prime minister. The Boer War that Wilson abhorred so much had ended in May 1902 with a British victory. The three explorers had their own momentous news: their discoveries and observations in the unknown south, their observations on the nature of the Great Ice Barrier. Many photographs were taken and they sat down to a huge dinner. Wilson did not want to rush his letters. 'I felt an absolute confidence that all was well with all that I cared for most at home'.[122]

Discovery was incarcerated in miles of ice. It was hoped that the ice would break up before *Morning* had to leave but this did not happen in spite of sawing and blasting. Winter provisions, fruit vegetables and mutton were transferred from *Morning* to *Discovery*. Scott sent Shackleton, amongst others, home on *Morning*. He thought that Shackleton was not fit enough for another polar winter and wrote officially, 'It is with great reluctance that I order his return and trust that it will be made evident that I do so solely on account of his health and that his future prospects may not suffer'.[123] Wilson wrote that the decision to send Shackleton back was because of his breakdown on the southern journey and that he, Wilson, supported the decision.[124] When *Morning* left for New Zealand on 2 March with Shackleton on board, Shackleton wept.

9

Paintings and Penguins

Wilson was unemotional about *Morning's* departure on 2 March 1903. He did not go to wave off the dejected Shackleton, but remained on *Discovery* and cleaned out his cabin and got everything ready for him to start work again. He painted skua heads, caught up with his correspondence and started working on pen and ink drawings from his southern journey sketches. This was a major and prolonged undertaking; the newly discovered Victoria Land coastline and the mountain ranges were of tremendous general interest and he eventually worked up 100 feet of drawings into a panoramic record.[1] Nothing was easy. The light in his cabin was so poor that painting had to be done in the mess and all the artwork cleared off the mess table for each 'prolonged' meal. But he managed '3 hours in the morning if one does not go out, in the afternoon 2 and a half hours and in the evening 7.30 to 11p.m. when the acetylene gas is turned off and only those with candles to spare can go on working'.[2] Lighting was a problem, not only for Wilson's painting but for the psyche of all on board – continuous darkness can lead to depression. Wilson thought that the lack of light would make their lives miserable in the long sunless winter. They had no lights in their cabins,[3] but Skelton had rigged up an acetylene light system, which ran through the inhabited parts of the ship for limited hours. This was a bonus for morale and better than smoky candles, which were in short supply anyway. But since Wilson's work was so dependent on light he made candles by melting old wax and pouring it into glass tubes threaded through with a piece of string fixed with a cork.[4] Three home-made candles equalled the light of one proper candle and lasted for eight hours.

After the southern journey Wilson's knee stayed stiff and swollen, 'a nice clean discomfort, not an illness, which needn't worry other people'.[5] He had to stay on the ship for six weeks until he was mobile. His appetite was enormous and he soon began to put on weight. His attack of scurvy does not appear to have affected his scarred lung. This is surprising because scurvy can cause the disintegration of old scars as the normal production of 'repair' protein is arrested and old 'repair' protein continues to be broken down. If the St George's diagnosis of tuberculosis was correct, scurvy might well have caused a recurrence of the disease; the organisms that cause tuberculosis can survive for years in scarred lung tissue and can become active again if a scar breaks down. But he seems to have had no chest problems whatsoever. He was not concerned by the thought of another Antarctic winter; in fact he wanted to stay on to continue his observations on bird and marine life. He wrote to his mother, 'A polar winter is not by any means the terrible experience we were led to imagine it was, but merely a period of rest and quiet and extra sleep' and 'I have no fear of the winter now, knowing what it means. The climate suits me down to the ground. I simply revel in it, bracing cold and clear air'.[6] His plan was to spend the winter months, March to September, working up his paintings, and painting new scenes. Here he succeeded. By the end of the winter he had a portfolio of 200 coloured sketches: panoramic views, paintings of the Aurora (a hugely luminous display of colours in the atmosphere).[7] Many of these were later reproduced in *Scott's Voyage of the Discovery*.

His main ambition for the spring in the coming September was to continue his studies on emperor penguins. He planned to study eggs at different stages of development and to capture specimen young chicks. Calculating from Royds' return with chicks in October 1902 he decided that this would mean two journeys to Cape Crozier: September for eggs and October to observe the chicks. He also wanted to find how and when the penguins went north. In the event he was able to make the

1. Working together

2. Wilson preserving pelts

3. A grouse dancing

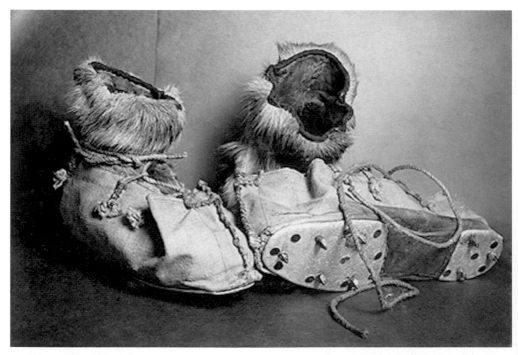

4. A pair of finescos

5. A pair of red grouse and chicks

6. An Alfred Stoord portrait of Wilson

7. 'Crippetts 1888' sketch at sixteen years

8. 'Fogbound on the Barrier'

9. Emperors

10. Formed sasturgi ridges on Barrier

11. Horses and dogs at sea, 1910

12. 'Man chased by dog' sketch at eight years

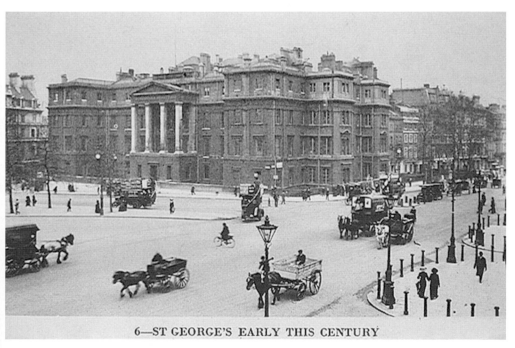

6—ST GEORGE'S EARLY THIS CENTURY

13. Hyde Park Corner, London, early 1900s

Cairn left by Norwegians - S.S.W. from Black Flag Camp
Jan. 16. 1912.

Amundsen's South Pole mark.   Jan. 18. 1912

14. Norwegian Polar Flag at South Pole, 1912

15. 'Peregrine Falcon' sketched in 1896

16. Oriana Souper

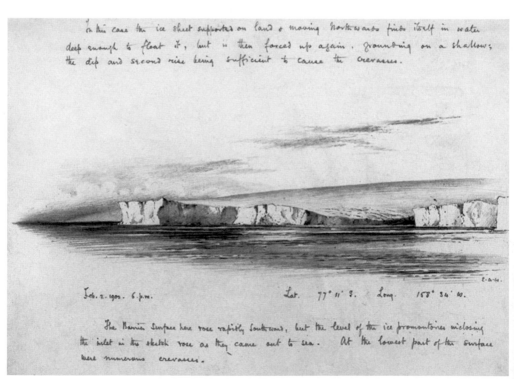

17. Panorama of the Barrier, 1902

18. Return from Winter Journey

19. 'Sea Ice Off Terra Nova'

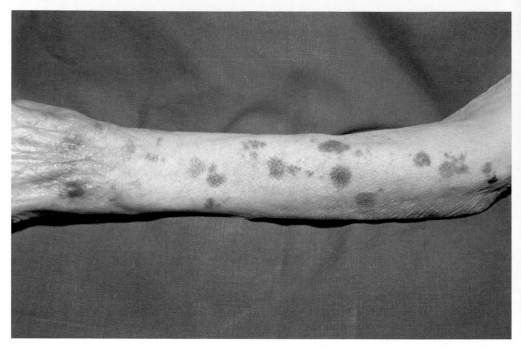

20. Scurvy

21. Sledge sailing

22. 'Terra Nova caught in Sea Ice'

23. Tabular iceberg, 1910

24. 'Three men in a tent'

25. Wilson and Oriana

26. Wilson at work

27. Wilson dressed
for expedition

28. Wilson inspecting a leopard seal

visits but failed in his aims because his calculations about the emperor's life cycle were wrong and he arrived too late. The eggs are laid in May and the chicks emerge about nine weeks later, in July. This disappointment was one of the reasons for his eagerness to return with Scott in 1910, when his return to the emperor colony of Cape Crozier was the subject of one of the most famous travel books ever written about Antarctica: *The Worst Journey in the World* by Apsley Cherry-Garrard.[8]

When he was able to walk he went alone, because, as he wrote to his wife, 'first I want to sketch and one cannot keep others waiting about in these temperatures and secondly, because it is the only time I get to myself to be alone with God and you'.[9] To sketch, he took his right hand out of his glove for a few minutes, sketching until 'you can no longer feel the pencil'. Then he put his hand back in his glove and 'the pain makes you dance on one foot and then the other'.[10] All pencils, soft or hard, made the same gritty marks. Throughout the winter, his body anticipated any coming storm, 'A coming blizzard is always heralded by a headache, migraine over one eye as a rule shading to neuralgia of the face and touches of rheumatism even of the legs'.[11] He suffered recurrent attacks of general 'rheumatic' pains throughout the winter and became certain that the problem was related to damp.

He had received many letters from home on *Morning*, but his father thought that he got the greatest pleasure from a letter from his contemporaries at St George's, a remarkably Edwardian epistle signed by 158 signatories.

Dear Wilson, the undersigned old friends and St George's men gathered together at the annual dinner presided over by Sir Clifford Albutt, send you their heartiest greetings and wish you a continuance of success in your great enterprise, fair weather, a pleasant journey and safe return. We all look forward to the pleasure of seeing you after such an eventful absence.[12]

He was pleased because there were Cambridge men amongst the signatories and the message showed that he was not forgotten.

He would also have been pleased and perhaps surprised by comments about him in the letters being carried to New Zealand on *Morning*. The Edwardians were great letter writers and to receive these missives must have been a comfort to Oriana, who had already sailed to New Zealand, anticipating that Wilson would be back there in 1903. The letters showed her how her husband was appreciated. Scott wrote that it was not a kindness but a pleasure to write to Oriana about her husband. He said that they had some trying times on the southern journey but if ever he had a repeat experience, he hoped to have a man like Wilson with him. Oriana had not seen her husband for almost eighteen months and anticipating her disappointment that Wilson had not returned to New Zealand after the first season, Scott continued, 'I feel confident he will get home safe and in better health than when he started and I trust it may comfort you in your disappointment to know how well he is and how we all esteem him'.[13] Others wrote; Royds said:

> Your old husband is one of the best and I missed him awfully during the long journey south and was so awfully glad to get him back aboard again. All during the winter I used to do drawing every Sunday under his able supervision. Life on board would have been very different without your husband. I feel much better for having been with him and he has my greatest admiration and friendship.

Barnes wrote:

> 'Billy' is the prime favourite on this ship there is no one who does not 'go all the way with him'. I hope he sent you some of his charming little sketches they are such perfect little pictures and his sun-sets and sky effects are I should think, as near an approach to the real thing as it is possible for an artist to procure.

Even Armitage, possibly the least contented of the officers, wrote 'Of course he is a great favourite on board and his sketches charm us nearly as much as he does himself'.[14] Hodgson wrote later that he had 'never met with a man so universally admired and respected in every way'.[15]

He had to consider his future after he returned to Britain. Clearly by now he thought that general practice, or any other conventional medical career was out of the frame. He wrote to Oriana:

Medicine and Surgery form a work that one should either give one's whole and undivided attention to from the first or leave strictly alone in practice: and I am afraid I have done neither for I have squandered my energies over various hobbies instead of making my profession my one object in life.[16]

His friend from St George's, Dr John Fraser, wrote later that if he had stayed in hospital work, research would have suited him best.[17] But clearly his real talents and enthusiasms were for becoming a naturalist with ornithology as his particular passion. However openings offering regular employment in this field were few and although he had hopes of returning to New Zealand to record the wildlife and flora there, no offer of financial support was made. His mind strayed over other vaguer options: he wondered about translating German scientific works into English and lecturing in Swiss sanatoria in German and English on his experiences in the Antarctic.[18] Both these options unsurprisingly came to nothing. At least by now he was slightly better off. The Antarctic Committee had increased his salary by £50 per year starting in March.[19] This probably made more difference to Oriana than to him, but he must have been pleased that his contributions to expedition life were recognised.

Avoiding scurvy remained a priority for the doctors. For the winter of 1903 the men harvested large supplies of seal meat and skua for the larder and occasionally fish was added to the breakfast menu. Food during the winter of 1903 was an improvement on the previous year The recalcitrant cook Brett, who had been carpeted by Armitage, had gone back to New Zealand on *Morning*. His replacement, a professional baker, produced tasty, appetising and (because of the predominance of seal and skua meat) healthier meals.

Activities were important to keep up morale. This winter there were fewer concerts and *The South Polar Times*, edited now by Bernacchi, had lost some of its sparkle; Bernacchi did not equal Shackleton in editing ability and Scott thought the second year was not as good as the first. Lectures were given. Skelton gave a magic lantern show. The men played hockey at temperatures that dipped to minus 39°F, only stopping because of poor light. Wilson played cards and read. The sailors also passed the time by making models out of the sledges' silver runners that had been discarded. Wilson was given a small model of a sledge and was delighted at 'the very pretty souvenir'.[20] Midwinter Day, the darkest day of the year, 22 June, with neither moon nor sun, was celebrated, but not as enthusiastically as in 1902. Wilson gave away the cigarettes sent to him on *Morning*. The ship was not decorated as there were no evergreens to cut, but they ate real turtle soup (also sent on *Morning*), large cakes (donated in New Zealand), halibut, a huge side of beef with artichokes, all topped off with devilled wing of skua as savoury and champagne. On 16 July, Wilson remembered his wedding anniversary, 'Two years now since Ory and I were married and we have had three weeks of it together'.[21] Oriana's health was drunk in the mess. During the winter the sledges and fur sleeping bags were overhauled, as Royds kept everyone busy preparing for the forthcoming sledging season. Today, scientists with all the advantages of electricity and communications still complain about the monotony of Antarctic winter. Perhaps in 1903 expectations were lower; whatever the reason, the ship's complement seem to have endured the long dark days without intolerable problems, on a ship lit by strictly rationed candles and variable acetylene light. But it must have been a relief when spring arrived in September.

Plans for the season included explorations to the west and south-west, but the paramount goal was to free the ship by any means available. Scott had decided that there was to be no further attempt on the South Pole.

From Wilson's point of view, the important journeys were his two expeditions to the Cape Crozier rookery. The first expedition was from 7–17 September 1903. This was the time that he thought that 'early' eggs would be available and was the first expedition in the Antarctic spring. Six men set out on skis, pulling two sledges and carrying 110 lbs each. As low temperatures were expected the men used the three-man sleeping bags, marginally warmer than single bags but more uncomfortable because the men were jammed in so tightly that anyone's movement inevitably disturbed his companions. Wilson wrote that he never got more than one hour's uninterrupted sleep and his sleeping-bag partners thought that they had not slept at all 'but from listening to the others snoring we knew that everyone else had'.[22] He dreamed vivid dreams, 'of home and warmth and England, far more vivid than any waking thoughts'.[23] The daylight was so poor that work in the camp had to be done by candlelight. When the team reached Cape Crozier on 12 September, they found dramatic changes from the previous year: a chasm had opened up and ice blocks now blocked the path to the rookery. They returned to camp. On the following day Wilson and two companions set out again, roped together, wearing crampons on their finesco and carrying one ice axe and a long ski pole. After two hours of climbing, step cutting, and dropping into cracks and crevasses, they reached the huge colony. Wilson was surprised and disappointed to find that the birds had already hatched their chicks and were nursing babies that looked as advanced as those that Royds had brought back in October (five weeks later), the previous year. He could not get early eggs. This was a setback and calculations for incubation times and hatching would have to be rethought; but he did have the opportunity to study the birds close up, putting up with 'vicious' pecking and slaps from their wings in the process. He described the pot-bellied babies, their silky white and silver-grey coats and their clumsy big feet that looked as if they were made of rubber; the parents' bulky flap of loose skin hanging down from the abdomen that protected their chicks; their leg-tied, shuffling gait as they carried their

165

chicks on both feet; and the way they balanced on their hocks and tails when not moving.[24] He was impressed by the birds' intense brooding instincts; adults would try to incubate dead chicks, deserted putrid eggs, or even balls of ice rather than be without. If a chick wandered from its parents, other adults, desperate for ownership, pulled and jerked at it sometimes so strongly that it got killed adding to the already high mortality.[25] He collected frozen eggs, dead chicks and two live chicks which the team somehow managed to keep alive in temperatures of less than minus 45°F by wrapping them in their sleeping jackets and feeding them on masticated seal-meat. When Wilson got back to *Discovery*, the chicks stayed in his cabin and caused great interest. The amount that they ate was enormous; they were like bottomless wells and the mess in the cabin can only be imagined. But they did not survive long though one kept them entertained for some weeks.[26] The frozen eggs did not add to his knowledge either; they were stinking and one was full of putrid fluid.

Two days after their return, there was an impromptu concert: Royds sang and played, Ferrar sang, the men sung and Bernacchi recited. The King's health was toasted with whisky. Wilson did not try to entertain though he thought the event was quite a success. It was Oriana's birthday, the third he had missed since they were married. 'What a husband, poor girl'.[27]

On 12 October Wilson was off again for the second expedition to Cape Crozier. He took with him two seamen: Cross, who had become his regular zoological assistant, and the stoker Thomas Whitfield. The outing lasted until 5 November 1903 and reinforced the men's perception of the discipline needed to endure life in the Antarctic. Wilson aimed to get to Cape Crozier by 19 October, the date that Royds and Skelton had been there the previous year, and they just did this, having had to relay on the way. When they reached the rookery Wilson thought that although there were hundreds of birds, there were fewer chicks than in September and, based on Skelton's report, than in 1902 and he estimated chick mortality at more than 70 per cent. He recorded again the penguin's determination to brood over something, anything would do. Six adults fought over a chick that had fallen through a crack in the ice 'though not one had the sense to help it out'.[28] He took photos with his old click-box. The three went later to the Adéle penguin rookery, updated the mail cairn and collected rubble for Ferrar to analyse. Because the cold was so severe they again had finesco rather than boots on their feet and unsurprisingly their feet got badly bruised and blistered. They found the little Adéle birds nesting. He decided to return later when the eggs were laid, to have a 'fresh egg feast'.[29]

But bad weather dogged them. They were marooned in their tent, 100 feet above the bay, for nearly a week, Wilson passing the wet miserable days by reading Tennyson's *Maud*, a favourite from his Cambridge days.[30] Lack of oil and food, those old familiar worries, surfaced again; a delay of this length had not been anticipated, so they killed seals to make up for both deficiencies and looked forward to the Adéle eggs. When at last the storm cleared they went back went on their egg-collecting foray hoping for six eggs each, more for the men on the ship and some for Wilson's collection. The Adéles were there, sitting tight on their nests, screeching and pecking furiously as the men pushed them off. But no matter how many nests they searched the men could not find a single egg. So they sat, eating dry cheese and biscuits watching as 'the Adéles made love to each other and stole each others nesting stones and stood bolt upright with their heads in the air chortling to themselves as they slowly waggled their flippers'.[31] They revenged themselves by taking three adults back for supper. 'Stewed, they were delicious, but fried in butter, in blessed mouthfuls, they were heavenly'.[32] As another storm held them up, they chipped bits off the remains of the frozen Adéle penguins with a geological hammer and fried the crumbs, which were excellent. Low on food and four days overdue, they finally got back to the ship on 5 November. Whitfield had a swollen and stiff leg which Wilson thought was due to scurvy, and his own feet were raw and bleeding.[33] He wrote home, 'Bird-nesting at -62°F is a somewhat novel experience. Those journeys to Cape Crozier were pretty average uncomfortable even for the Antarctic. It has been worth doing – I feel that, but I am not sure I could stand it all over again'.[34] But he had achieved a great deal: apart from studying penguins he had collected rocks and made geological notes and diagrams, notes on the pressure ridges (those masses of ice forced up into lines and separated from each other by deep valleys) and notes on the ice-cliffs which changed from white at the top of the cliffs, to blue, grey and then dirty grey.[35]

In this second season Wilson went on two other expeditions. With Hodgson and seaman Croucher, he went to the south coast of Ross Island on a 'picnic trip', making comprehensive sketches of the glaciations of the volcanoes Erebus and Terror and investigating the tide crack between the island of Erebus and the Barrier. This was an important investigation; the tide crack is the gap between land ice and floating ice and part of *Discovery*'s brief was to investigate whether the Barrier was afloat or grounded. Wilson seems to have thought that there was indeed a tide crack masked by pressure ridges, and the Barrier was therefore floating.[36] This party returned to *Discovery* on 22 November in time for the usual Sunday breakfast of seal liver.[37]

After four days he was off again. He went with Armitage and Seaman Heald to the western side of the strait for a fortnight's exploration of the geology and ice formation at the foot of Mount Discovery. They took an eleven-foot sledge and three weeks' food. This expedition too had its problems. On 30 November the snow surface was too bad for pulling and even after dividing the load they made a mile only after five hours' struggle.[38] In the fortnight however they managed to collect rocks, examine the glacial bed and complete a topological survey. As they returned to the ship on 12 December Wilson saw a little black cross – the second emperor penguin, brought back from Cape Crozier, had died.

With Scott away on an expedition Armitage organised the attempts to break up the ice incarcerating *Discovery* so that she could escape to the sea. Scott had decided that a path should be cut in from the sea edge and that sawing should

begin soon after 12 December. Crew, scientists and officers were divided into three shifts and work went on around
the clock. A tent city, 'Saw Camp', was erected close to the
work. Officers and men were separated in the tent; three crewmen sleeping together and officers in separate sleeping bags.
Wilson describes his shift from midnight to 4a.m.: two hours
sawing and two hours using gun-cotton explosive to try and
break up the ice, then back to his tent until 10a.m. to start
again. No washing, no change of clothes, sleeping bags and
the other watches eating and talking all around the sleepers.[39]
The teams only managed to loosen about forty feet of ice in
their four-hour shift and Wilson, and others, saw that the
whole process was a complete waste of time. But he wrote,
'there never was a healthier crowd of ruffians than the thirty
unwashed, unshaven, sleepless, swearing, grumbling, laughing, joking reprobates than lived in that smoky Saw-Camp'.[40]
The ice was seven to eight feet deep and it was calculated that
it would take approximately 220 days to open up the miles of
ice between ship and the water, that is, through the remainder
of the summer and through the remaining winter.[41] The official
reports sent back to the ship indicated that all was going well
and Scott, back from and exhausted by a two-month expedition to the western summit, remained on the ship for a week
before going to see the progress for himself. When he visited
on 31 December he saw the futility of it all and he gave all
hands New Year's Day off. Scott had a small tent and Wilson
slept with him. No doubt they discussed the situation. Work
was resumed for a short while and then finally abandoned.

On New Year's Day Scott asked Wilson to go with him to a
small camp on Cape Royds so that he, who was suffering badly
with indigestion, could rest away from the ship and Wilson
could study the Adéle rookery nearby. They had much to consider: the ship had only fifty tons of coal left in addition to a
little oil and acetylene,[42] the ice showed no signs of breaking
up and the possibility of a third winter in the Antarctic, with its
attendant financial implications for the expedition, must have
weighed on Scott's mind. At Cape Royds Scott asked Wilson

if he would stay on for another winter unless news from home made this impossible and Wilson agreed. On 5 January, when the two were sitting in their tent looking out to the distant sea, Scott suddenly saw a ship. He thought it was the whaler *Morning* (it was actually another ship, *Terra Nova*). Soon Wilson saw another.[43] They did not know what this meant; they could not guess that the saga of the relief expedition had reached a point that stripped Sir Clements and Scott of the control of the *Discovery* expedition.

Because *Morning* had not got through to *Discovery* in 1902 a further attempt was needed in 1903. Demands for yet more money were not enthusiastically received although Sir Clements argued that the *Discovery* expedition was a national endeavour and that Parliament, representing the nation, was responsible for her relief. After considerable behind-the-scenes bargaining, His Majesty's Government came to the expedition's aid, but at the price of taking control of the relief expedition and the ownership of *Morning*. Sir Clements was furious, but with no alternative financial backing he had to agree 'under protest'. He had worked and schemed for the expedition for years and this was a terrible blow to his authority.

A naval committee bought a second ship to go to the Antarctic along with *Morning*. This ship was *Terra Nova*, a whaling ship that was to carry Scott and Wilson back to Antarctica in 1910. Instructions were that all personnel were to be brought back to England. If *Discovery* could not be freed, the men and equipment were to be transferred to the rescue ships and *Discovery* abandoned to the mercies of the Antarctic.

When Wilson and Scott saw the ships they reasoned that they could at least be sure of sufficient provisions for another winter. The thought of abandoning *Discovery* had not been seriously considered. They crossed to the ships together. Wilson wrote that the whaling men on *Terra Nova* 'spoke such perfect Dundee that we could hardly understand a word they said for a bit'.[44] The sailors too probably had difficulty in recognising the unwashed, unshaven duo as officers. On board Scott came to understand the details of his orders. He was dumfounded;

he said he could scarcely grasp their true meaning.[45] When he addressed the crew, he had tears in his eyes. Armitage wrote that he was confident that there was not a single man on board who, given the chance of staying another two years on *Discovery* ice-bound, or of deserting her to return safe home, would not have chosen the former course.[46]

Morning carried mail. Since Oriana was in New Zealand, Wilson had her news at once. He went back to Cape Royds to relish her letters slowly in addition to a year's family and general news. He hated the thought of abandoning *Discovery* but since neither explosives, sawing nor *Terra Nova's* ramming of the ice helped, he did not waste time bemoaning his fate but calmly collected more geological specimens, made observations on the tide using a tide pole and killed a male sea elephant, the first seen in the Antarctic. He wrote:

> We took guns knives and cameras. . . . He was in the same spot and asleep . . . when we had to show ourselves on the sandy beach, he woke at once and raised himself on his flippers showing a hideous great muzzle. He was about as ugly a beast to walk close up to as I had ever seen outside a cage, but I wanted to get him . . . I fired both barrels at the back of his head and he rushed into the water . . . the next charge turned him over dead.[47]

It took six men to haul the enormous animal up the beach and Wilson was proud of the catch. The sea elephant was twelve feet long and ten feet in girth around the shoulders with an enormous head and neck. It was covered in two or three inches of blubber.[48]

When the relief ships arrived, *Discovery* was encased in solid ice ten miles from the sea edge. The barrier had been much less the previous year but impossible to escape from, so Scott prepared to abandon ship. He arranged for his officers, crew and scientific equipment to transfer to *Morning* and *Terra Nova* so that ships could leave by late February. But such are the vagaries of nature that in 1904 the ice did break up. By 3 February Wilson wrote that only seven miles separated *Discovery* and

Morning. On the 11 February the ice was breaking up rapidly and yielding to the combined onslaughts of the ongoing blasting and ramming. There was only four miles between *Discovery* and open sea. By 14 February the relief ships could approach rapidly; they rammed the ice again and again until at last they broke through to the Hut Point basin.[49] On 16 February the last gun-cotton charge freed *Discovery.* She shuddered and floated free for the first time in nearly two years. The crews of all three ships went wild with excitement, cheering, all round congratulations and rejoicing that *Discovery* had avoided a ghastly and ghostly end in the Antarctic.

But nothing was easy. Wilson recorded 17 February as a day 'we shall none of us forget as long as we live'.[50] As *Discovery* moved out into the water, strong winds forced her onto the shore at Hut Point Bay where she stayed, grounded by wind, waves and tide for more than eight hours. Her timbers creaked loudly; bits of keel were ripped off and drifted to the surface. It was heartbreaking. Wilson thought the ship could not survive such strains. Scott had told him that he thought the ship was done for; she was so badly grounded that she would not get off even if she survived until the wind dropped. Wilson wrote: 'at dinner we were as glum a party as could well be got together'.[51] Finally the tide changed and the wind dropped. The engines were started full steam and *Discovery,* against expectation, backed off the shoal into deep water. She was afloat again.

Discovery crossed the Antarctic Circle after an interval of two years and sixty-two days, on 5 March 2004. Wilson skinned birds all day. By now he was absolutely sick of this occupation and said that he sometimes skinned birds all night in his sleep. He had however seen or preserved a significant collection of birds: falcons, a parson bird or tui, bellbirds, white-eyes, yellow breasted tits, groundlarks, a parakeet, terns, sheerwaters, petrels, cormorants, penguins, ducks and blackbirds. Also, he had seen and described gulls, giant petrels and cape pigeons, and killed a sea elephant. On 7 March they saw the last iceberg, 'Thank God'. *Discovery* continued to roll like a thing possessed and there were some wonderful crashes; one man got a bowl of sugar, a plate of stewed plums, a glass of port and a pot of coffee in his lap.[52] But soon all reminders of the Antarctic faded as *Discovery* arrived at Auckland Island, a beautiful sight, covered with russet scrubland bathed by warm breezes, and, a novelty, bluebottle flies which were soon buzzing around the wardroom.[53] Here the ship was prepared for her return to civilisation. A government ship was also there, searching the islands for shipwrecks, and when their crew came on board the explorers would have heard more details of things that had happened in their absence: Edward VII had been acclaimed Emperor of India, Mrs Emmeline Pankhurst had set up a militant feminist movement and Marie Curie had become the first woman to win the Nobel Prize.

When they reached New Zealand on 31 March, *Discovery* remained off shore so that all three ships could enter port Lyttleton together, but Oriana got onto the ship by tug. She was first on board 'looking not a day older than when I left her and far more beautiful'.[54] She had been woken with the news of the ship's arrival and rushed for four miles to get to the harbour. 'When Ted at last appeared beaming and I was helped on board, then indeed all was well'.[55] 'What a day it was, a brilliant sunshine and as still as possible. What a day indeed! We both felt it'.[56]

The ships tied up in the dock to the strains of 'Home Sweet Home', and an enthusiastic reception from the Christchurch residents 'who treated the men like relatives'.[57] No one was sorry to be back. They had arrived on Good Friday 'and a very good Friday indeed'.[58] *Discovery* stayed in New Zealand for more than two months and for Wilson and Oriana their honeymoon proper began. Their concentrated steady regard and love for each other had not faltered, the harmony of their partnership continued. They stayed with Oriana's aunt and then with the hospitable Dr Jennings in Christchurch. They visited and stayed with friends, good friends like Sir Joseph and Lady Kinsey whom Oriana had stayed with whilst waiting for her husband, a couple who shared their passion for the natural sciences. They attended official functions; Wilson worked on his specimens. They took a boat to Wellington and toured the hot lake districts of North Island. These had a huge effect on Wilson who was unendingly impressed with the enormous possibilities of the country as an untapped source of scientific and naturalistic possibilities and conscious that many aspects of the life were rapidly disappearing. He wrote to his father:

> New Zealand hasn't woken up to the fact that it is a ready-made world's Sanatorium, with the most astounding variety of springs at all temperatures and of all chemical combinations, all handy and workable. I had no notion of the wealth of this country from the therapeutic point of view. . . . In a century or less, all or most of this unique flora and fauna will be extinct – they are dying out before one's eyes. I could spend a few years here with advantage on a really classic piece of work.[59]

After he had left New Zealand he wrote to Kinsey emphasising his enthusiasm to return,

> if only your blessed government would take the hint and give a willing worker a chance of doing a job that really wants doing, for the opportunity will be clean gone forever before long. The more I think of what there is to do out there the more keen I am to come out and do it only they must give me enough to live on – that's all. I know it can't be a paying job but it must be enough for bed and breakfast.[60]

He also wrote to Sir Joseph Ward to request that he be considered for the post of caretaker of the Sanctuary Islands. His ambitions were to remain unfulfilled. No funds were forthcoming.

After a short stay in Wellington they returned to Christchurch for a ball given by the officers for the people of the city. Oriana and Scott received the guests for *Discovery*. Wilson wrote home, 'I could only stand in the crowd and admire her and wonder how the deuce such a girl came to give herself to me'.[61]

The last few days were spent with the Kinseys, packing rocks, bones, skulls and ferns and attending a farewell dinner for the officers at which each man had to speak. Wilson's was said to be the 'speech of the evening' because he had them all laughing. Then he and Oriana were set for home: he on *Discovery,* she on a cruise-liner. As he thought of home, anticipation grew. He wrote to his father:

> I think that few men have stepped into life with a better all-round education than you have given me. I don't mean so much my year at Clifton though that was worthy a mint of money to me, nor the Public School nor even the University though I realise their value, nor even the Hospital and you know how I value that; but what I marvel most at now is that you saw the reasons for giving me those walking tours in Wales before I left school, do you remember? And all that bird-nesting regardless of schoolwork, Sundays or even meals . . .[62]

The last part of the journey home was stormier than ever. Sheep, a final gift from the people of New Zealand, were drowned. The ship flew through the water

> now on her beam ends, now coming up to windward with a roar, now plunging into a hollow depth of darkness to drown the fo'c'sle in a green sea, now lifting with a twist that throws one off one's feet in a half circle and help the man who tries to move without hanging onto something.[63]

The sea-elephant skin survived these traumas and was forgotten until the ship arrived in the tropics when it began to smell overwhelmingly; as Scott remarked 'shift it from place to place as you would, it made its presence felt everywhere'.[64]

When names for the landmarks in Antarctica were suggested Wilson put in a plea for Cambridge to be given something, as there were Cambridge men on the expedition. Scott agreed to mention this and also informed him that the elusive cape on the southern journey was to be named after him.

On 10 September 1904, thirty-seven months after leaving Southsea, *Discovery* docked. The Wilson family was well represented in the happy welcoming groups. Parents, brothers, sisters and Uncle Sir Charles were there to greet him.[65] The voyage of *Discovery* had ended.

10

The Grouse Challenge

The *Discovery* expedition could claim success in terms of magnetic research, geology, biology and meteorology; the scientists had gathered a large body of material about Antarctica. Although the official report, published later in 1908, contained criticisms of the meteorological observations – potentially damaging at a time when Scott was seeking financial backing for a second expedition – in 1904, Sir Clements could rightfully state that the expedition had resulted in greater understanding and knowledge about the Great Ice Barrier, the vastness of the inland of East Antarctica and the discovery of King Edward VII Land. The extraordinary mountains and skies had been recorded and photographed for all to see and Wilson had recorded them for posterity in his sketches and paintings.

British experiences in the Boer War had produced, at least temporarily, a sense of diminishing national greatness and the nation was ready for heroes. Scott's officers and men were regarded with an awe that amounted to reverence when details of their daring, endurance and courage became generally known. Shackleton was one of the first to greet the *Discovery* men. He had already created enormous interest in the expedition and its achievements and the ship's return was a public relations success that not even Sir Clements could have anticipated.

The months that followed the return were full of activity for Wilson and Oriana. There was no further talk of him returning to a medical career; his ambition was to be a writer and illustrator of wildlife. If only he could have gone back to New Zealand as a government scientist or a warden in one of the wildlife sanctuaries, he thought, he could have produced a classic piece of work that very few others could have achieved.

> It is a pretty ghastly fact that from a luxuriant sub-tropical forest-clad country with as unique a flora and fauna as any country in the world, New Zealand is being turned into a beastly, uniformly grass-covered, sheep-run with a mixture of the commonest birds in Britain, Australia, India and other countries and a travesty of Spring and Autumn faked up out of British introductions in the way of deciduous trees. Isn't there work for anyone who will take it up?[1]

He wrote, 'I look on things in this way, that now while one has health and activity and can stand roughing and travelling one should be collecting 'copy' so to speak for oneself, not settling down to collect copy that other people are collecting'.[2] Meanwhile he worked in the British Museum's History Department for four days a week and, predictably, he undertook a daunting amount of other work: copying his Antarctic pictures, illustration of Scott's book in colour, work on Armitage's report (for which he produced fifty pen-and-ink drawings), work on *The South Polar Times*, lantern slides for Royds and collaboration with Skelton on a publication for the Royal Society. The public had an insatiable interest for all things Antarctic and he received a flood of requests for lectures to scientific societies, his medical school and public schools. There were also many invitations to social engagements; the festivities began with a lunch party for more than 150 guests including Wilson and his father at the East India Dock on 16 September. The lunch, hosted by Sir Clements Markham, boasted representatives from no less than fifteen newspapers including the *Daily Mail*, *Standard* and *Daily News*. Wilson also had the doubtful joy of being the 'hero of the moment' at a dinner in Cheltenham.[3] His greatest energy and interest however was focused on his scientific papers. His report on mammals and birds was to be published by the Natural History Department and he wanted his report on emperor penguins to be a classic.[4] There were other scientific papers. His father read them and made suggestions.

In November 1904 his Antarctic pictures, advertised as being by kind permission of Sir Clements Markham and Scott, were exhibited in the Bruton galleries in Bond Street, Mayfair, a very fashionable area of London. As well as Wilson's paintings, nearly 200 of Skelton's photographs, a model of *Discovery's* sledging equipment and flags were on show. Burroughs Wellcome advertised that they had provided the medical equipment for the expedition and Burberry showed its lightweight tents and clothing. Orders could be placed for Scott's book, which was to be ready in early Autumn 1905. Wilson's contribution was impressive: eighty-eight watercolours of birds, 129 scenic watercolours, thirty-four pencil drawings and twenty-nine topographical sketches. The exhibition attracted an estimated 10,000 visitors and, as the opening coincided with a lecture by Scott in the Albert Hall, Wilson's fame was assured. Visitors were anxious to see for themselves the actualité of the Antarctic and eager to buy copies of Wilson's pictures (he thought that the Royal Geographical Society had the claim to the originals and many of the watercolours are still there). The paintings were described as reports of enduring value, showing throughout the personal joy of the author. Amongst the visitors was Sir Joseph Hooker (1817–1911), the grand old man of Kew, and the man who had suggested balloons for the Antarctic. He took great interest in Wilson's work. By now nearly ninety, as a young man he had spent four years in the southern oceans as an assistant surgeon on *Erebus*, under Sir James Ross Clark's command, and he showed Wilson pictures of that expedition. Age had not lessened his enthusiasm for the Antarctic and he wrote, in words that would have been intensely gratifying to Wilson:

> I made an effort to see the Antarctic sketches with my legs bandaged up to the knees (but not painful). They are marvellous in

number, interest and execution. No naval expedition ever did the like. The heads and bodies of the birds by Dr Wilson are the perfection of ornithological drawing and colouring. They are absolutely alive.[5]

The exhibition was an artistic success. The public was absorbed and particularly fascinated by the first drawings ever of emperor penguin chicks. Wilson's pleasure in this interest was tempered by his agreeing to produce 'upwards of forty' copies of the drawings. Although each picture sold for twenty to thirty guineas,[6] making a good commercial profit, the commission taken by the gallery left very little over for him and probably confirmed his distaste for commercial transactions.[7] However he would have been delighted to know that the pleasure and interest in *Discovery* paintings continues. His watercolour, *Emperor Penguin Rookery, Cape Crozier*, was sold at Christies in London for more than £9,000 in 2003 and *Last view of Mount Discovery* was bought for over £5,000 at the same auction.

He saw his family and friends less than he would have liked, but his friendship with Scott continued. When Scott went on his national speaking tour he stayed at Westal when lecturing in Cheltenham. He spent the evening with the Wilsons and no doubt praised their son highly. Jim, Wilson's young brother, thought that Scott must get bored, having to talk continually about the Antarctic. Meanwhile, since Wilson and Oriana needed to be close to London, they rented accommodation in Bushey, a village close to north London. It had a rural environment which suited him better than London itself, but was close enough for him to work in the British Museum and on his expedition reports. Bushey had the added attraction that one of his sisters, Mrs Godfrey Rendall, lived there. In Bushey he worked on a picture for presentation to King Edward and in Bushey he narrowly escaped a premature end to his career: a wasp stung him on his temple. This caused an anaphylactic reaction, a serious allergic-type reaction that can lead to death. Within minutes of being stung he suffered generalised itching, wheezing and coughing and could hardly breathe, with pains in his chest and a racing pulse. He felt faint and became confused, probably related to low blood pressure and lowered oxygen levels. His father wrote that he would have died without prompt treatment.[8] The immediate lifesaving treatment was (and still is) adrenaline and the man who saved his life was by chance Ernest Shackleton's cousin, a Dr Shackleton, who practised in Bushey. Although he improved slowly, Wilson's chest went on rattling and wheezing for hours and the white wheals on his bright red skin took days to resolve. He had a narrow escape.

Lecturing and after-dinner speeches did not come naturally, though he agreed to talk to colleagues at St George's, the Royal Geographical Society, the Cambridge Philosophical Society, the Royal Institution and schools. At St George's, having been eulogised, he stood up, suffered stage fright and could not continue; very unpleasant, but he hoped it did not 'live in others' memory as long or as lively as in his own'.[9] Early on he read his lectures from carefully-written (and rewritten) notes, but as he became more confident, and with repetition, he began to speak directly to his audience. He spoke with humour rather than didactically and he often made his audience laugh, always a successful ploy for a lecturer. On scurvy his message was clear: fresh meat was preferable to lime juice, that there was no associated anaemia or arthritis, but that muscular pains were common. He wrote that the taste for alcohol became less as the cold became more intense.[10] When he was due to address the Society for the Protection of Birds, he warned his father that he was going to speak on a topic that outraged him: thousands of penguins were hunted into red-hot cauldrons and boiled down for oil extraction on Macquire Island. He thought this practice appalling and thought his audience would too. After his death, others, including his friend, Apsley Cherry-Garrard, who wrote about his experiences with Wilson in his book *The Worst Journey in the World*, took up the crusade. Eventually the practice was forbidden by Parliament.[11]

In mid-December 1904, Wilson presented his Antarctic watercolour to the King, who in turn awarded him with a Silver

Polar Medal, along with more than forty of his colleagues. He also met a number of people who would have been of interest to him and whose interest in him would have been gratifying. He met the well-known older artist, Sir Hubert von Herkomer (1849–1914),[12] who actually lived in Bushey and had opened the successful Herkomer Art School there in 1883: a man 'with a big ascetic nose in the middle of a refined clean-shaven face'. Herkomer was probably at the height of his fame in 1905. In 1901 he had been asked to paint Queen Victoria as she lay on her deathbed, an unheard-of concession to a commoner (albeit one of German descent),[13] and his friendship was gratifying. Herkomer was a portrait painter (he painted Ruskin), and a freelance artist for *The Graphic* magazine. Many of his pictures illustrated poverty: *The Old Village Nurse*, painted in 1892 and depicting the death of a child, shows a road in Bushey that Wilson would have known and he would have empathised with the content. Wilson also met John Macallan Swan (1847–1910), 'the finest animal painter going – such a fine old chap with a colossal head and a mass of grizzled curly grey hair',[14] and the brilliant zoologist Sir Ray Lankester, (1847–1929), who advised him to make himself *the* foremost authority on seals.[15]

He would have been happy also to re-meet the Duchess of Bedford who had been at school in Cheltenham and knew his sisters. The 'Flying Duchess' had been dissuaded from training as a nurse by her father but the interest remained and as Duchess she designed and went on to build a cottage hospital in the grounds of the Bedford's ancestral home, Woburn Abbey, not far from Bushey. She discussed her plans with Wilson and gave him access to roam in the 3,000-acre estate. Wilson also met John and Hallam Murray of the publishing house 'John Murray'. Their names would have been familiar. Their company had published – amongst other successes – the works of Charles Darwin and Jane Austen as well as Lord Byron's *Childe Harold's Pilgrimage*. They had also published one of the first cookery books for housewives, Mrs Rundell's *Domestic Cookery*. Byron had been delighted by the second

John Murray's pleased observation that both *Harold* and *Cookery* were much wanted. Wilson must have been pleased and flattered when the Murray brothers advised him to write and illustrate for publication. '[They] gave me to understand that they would be pleased if I came to them for an offer first'.[16] Hallam Murray went with him to his Antarctic exhibition. Wilson wrote: 'I have rarely met such a charming man or one so courteous and full of help and sympathy. He told me of several faults that run through all my paintings – easily corrected, I am glad to say, now my attention has been drawn to them'.[17]

Another publisher, Reginald Smith (1857–1916) of Smith, Elder and Co, was to become a lifelong friend. Wilson first met Smith when he went with Scott to the Smith, Elder and Co offices to discuss the book of the expedition, which was to be published by the firm in October 1905. Smith was intelligent, thoughtful and highly principled and had a big enough private income for him to pursue 'quality rather than profit in his professional life'.[18] He headed the London firm of the Smith, Elder and Co publishing company, which vied with John Murray publishing for the distinction of their authors: Trollope, Browning and Thackeray were amongst these and Smith's father-in-law had discovered Charlotte Brontë. He was a man who encouraged his authors and in turn inspired their admiration and gratitude; several dedicated their books to him.[19] He and Wilson were both meditative men with tastes in common. They became good friends, a friendship that would endure for the remainder of Wilson's life. Before Wilson's final expedition, Smith gave him a watch on which he had engraved 'From now onward till we return . . .'.[20] Wilson, thanking him, wrote:

> not a single day will pass but I shall be reminded by the simple inscription on the back of the watch of the friend whose friendship has made all but the very highest principles in life, impossible. It is a very great thing to have a friend like that and we feel that to possess the friendship of yourself and Mrs Smith

is to possess something that will outlast watches, and will be still going when the last of them has stopped.[21]

They were to become particularly close over the Smith's publication of what was to be Wilson's magnum opus, his report on *The Grouse in Health and Disease*. When Wilson died, Smith wrote that to have known Wilson was a lifelong possession, as to have lost him was a lifelong regret.

It is ironic that, in relation to his feelings for animals in the wild, his next big undertaking was related to field sports. It was however another unlooked-for opportunity for work in an area peculiarly suited to Wilson's training, experience and interests. After he made a presentation to the British Ornithologists' Union in March 1905, he was introduced to Lord Lovat (1871–1933),[22] who was chairman of a commission investigating a disease that was decimating grouse on the moors. This was no small matter. Gross rent from grouse moors alone in the early 1900s was approximately £1 million a year in Scotland, and £270,000 in Wales and northern England. In addition, wages and earnings added a big direct and indirect boost to the economy.[23] This was threatened by grouse disease, which had already been investigated by both eminent and considerably less eminent scientists and landowners. There was no generally-agreed policy for attacking the problem because there was no consensus as to the cause; the conclusions of the grouse inquiry (which took six years) were the springboard for accepted changes in moor management. At Lord Lovat's invitation Wilson went to Carlisle in northern England to attend a meeting on the disease. He found the problem absorbingly interesting, a scientific thriller. He thought that 'a nicer piece of work can hardly be imagined nor one I should prefer to take up'.[24] He accepted the appointment of field observer to the inquiry in November 1905, for the remuneration of £150 plus travelling expenses.[25] He was the third field observer; two respected scientists had previously investigated, but not solved the problem. As field observer he travelled widely; to Scotland, the Lake District and northern

England and though it was originally thought that the work could be done in six months of each year, so leaving time for writing and painting, it was obvious almost immediately that full-time input was needed. Thoughts such as 'he couldn't imagine anything nicer' became lost in a blur of dissection, microscopic work, travelling and writing. Typically he began with the basics and studied the feeding, moulting and other characteristics of the normal grouse before moving on to dissect hundreds of birds that had died of the disease. Apart from tramping the moors, and slowly gaining the active cooperation of the keepers who grew to respect his knowledge, he consulted with his colleagues and took part in experiments in the observation area, where bacteriology results were tested. His contribution to the final report is impossible to overemphasise. This report not only proved the cause of the disease conclusively, but also, with its practical advice on management, saved a sport estimated to add in total over £2 million to the economy.[26]

The report was issued in 1911, long before Wilson's fate was known, so that Lord Lovat's comments on Wilson's contribution can be taken at face value. Lord Lovat was almost fulsome in his praise of Wilson (designated in the report as M.B., F.Z.S., M.B.O.U.).[27] He wrote that it was 'difficult to speak highly enough of Dr Wilson's services, for not only was he an indefatigable worker in the field, but his ornithological knowledge, his scientific training and his artistic skill, have been of the utmost value in every branch of the inquiry'. He went on to say that Wilson had 'written or aided in writing ten out of the first fourteen chapters of the book and has not only fully illustrated his own contributions, but he had placed his artistic skill at the disposal of nearly all the other writers'. He concluded that 'Dr Wilson's personal qualities secured for him the willing assistance alike of Local Correspondents and Scientific Staff and went far to ensure whatever success the committee has achieved'.[28]

Along with the grouse work Wilson, perhaps inevitably, took on too much. Even his father reflected that he had taken on more than he could cope with.[29] His defence would have been that the commitments were taken on when it was thought that the grouse work could be done in six months of the year. He would have been determined to continue financially independent; the social norms of the time demanded that a married man support his family, also he and Oriana might have children. So in addition to his own illustrations for the gallery, Scott's and Armitage's books and work on the National Antarctic Expedition's report, he agreed to illustrate a new edition of Bell's *A History of British Mammals* for a friend from Cambridge, Gerald Barrett-Hamilton (1871–1914). The work needed for this publication was prodigious: full-page colour plates, fifty-four black and white plates and more than 200 smaller sketches. So his agreement to do yet more coloured illustrations for the appropriately named Dr William Eagle Clarke (1853–1938), of the Natural History Department in Edinburgh, for a publication, *British Birds*, underlines his inability to prioritise.

Of these two commissions the first number of *British Mammals* was not actually published until 1910, after which Wilson's work appeared in many further editions. By the time the fourteenth was published in 1913, Wilson's fate was known and the edition included an appreciation of Wilson by Barrett-Hamilton. Edition number fifteen, printed after Barrett-Hamilton himself had died, included a further appreciation by a mutual friend. 'Wilson has gone. His long lean figure will no longer stalk down the galleries of the British Museum of Natural History. . . . But we, his fellow workers, will treasure his memory, proud that for a brief space he journeyed with us, lightening our labours with the truest good fellowship.'[30] The commission for Dr Clarke's *British Birds* was withdrawn after Wilson had finished many of the illustrations; Dr Clarke said that they were 'not satisfactory' and, more believably, that the work would not be finished on time. This was very galling to such a careful worker, particularly when Eagle Clarke had told Wilson that he was pleased with the work and Wilson had thought there 'was no shadow of doubt about his appreciation'.[31] Wilson's efforts were not entirely wasted; some of the work was eventually reproduced in *Sport in Wildest Britain* in 1921. But Eagle Clarke had a valid point. Because of Wilson's conflicting priorities, he often finished his commissions late and delivered them with long apologies.[32] In addition to illustrating, his lectures continued. He remembered his old friends: the forty-pound profit for his lecture at Queen's Gate Hall in South Kensington, London – advertised in a way that must have shaken him: five shillings for a reserved seat, half-a-crown for an unreserved seat – went to the Caius Mission.[33]

Wilson and Oriana stayed in Bushey for five years. In summer 1905, they moved to a small house, near to the almshouses. The house, formerly 'Tynecote' now 'Bourne Hall Cottage', is still there and was represented in an embroidery made by the Bushey Museum as part of the millennium celebrations. In 'Tynecote' the young couple put their theory of not allowing the less privileged class to give up precious time to look after the privileged minority, in this case the Wilsons. He wrote to one of his aunts:

> How we wish you would come and see us and have a look at our cosy home. We are down at six every morning. O. does all the cooking and house cleaning, and I do the kitchen grate and light the fire and do the flue. I don't smoke and I don't drink and I have to swear horribly to prevent myself becoming a little angel and flying away.[34]

This gesture, although altruistic, could be considered naive and simplistic. There were no children, he and Oriana were young and well and, presumably, the liberated servants had to earn their wages from less enlightened employers. The decision could cause little change in wealth distribution; this would take years. But he was absolutely sincere in his vision of equal opportunity, though the tension between his ideals and his middle-class identity was demonstrated when he went to join his family in Ireland for a month's holiday; an impossibility for most workers. In Ireland he painted some of his best landscapes of the beautiful scenery around Killarney.

Work began in earnest on the grouse project in the autumn of 1905. The red grouse is unique to the British Isles. It is a subspecies of the willow grouse, but while the willow grouse are sprinkled around the Arctic tundra, the red grouse thrive, in hundreds and thousands, on Scottish and northern English moors. Grouse shooting is an exciting field sport. The birds do not fly high, but skim the contours of the hills with an accuracy of cruise missiles, flying a few feet above the heather in order to outwit their main predator, the falcon. They can navigate the moors at sixty miles per hour or even faster with a following wind. On a shoot, the beaters launch them into the air by crying, whistling and banging.

Nowadays the heather is carefully managed to give the grouse food and shelter and the keepers protect them from predators. In the early 1900s the heather was managed with equal interest but with less success. Grouse disease had been an intermittent problem for years and causes varying between poor drainage of the moors, starvation of the birds, infection and damage by predators had been considered. The two previous field observers had reached conclusions that were strikingly at variance with each other, a result that could only add to the general uncertainty. Dr Thomas Spencer Cobbold (1828–86) concluded that the disease was entirely due to hundreds and thousands of tiny worms, *Trichostrongylus perigracilis*, in the grouse intestine. By contrast, Professor Edward Emanuel Klein (1844–1925) stated that the disease was due to an acute infectious pneumonia due to a bacillus that attacked healthy birds and killed them in their prime. Faced with these conflicting views, with hundreds of dead birds and a potentially catastrophic loss of income, Lord Lovat's commission aimed to investigate which (if any) of the theories was correct, how birds actually became infected and what, practically, to do about it. The work was to take six years.

The pivotal part of Wilson's work was the investigation of healthy birds. Much of this work was done in the observation area in Surrey, which had been granted a Home Office licence[35] for grouse to be kept in captivity. His observations allowed

Wilson to state categorically that variations in, for example, the birds' plumage, that had been previously considered a marker of disease, were in fact normal and that plumage could vary in healthy cocks and hens at different times of the year and in different locations. Also the weights of the birds could vary significantly in health.[36] In the final report Wilson wrote or contributed to chapters on the normal grouse, its life history, its plumage and its food, and the grouse in disease.

It was agreed that the first priority was to find the cause of the disease before a cure could be attempted. It was entirely unclear whether Dr Cobbold and Professor Klein could both be correct and that the two presentations (of acute pneumonia or emaciation) were actually forms of the same disease, or whether there were two (or more) distinct entities. The inquiry conclusion was that was that there was only one disease, due to the microscopic threadworm, *Trichostrongylus*. It was found that the threadworm crawls up the fronds of the heather, infests the dewdrops on the ends of the young shoots, which the grouse feed on and so infects the birds with the lingering symptoms of grouse disease by damaging the delicate lining of the gut and interfering with absorption. In relation to the Klein hypothesis, Wilson and his co-workers found no cases of 'well' birds dying suddenly, as might occur with pneumonia. They found however that the pneumonic changes seen by the professor were, in fact, post-mortem changes, similar to changes found in perfectly healthy birds some hours after death.[37] No criticism was made of Klein's work; the professor had made his observations when bacteriology was in its infancy,[38] but the report clearly states that the conclusion that pneumonia was the cause of grouse disease was a misconception.[39] The conclusion was backed by experimental evidence. Wilson was able to reproduce the disease at the observatory when he fed grouse with contaminated food.

The investigation was so authoritative because every dead grouse picked up on the moors in Scotland, Ireland and England was sent to Wilson, who dissected and examined them all. Already by 1906 there were daily deliveries. Wilson eventually dissected nearly 2,000 birds and made a skin of every one. He said that he continued to skin them in his sleep. In addition to dissection, the birds were weighed and measured, and the crop contents and intestines examined and analysed. He worked at home, in makeshift laboratories and in hotel rooms up and down the country, where unsurprisingly he was not popular. Even Westal became filled with grouse feathers.[40] He often wrote his notes up on the train. The work gradually took over his and Oriana's lives. She became his assistant, writing to his dictation, or reading to him, whilst he sketched and skinned. It is remarkable that, out of all this messy and confusing work, Wilson was able to come to such lucid, definite and unambiguous conclusions. Also that his wife – unexpectedly plunged into the morass of unfamiliar, repetitive and unpleasant work, accommodation in strange hotel rooms and frequent exhausting travel – seems to have taken to the work with interest and with no complaints or recrimination. Truly, a marriage of minds.

The work took so long because not only did the cause of the disease have to be established but also the mechanisms of infection had to be worked out. Life was a round of grouse-moor inspections, examination of the heather, dissecting grouse, looking at microscopic specimens, having interviews with colleagues on the Committee, correcting proofs and continuing his correspondence. In the summer of 1906 Wilson moved to Scotland to be close to his work. He often sat up all night on the moor to obtain a better understanding of the grouse and her chicks, or to collect early morning dew. He and Oriana continued without servants. 'Servants seem to be everyone's chief anxiety and we are spared much by having none'.[41]

As he was unravelling the scientific mystery, an unexpected letter arrived from Ernest Shackleton dated 12 February 1907. This announced Shackleton's intention to lead his own expedition to the Antarctic and he invited Wilson to join him as second-in-command. Shackleton's plans had been released to the press two days earlier; a flood of volunteers followed the announcement immediately, but Shackleton wanted Wilson.

He suggested that if his own health stopped him from attempting a polar journey, Wilson should take this prize on. Wilson responded to this invitation with a regretful 'no'. Oriana would have supported a return to the Antarctic, but he could not allow himself to abandon the grouse work at such an important stage. A flurry of letters between Shackleton, Wilson and members of the Grouse Inquiry Board followed Wilson's disappointing reply and although Shackleton offered to help speed up the grouse work with secretarial assistance, his offer was turned down. Lord Lovat and other members of the Board by now thought that Wilson's contribution was indispensable and Wilson was not about to abandon it.

> My Lord . . . I write to say that I have refused the offer (of the expedition) and that I am quite prepared to stand by the Grouse. For many reasons of course I should like to have gone, but I feel it would be absurd and unfair to throw up the Grouse Inquiry work just when I have begun to get a grip of it. . . . Shackleton is of course a great friend of mine as we were together in the *Discovery*, and in refusing to go with him I told him it was a great disappointment. Under the circumstances I should be equally sorry now not to see the Grouse Inquiry through to the end.[42]

Shackleton thought the decision was almost as bitter a disappointment as he had felt when he had had to leave *Discovery*. He wrote to a senior member of the committee, 'the loss is the Expedition's and to me personally, that of a good friend and adviser'.[43] He wrote to Wilson, 'Heaven knows how I want you – but I admire you more than ever for your attitude. A man rarely writes out his heart but I would to you. If I reach the Pole I will still have a regret that you were not with me'.[44] Almost until he left, Shackleton was asking for Wilson's advice on any number of matters and hoping that he would change his mind.[45]

Scott remained a friend. He corresponded with Wilson regularly but he only heard of Shackleton's sensational plans for an independent expedition on 12 February, days after they had been announced, and when he was sailing with the Atlantic

Fleet on *Albemarle*.⁴⁶ He had already written to the Royal
Geographical Society seeking financial assistance for a further
expedition and the news that Shackleton had already obtained
sponsorship (from the shipbuilder William Beardmore, to be
repaid on Shackleton's return by writing a book, lecturing and
selling articles) and was also approaching the Geographical
Society for support, was a serious blow. He thought that
Shackleton was trying to subvert his own plans for a return to
the Antarctic. *Discovery* officers were aware that Scott wanted
to return, but that his plans depended on naval support and
pay. Scott was helping his mother and younger sisters financially; in addition he needed more sea experience before he
could apply to go on half-pay and so have the time to pursue
his Antarctic ambitions. He felt that Shackleton had cut into his
life's work and that Shackleton's plans to aim for 'his' part of
the Antarctic in McMurdo Sound were dishonourable. He felt
it was 'the natural right of his leadership to continue along the
line which he had made'. Out with the Atlantic Fleet he wrote
to Shackleton that his announcement 'cut across my plans' and
that he was sure that only Shackleton's entire ignorance of his
plans could have 'allowed him settle on the *Discovery* route
without a word to me'. He was sure that 'with a little discussion
we can work in accord rather than in opposition'.⁴⁷ Scott had
not thought that Shackleton, who was now married and out
of the Navy, would consider another Antarctic adventure and
he thought he had the right of leadership to McMurdo Sound.
He wrote that two expeditions could not go to the same spot
within years of each other. He appealed to Wilson, a man 'who
commands our respect and who could not be otherwise than
straight',⁴⁸ and said that he would suggest that Wilson commu-
nicated with Shackleton. So Wilson found himself, in addition
to all his other duties, in the role of peacemaker between the
two ambitious, determined men.

Shackleton wrote to Wilson that he was sorry that he was
having so much worry but that 'this was the penalty of being
considered capable in judgement'.⁴⁹ Scott wanted Shackleton
to change his plans, or at least to agree to avoid McMurdo

Sound and 'his' base. In March Shackleton travelled to Westal to thrash out the problem. Wilson thought initially that he should simply leave the field open to Scott but failing this, he thought that Shackleton should definitely avoid the *Discovery* base. He wrote later that even if Shackleton succeeded in getting to the Pole 'the gilt would be off the gingerbread' if he had gone from McMurdo, 'because of the insinuation which would almost certainly appear in the minds of a good many that you forestalled Scott who had a prior claim on the use of that base'.[50] Once Wilson was sure of Scott's plans, his high-minded loyalty made him feel that Shackleton was 'intruding' into Scott's Antarctic. But Shackleton, having convinced him that he had had no idea of Scott's plans, eventually departed with Wilson's blessing, with the agreement that he would not use McMurdo Sound as his base.[51]

In fact, even if Wilson had felt able to leave the Grouse Inquiry in 1907, he probably would have refused to go with Shackleton once he was certain that there was a probability of Scott's returning to the south. By the end of March1907, he had accepted Scott's invitation to return with him to the Antarctic, on the proviso that he would not be available until the end of 1908.

Shackleton sailed off on *Nimrod* on 30 July 1907. Wilson wished him well, but his mind was not on the expedition. He had other more pressing concerns. He had lost his notes. He always took relevant papers to meetings and the loss of two years of dissection records (his father wrote that his suitcase was stolen) on a Glasgow railway station, was a major blow.[52] He had kept rough notes but much of the work had to be repeated. The 1907 Grouse Committee meeting opened with the statement that the most important decision to make was that 'Wilson must have a holiday'.[53] Over the following months the Commission went on to decide on and to recommend stratagems for keeping the birds healthy. A regular cycle of burning bracken and undergrowth and cutting the heather back was advised. The numbers of birds in any particular area was matched with the amount of food available so as to reduce overcrowding and infection. The advice was practical and efficient and quickly adopted. The grouse industry was saved for an outlay of £4,366, an average of £727 a year.[54] Red grouse are still carefully monitored along with the worm burden; the worms survive worst in dry cold conditions.[55]

Wilson and Oriana, along with Scott, were regular guests of the publisher (and now friend) Reginald Smith and his wife in their shooting bungalow in Scotland. Here he could relax and be brought up to date on Scott's plans for a second expedition. It was here that in 1908 he met a young man, Apsley Cherry-Garrard (1886–1959), whose future he was to dominate. Cherry-Garrard was Reginald Smith's first cousin although thirty years his junior. When he met Wilson he was 22, the hugely wealthy owner of estates in Hertfordshire and Berkshire (his father had died less than a year previously in 1907), but a man uncertain of himself and without a definite sense of purpose. Two years after their first meeting he heard that Scott and Wilson were going south again and he was sure that this was the adventure he wanted. He wrote to Wilson to suggest that he volunteer. Wilson already liked him, and would anyway be biased in favour of a relative of Reginald Smith, but he knew that 8,000 had already applied and he was cautious about offering encouragement. When Cherry-Garrard wrote to Scott, he was turned down initially; he was young and had terrible eyesight. Wilson had suggested that Cherry-Garrard should subscribe as a volunteer and give £1,000 to help with expedition expenses[56] and Cherry-Garrard impressed Scott by sending the money independently of his being accepted. Cherry-Garrard was not alone in donating money. Captain Laurence 'Titus' Oates (1880–1912), another wealthy young man, had already agreed to donate the same amount. Cherry-Garrard was eventually included as assistant zoologist after being interviewed by Scott although he almost failed his medical being only able to see people on the other side of the road 'as vague blobs walking'.[57] In a letter to Cherry-Garrard, Wilson wrote of Scott, 'I know Scott intimately as you know. I have known him now for ten years and I believe in him so firmly that I am often sorry when he lays himself open to misunderstanding.

I am sure that you will come to know him and believe in him as I do'.[58] Cherry-Garrard felt much the same about Wilson; he absolutely believed in him. After the 1910–12 expedition he went on to feel a guilt and oppression about the death of the polar party, that coloured the remainder of his life. His book on some of his experiences in the Antarctic, *The Worst Journey in the World*,[59] was written with help from Bernard Shaw. It is a book written without the usual constraints of the period and it touched the hearts and imagination of thousands of readers. On publication it was called 'the most wonderful story in the world'.[60] It has been voted the best travel book ever written.

Wilson continued his relentless itinerary. His grouse work was reaching a conclusion, although the report was not published until 1912, but other work continued. Some of his illustrations had been seen by publishers in Edinburgh, Oliver and Boyd, who were enthusiastic about his painting, saying that they had been advised that Millais[61] could not have done better pictures. This appeared to be high praise, but Wilson wrote to his father that 'this was humbug'[62] and so it seemed to be; the comment had been made by the same Dr Eagle Clarke who had praised his *British Birds* before ditching him and the work, without pay.

When in Scotland he sometimes stayed in Lord Lovat's shooting lodge. However busy, his religious convictions coloured and infiltrated his existence and on one of these stays he visited the monks in the nearby St Benedict's Monastery. He wrote to Oriana:

Here we have no abiding place. I feel it more as I get older. . . . It is amazing and most puzzling when one tries to think what is the object of our short life on earth – a mere visit – and how desperately this must represent our effect on the little part of the world with which we come into contact. I get such a feeling of the absolute necessity to be at something always, and at every hour, day or night, before the end may come or I have done a decent portion of what I was expected to do; each minute is of value, though we often waste hours and hours, not because we want rest, nor because as sometimes it is a duty, but out of sheer

want of application. . . . The more one does the more one wants
to do. . . . I want to be able to feel and to make *you* feel, that
when my end comes, that I couldn't have done more – and then
I shall die quite happy . . .[63]

A pertinent comment in view of his early death, and he continued to put his ideas into practice. When Seaman James William
Dell of *Discovery* days could not work because of the infection
in his arm and his family struggled to manage on the £26 a
year (half the usual pay) awarded, Wilson busied himself getting further medical opinions for Dell and planned to get him
treatment in a sanatorium or a London hospital rather than in
the naval hospitals.[64]

He kept up regular contact with Scott. From August 1907
Scott was finally on half-pay for a few months and able to concentrate on Antarctic plans. He was also able to socialise for
the first time in years and he met the sculptress, Kathleen Bruce.
Scott saw in her 'a passionate commitment to work, to life and
to living' that was a happy contrast to his own puritanical
and duty-filled dedication'.[65] The couple were engaged within
months and married in the Chapel Royal at Hampton Court
Palace on 2 September 1908. When Wilson helped organise
the wardroom wedding gift, clearly still ambivalent about
Shackleton, he was uncertain as to whether he should include
Shackleton on the donor list and decided that he should, if only
for the sake of Emily Shackleton. Kathleen was to become a
forceful advocate for the expedition. In relation to her work
and the Antarctic expeditions, she made sculptures of her husband; a bust is in the Scott Polar Institute, a statue in Waterloo
Place, London and the memorial image of Wilson that stands
in the main street of Cheltenham. She also sculpted a nude 'victory' figure of T.E. Lawrence of Arabia's brother, now behind
a decorous hedge in the grounds of the Scott Polar Research
Institute in Cambridge.

Shackleton made a triumphant return to London in June
1909 having crossed the Ross Ice Barrier and found the
way up onto the polar plateau through a pass he named the

Beardmore Glacier, after his sponsor, William Beardmore.[66] He had made the most significant advances and reached to within ninety-seven miles of the Pole. But in spite of these great achievements, he had perpetrated a cardinal sin in Wilson's eyes by landing on McMurdo, as he could not get through the ice pack around King Edward VII Land. Scott felt that this had always been his intention and felt betrayed. Wilson never forgave Shackleton in spite of being familiar with the conditions that Shackleton would have met and being aware that exploration costs made it important that sponsors got a good return for their money. He felt that the compromise that he had bartered had been broken and his deep and intransigent sense of right and wrong was affronted. He wrote to Shackleton to say that he was glad that they had been able to meet and talk in a friendly manner but giving his uncompromising opinion that Shackleton had broken his word. He said the Shackleton had taken Scott's job practically out of his hands, against his wish and knowing that Scott was hoping to finish it. He wrote that he thought that Shackleton should not have gone, but since he had, the correct course now was for him to be as generous to Scott as Scott had been to him, by stating publicly that he had had his turn at the Pole and that the field was now open to Scott 'to take up his own work again'. He told Shackleton to 'play the game now by him as he has played the game by you'.[67] He finished the friendship.

Scott knew that Shackleton's return without a polar 'hit' had reopened the door to his own ambitions. His plans solidified. Having obtained the necessary assurance from Shackleton that he had no objection to the next Antarctic adventure, he sent a telegram to Wilson on 16 September asking him to organise and lead the scientific staff for the expedition due to leave England in June 1910. Wilson accepted, writing to his father in September, 'Scott is a man worth working for as a man'.[68] He wrote to his mother,

> For my own part I have long been convinced that the first principle of right living is to put one's life into the hands of God

and then do the work he gives one to do. I know one sometimes has to make a choice between two pieces of work which offer; but when one alone is offered one is meant to do it trusting it will turn out all right in the end. . . . There has been no choice and therefore no difficulty to my mind in deciding and I am to go as 'Leader of Scientific Staff', a high sounding title with the disagreeable duty attached to it of having to reply to toasts on behalf of the Scientific Staff at the Send-off dinner.[69]

So began further, seemingly endless work. He had to complete his writings on grouse disease. He was still working on *British Birds* and *British Mammals* and the preparations needed for the expedition were formidable. He was consulted on details of every department in addition to his own. Most importantly he had to select his staff, inspect the scientific instruments, calculate food values and quantities for men and animals, consult on details for depot laying and keep up with his correspondence. He wrote, 'My work is endless; it seems as if I could not possibly get through it all, and yet bit by bit it gets done'.[70] He had to work standing up to keep awake. Probably at the suggestion of his wife, he tried to introduce some balance in his life and had his portrait painted. The portrait, now in the Scott Polar Research Institute at Cambridge, shows a strong face, a man of purpose and determination. The commission was done by Alfred Soord (1868–1915), a pupil of Wilson's famous artistic neighbour, Herkomer. Soord went on to paint both of Wilson's parents and 'Titus' Oates' mother, Caroline. He also prepared, from her description, a 'portrait' of a lady's dead father. She had no photographs to show him. On being shown the result, she shook her head sadly and commented on how he had changed. Wilson enjoyed the enforced relaxation and wrote to Soord:

I too learned a lot from our conversations. You have done a great deal more than to paint a picture which will be a great comfort to my 'grass-widow'. . . . My character is weathered or ought to be as you have painted it, and I pray God it may be increasingly to the end . . . for 'here we have no abiding place and this is not our rest'.[71]

He spent his last English Christmas at Westal with his family. His father recorded that he was the gayest and liveliest of the family. He gave a copy of *The South Polar Times* to his godson, the son of his St George's friend, Hugh Fraser. He visited his brother-in-law Bernard Rendall's school in Sussex and thanked the boys for their help in providing a sledge for the expedition and contributing to the purchase of scientific instruments, (support equalled by donations from all over the country). Before he joined Scott's new ship, *Terra Nova*, in June 1910 he had one further experience to cram in.

For years he had wanted to go on a whaling boat from the Shetland Islands in Scotland. He wanted to update his knowledge on whales and whaling techniques and if possible to obtain the services of a Norwegian whaling gunner. It was 'now or never'. He travelled to Scotland arriving in Orkney on 1 June. Here he was enthused by the herring-fishery industry, the steam trawlers, the tugs, the harbour, the lighthouse, the seabirds and the sheep. He went to the cathedral and sketched the monument of Dr John Ray, who had investigated the loss of Franklin and his crew in the Arctic and who had found the remains of bodies, identified by their possessions, as part of that ill-fated expedition. In his report to the Admiralty, which was published in *The Times* in July 1854, Ray had written that the survivors had been driven to cannibalism.[72] This had attracted much hostility and he was ostracised. Wilson wrote that he 'lay asleep wrapped in a buffalo sleeping bag with moccasins on, and just a book open by his side . . . [He] sleeps soundly in this little out-of-the-way Cathedral honoured by his own people and caring nothing for the rest'.[73] On this northern visit Wilson met a future companion, Edward W. Nelson (1883–1923), the biologist on *Terra Nova,* 'who has known the Shetlands all his life and will one day own half of them'.[74]

Whaling was a lucrative, very dangerous business. Oil was needed for fuel, and bones for corsets, hairbrushes and whips.

Whaling ships were fast and rugged; the one that Wilson was on rolled from side to side and twisted and untwisted unendingly. Its deck was awash with water that reached to his knees and at first he 'wasn't sure he could go on'.[75] It was a day or two before he could stagger on deck to breathe air instead of 'concentrated Chief Engineer and whale oil'. The Engineer was 'a perfectly hugely fat pendulous man, who always came down the gangway backwards and squeezed into his cabin door sideways'.[76]

The Captain was a 'Viking' of a man' who had killed almost every species of whale. Harpoon guns were used to kill the whales. These were often shot from small wooden whaleboats that trailed the whales as the huge sea monsters moved underwater, to be close enough to kill the beasts as they slowly rose out of the sea, blowing out huge spouts of spray. The harpoon carried lines that anchored the poor beast, and the whaleboat crew could be treated to a 'sleigh ride' as the whale dragged its hunters through the sea, often for hours, in its attempt to escape. Eventually the whale was winched back to the ship. It was essential to prevent damage from the immense flaying tail and any residual signs of life were extinguished by a *coup de grâce* from a long lance thrust through the heart or chest. The body, belly up, floated high in the water and was kept on the surface by having air pumped into it. Wilson thought it a 'great and thrilling sport, no more cruel in proportion than the shooting of a stag'.[77] He had clearly moved on from his complete allegiance to St Francis.

Returning to Cheltenham, he valued Oriana more and more. She had carefully prepared his possessions for the Antarctic and the ports of call on the way. He had to continue working late into the night on his last days at home, but Oriana insisted on staying up with him. He wrote, 'we were both tired out and dreadfully short of sleep but I remember these last days with her as days of the most perfect companionship I have ever known'.[78] He wrote to Dr Fraser that Oriana took the place of all friends and rendered him independent of them though not indifferent:

My wife is all my friends and all my relatives and I often wonder why she has never been taken from me, as good things so
often are when they become the breath of one's very existence.
My religious convictions are precisely what they were when you
knew me at 'The Corner' [St George's at Hyde Park Corner], but
they don't show so much.[79]

The final few days before departure were truly chaotic. On
Monday 13 June Wilson and Oriana travelled to London; he
was still writing up a paper for the Zoological Society and doing
more illustrations for *British Mammals*. In London he arranged
for whaling equipment to be taken down to Cardiff (the starting port for *Terra Nova*), purchased scientific equipment, said
his goodbyes to friends and continued with the grouse report,
which was finally to be sent back from South Africa. They travelled to Cardiff on 15 June. Oriana and his parents stayed on
board for the first thirty miles or so of *Terra Nova's* voyage.
They parted without anguish. Oriana was to meet him in South
Africa. He went 'full of hope for their next meeting'.[80] And so
to his bunk for the first good sleep in days.

II

Terra Nova

Scott said, 'A true sportsman is not jealous of his record or slow to praise those who surpass it',[1] but there was surely schadenfreude behind these generous comments; he must have been secretly relieved that the South Pole still remained unconquered and within his grasp. He must have been delighted that Wilson had chosen to go with him.

Terra Nova, a three-masted, scarred, worn, wooden whaling vessel had been purchased for £12,500. (*Discovery* was by now owned by the Hudson's Bay Company who refused to give her up). *Terra Nova* had already been in action in the Antarctic during the *Discovery* rescue of 1904. In 1910 she left the London docks in early June, so as to be in New Zealand by mid-November.[2] This meant, it was hoped, that she could force her way through the pack ice earlier than usual and that the expedition could set up a base in the Antarctic by the beginning of 1911.[3] *Terra Nova* sailed round the south coast of England to Cardiff which was to be her final leaving point, eleven days after the burial of that royal Antarctic sponsor, King Edward VII. The beginnings of both Antarctic expeditions were overshadowed therefore by the death of the reigning sovereign.

She sailed under a White Ensign; the Admiralty had relented since *Discovery* days and *Terra Nova* was allowed to fly the naval flag. Cardiff was chosen as her leaving port in appreciation of the support given by the Welsh to the expedition in terms of cash donations, coal, oil and scientific equipment. Scott announced that Cardiff would be the first port of call on returning to England. Indeed three years later, in June 1913, she sailed into Cardiff again, to be paid off.

Terra Nova sailed from British shores on 15 June. The usual bands, flags, gun salutes and cheering crowds were there to send her off. Wilson wrote that the steam sirens and hooters 'of which Cardiff seemed to possess an infinite number, made a perfectly hideous din'.[4] His parents, sister and Oriana stayed on board for a short while. They were excited by the noisy bustle and his father wrote that when the ship got out of the dock 'the rocks, quays and every corner was occupied by people cheering like mad'.[5] He said that when he got back to Westal, the house felt 'dull and flat' without his son. But he proudly wrote that Wilson was 'very bright but fearfully busy . . . being wanted in every direction as head of scientific staff'.[6] Scott planned that *Terra Nova* would berth in Madeira, South Africa, Australia and New Zealand on her way to the Antarctic but he himself was not on board for the early part of the voyage; he stayed in England to continue fundraising (the expedition was still £8,000 in the red). Lieutenant Edward Ratcliffe Garth Russell Evans (1881–1957), second-in-command and navigator, was master. Scott with Kathleen, Oriana and Hilda Evans, Lieutenant Evans's wife, were to meet the ship in South Africa.

Although opinions varied as to the value of polar exploration and its results,[7] 8,000 had applied to join the expedition, eager to 'reach a spot on the surface of the globe which has hitherto been untrodden by human feet unseen by human eye'.[8] The President of the Royal Geographical Society opined that the expedition was 'going to prove once again that the manhood of the nation is not dead and that the characteristics of our ancestors, who won this great empire, still flourish amongst us'.[9] The ship's complement was listed as officers, scientific staff (Wilson, as chief of scientific staff and zoologist, amongst these) and men, and divided into 'Shore Parties' and 'Ship's Party'.[10] Wilson was listed amongst the Shore Parties. The seamen were nearly all from the Royal Navy and three of them – William Lashly the chief stoker, Tom Crean and Edgar Evans, both petty officers – were ex-*Discovery* sailors. The 'Scientific Staff' included the ski expert Tryggve

Gran (1889–1980), a sub-lieutenant in the Norwegian Royal Navy and 'a delightful young Norwegian giant',[11] and Wilson's protégé, Cherry-Garrard, who sailed under the impressive title of 'Batchelor of Arts, Assistant Zoologist'. The horribly over-loaded ship carried amongst all the tons of essential equipment, 1,200 lbs of tobacco and 30,000 cigars. More personnel, dogs and horses were to be squeezed on in New Zealand.

For Wilson most of the ship's complement were new acquaintances though he was of course close to Scott and Cherry-Garrard and had met Edward Nelson, *Terra Nova's* biologist. He would have remembered Lashly and Crean as well as 'Swansea's Antarctic explorer', the big Welshman, Petty Officer Edgar Evans (1876–1912). Before the ship's departure Evans had been a speaker at a banquet held in honour of the expedition in which he said that no one else would have induced him to go to the Antarctic again but if there is a man in the world who could bring this to a successful conclusion Captain Scott was that man. Evans had a tendency to drink but Scott described him as 'A giant worker with a truly remarkable headpiece'.[12]

Wilson was hopeful about the expedition. He had written to his father:

> As Scott's only companion on the previous voyage I shall have a good position in the Expedition from the first. . . . As leader of Scientific Staff I shall have a wider opportunity of making a success in that if possible, so that no one can say it has only been a Pole hunt, though that of course is *sine qua non*. We *must* get to the Pole; but we shall get more too and there shall be no loop-holes for error in means and methods if care in preparation can avoid them. I can promise you it is a work worth anyone's time and care and I feel it is a really great opportunity.[13]

Wilson's role before departure had been to help fulfil Scott's aim of continuing and developing the scientific work started on *Discovery*. He helped appoint the largest team that had ever gone with a southern expedition. He chose as meteorologist George Clarke Simpson (1878–1965), on loan from the Indian Weather Bureau, who was to become 'the father of Antarctic meteorology'. Simpson had been turned down for the 1901-4 expedition on health grounds but was keenly accepted this time. In later life he became Director of the British Meteorological Office. Wilson wrote that Simpson was their only real socialist, anti-everything and a firm believer in the *Manchester Guardian*.[14] Simpson's assistant was Charles Wright (1887–1975), a 23-year-old Canadian Physicist who had also been an undergraduate at Gonville and Caius. The scientific party included three geologists, two from Cambridge: Australian-educated Griffith Taylor (1880–1964) and Raymond Priestley (1886–1964). Taylor and Priestley joined the ship in New Zealand along with a third geologist, Frank Debenham (1883–1965), another Australian who went on to establish and become first director of the Scott Polar Research Institute in Cambridge and to become a Fellow of Gonville and Caius.

The scientific staff included two marine biologists from the Plymouth Marine Laboratory. Dennis Lillie (1884–1963) was at that time a frail, 26-year-old. He was predominantly concerned with deep-sea work and wrote the expedition's official report on whales. He was also a caricaturist. Wilson liked his work and redrew some of his caricatures for *The South Polar Times*. The second biologist was Edward Nelson, who Wilson had already met in Scotland. Kathleen Scott described Nelson as a man who 'spends all his time on shore being a man about town which makes him look exceedingly tired'.[15] Nelson was known as, amongst other things, 'Antonio the Immaculate', because he always wore a clean collar at dinnertime,[16] or Marie. The engineer in charge of the motor sledges, Bernard Day (1884–1935), had been to the Antarctic before, in 1907. He was also listed as a scientist.

Wilson had at least one detractor. The experienced Australian geologist Douglas Mawson (1882–1958), who had made major contributions to Shackleton's expedition, was approached by Scott to return to the Antarctic with him, but would only accept if offered the role of chief scientific officer, a position clearly not vacant. Perhaps predictably he noted later, 'I did not like Dr Wilson'.[17]

The officers were the Second in Command 'Teddy' Evans who in later years was promoted to Admiral and made Lord Mountevans. Evans was a skilled navigator and a man of energy and enthusiasm who had taken part in the relief of Scott's *Discovery* expedition in 1902. Early in the expedition he painted out the Plimsoll line[18] on the ship to avoid drawing the attention of the authorities (who might have prevented sailing) to her overburdened state. The mate was an old Etonian,[19] Lieutenant Victor Campbell (1875–1956), who had lived in Norway and could ski well. As on *Discovery* there were two doctors, Murray Levick (1877–1956) and Edward Atkinson (1882–1929), both London graduates. Wilson had no problems with them although both were more experienced in medicine than him. He said that Atkinson did nothing without informing him and asking for his approval.

The officers included two men fated to pass into the annals of Antarctic legend: Lieutenant Henry Robertson Bowers (1883–1912), gentle and honest with unquenchable spirits and energy, was accepted by Scott, sight unseen, on the forceful recommendation of Sir Clements Markham. Wilson must have been as startled as most people at his first sight of the plump little man with an immense nose and red bristly hair who was immediately called 'Birdie'.[20] The other was another old Etonian, Laurence Oates (1880–1912), who had given £1,000 towards the expedition and who signed on as midshipman at one shilling per week. He was called Titus, after the seventeenth-century anti-Catholic conspirator Titus Oates, or Soldier, because of his military experience in the Boer War when a bullet had sliced through his left thigh and fractured his leg. Oates was a captain of the 6th Inniskilling Dragoons[21] and the first soldier to join a British polar expedition. At his interview, he told a friend afterwards, he had said that he had no intention of being left at base and that he wanted to be in the party attempting the Pole.[22] His final words, before crawling out of the doomed tent to his death in 1912, were to become permanently famous: 'I am just going outside and may be some time'.[23]

The photographer or 'camera artist' was Herbert George Ponting (1870–1935). He was to create the most beautiful black and white stills (the originals are in the Scott Polar Institute) and a film of the early part of the expedition. Wilson described his work as 'beyond all praise' and planned a joint exhibition with Ponting after his return.[24]

The ship was slow. Wilson described her as having two speeds, slow and slower, and she took two months to get to South Africa, but the routine of regular work was soon in place, four-hour shifts, stoking the boiler, trimming the sails. Wilson maintained a busy schedule. He was woken at 4a.m. with a mug of cocoa. His duties included overseeing the scientific programme, completing commissioned sketches and paintings for the journals, writing up his whaling notes and finishing the grouse paintings (entry after entry in his diary records the hours he spent on these). He did a few medical duties though: diagnosing measles in Lillie and operating on Dr Atkinson's infected finger. He did not just limit himself to his scientific work but took part in the three-hour coal-trimming rota, moving coal from the main hold to bunkers to feed one of the three furnaces. He wrote to Oriana, 'in ten minutes we are streaming with sweat. . . . The air in the hold is always tested first to make sure it is breathable'.[25] The heat of the furnaces burnt their eyes. As the ship progressed into the tropics the conditions were to get worse; 'stoke-hole flies', drops of hot oil from the engines, stung the men's skin continuously as they worked in the hold.

Terra Nova arrived in Madeira after an eight-day sail. Wilson thought it 'grand'. But he still was behind on his commissions, particularly the grouse report. He took the grouse paintings on shore and set up in a café where he finally completed them, having worked through most of the night. He received 'two letters and a wire from Ory whereas poor Campbell and Evans did not hear from their wives at all'.[26]

He was permanently busy. He said a few hours rest at sea went a long way, but he still had to work standing up to stop falling asleep. He commandeered a corner of the baggage-room cabin and wrote on a suitcase perched on top of a washstand and was at his 'desk' most mornings from 4 until 6a.m. or on until breakfast. He could not work in his cabin, which he shared with Evans.[27] It was small, with little light, less air and no table or chairs. If he ever left papers out there they invariably landed on the greasy floor as the ship rolled along. But the voyage showed him nature at her attractive best and there was always someone about with expert knowledge to explain her mysteries.[28] It is difficult to imagine how beautiful even the most common animals are until they are seen fresh-coloured from the deep sea. As they went along constant cries rang out: whale, whale, new bird, dolphin. Wilson painted them all.

Terra Nova crossed the Line on 5 July. As on *Discovery*, Neptune (Seaman Evans) and his attendants arrived to initiate those men crossing for the first time. Wilson having been 'done' on *Discovery* watched as the hapless initiate was made to swallow a soap and tallow 'pill', as big as a golf-ball, washed down by a vinegar/cayenne mixture and lathered with flour, soot and water, shaved to the waist with a great wooden razor and dropped backwards into a bath. He had thought the performance barbaric on *Discovery* but now, as an onlooker, he was definitely more tolerant of proceedings.[29]

On Saturday 16 July, his wedding anniversary, he painted a 'sunrise' for Oriana. Seven days later, his birthday (he was thirty-eight) was celebrated in the middle of the night with dancing and singing on the main hatch dog kennel by his friends who had managed to forget the date in their busy schedule. Wilson wrote that 'everyone was overflowing with good nature'.[30] He was one of the oldest aboard and was called 'Uncle Bill' but he wrote enthusiastically to Sir Clements that he could not find the words to say how lucky they were with the choice of officers and civilian staff and how well they got on together and how they were bursting with health and spirits.[31] The feeling of being old soon wore off. He enjoyed the atmosphere on board which he described as being like an undergraduate outing with plenty of horseplay.

'Birdie' Bowers was also appraising his new companions. Of them all, the man who impressed him the most was Wilson. He wrote to his mother:

He is the soundest man we have, a chap who I would trust with anything. I am sure he is a real Christian [as was Birdie]; there is no mistaking it – it comes out in everything. Of course he has more presence than anybody in the mess, being the oldest and certainly the wisest.

He wrote later, 'I still think him the most pre-eminent chap – the perfect gentleman – the most manly and the finest character in my own sex that I have ever had the privilege to meet'.[32] The admiration was mutual. Wilson wrote that Bowers had 'the most unselfish character I think I have ever seen in a man anywhere'.[33]

The sailing track of ships from England ran out towards South America and, as on *Discovery* in 1900, the itinerary included a stop in South Trinidad. When they arrived on 26 July, Wilson and some others went ashore. South Trinidad was very interesting to Wilson. The birds, having rarely seen humans, were fearless and their variety was remarkable. With Cherry-Garrard he collected Trinidad petrel birds, white terns and 'handsome' gannets. Wilson himself wrote that the petrel named after him after his visit in 1901, and the other Trinidad petrels, were in fact all varieties of the same species; a fact confirmed later. The land crabs remained as nightmarish as in *Discovery* days. Their dead staring eyes followed the men as if willing them to fall down. They pecked at the men's boots hopefully. When the men returned to the shore to go back to the ship, they found themselves trapped by thirty-foot waves. The pick-up boat could not get through and they all had to haul themselves to the ship on a lifeline, pulling through the raging water and mindful of the fourteen sharks that had been seen in it that very morning. One sailor lost the rope and was battered to and fro onto the rocks. He eventually managed to get a hold, though underwater for 'an impossible length of time'.[34] Wilson's reaction to the whole incident was unruffled. He sat on the top of a rock coolly eating a biscuit. He thought that 'only the British temperament, (knowing there was nothing they could do), could quietly watch a man fighting for his life'.[35]

From South Trinidad onwards, Wilson stopped sketching to finish off the written parts of the grouse report, a task that must have seemed never-ending. But he thrived on the atmosphere on *Terra Nova*. He wrote to Reginald Smith: 'there hasn't been a single quarrelsome word on the ship on the way to the Cape'. He was pleased too that Cherry-Garrard, his protégé, was a success and wrote that Cherry-Garrard was flourishing, was as strong as a horse and popular; he had never seen anyone enjoying life more. Cherry proved to be a conscientious assistant zoologist; he skinned birds all of one night to save them from decomposing in the heat.[36]

Terra Nova arrived in Simonstown on 15 August. Oriana, her sister Constance and Teddy Evan's wife, Hilda, were waiting. The arrival was newsworthy and the *Cape Times* reporters were there. Wilson had finally got his grouse report finished. This was an enormous relief though he felt sorry for the poor proofreader, as the papers had been written in pencil on a heavily rolling ship. He and Oriana visited a whaling station and then felt free to devote themselves wholeheartedly to flowers and birds.

We were in a sort of enchanted land where the commonest things were all new and beautiful and one's foot crushes new beauties at every step. The variety of lovely Irises and small lilies and daisies and marigolds and heaths and geraniums and Heaven knows what, was quite bewildering and unreal.[37]

The birds were equally fascinating: on a hilltop he saw a black and white buzzard with a red-brown tail, perched on its eyrie on a rock, looking like a monument.

When Scott, having travelled independently to South Africa, arrived on board, Wilson was dismayed to be ordered to leave *Terra Nova* and to sail to Melbourne on *Corinthic,* a steamer. Scott wanted to get to know the crew and he moved into Wilson's cabin with Evans.[38] Wilson's orders were to go ahead to organise expedition matters, appoint a third geologist and to travel to Sydney to make a presentation for a Federal Government grant towards the expedition. He was to travel with Oriana, Kathleen Scott and Hilda Evans. Neither Wilson nor Lieutenant Evans was happy with the decision, 'for we felt there would not be lacking people who would put their own construction on such an unexpected change of plan at the first opportunity' (i.e. a lack in confidence or even an envy of Evans).[39] For himself, Wilson thought unhappily about the undesired comfort of a liner, rather than the happy-go-lucky attractive discomforts of the *Terra Nova*. He knew also that speeches and money-raising were not his forte. But he had no choice and he wrote to Sir Clements that it would give Scott a chance to get to know the 'first rate lot of men he has to work with him'.[40]

In the event the quartet that travelled together was an uncomfortable mix. Kathleen was probably too exciting and flamboyant for her companions and did not easily get on with any of them. She thought Wilson humourless, as probably he was in her presence. She later described Oriana, who had the ability to behave with someone she did not like as if that person did not exist,[41] as 'a absurd prig'.[42] She was later to have a furious row with Hilda Evans.

The uneasy quartet arrived in Melbourne ten days before *Terra Nova*. On a depressing, rainy 12 October, Wilson spent the afternoon in a motor launch, saddled with wives and mail-bags, searching the bay for news of the vessel. When the ship was eventually sighted Kathleen demanded that they set off again in total darkness and a rough sea. 'Ory behaved like a brick all through our difficulties in the bay, but in future I hope it will never fall to my lot to have more than one wife at a time to look after, at any rate in a motor launch, in running sea at night time'.[43] However the main reasons for him going to Melbourne, money-raising and appointing a geologist, went well. Asking for money was a disagreeable business. Seeing so many senior state officials every day and agitating important ministers, including the Federal Prime Minister, the Rt Hon Andrew Fisher, for a grant was a trial, but he was rewarded with £2,500 from the

Federal Government and £2,500 from a private individual. Appointing Raymond Priestley as geologist was, by contrast, a pleasure and he wrote to Sir Clements that the excellent crowd on *Terra Nova* would manage the Pole before anyone else, whether Japanese or German.[44] Invited to a Lord Mayor's Ball given in honour of Dutch ships also visiting Melbourne, he was unimpressed by the Dutch officers; the older ones were 'stout, bald and ugly, the younger officers with one or two exceptions were well on the way to becoming stout, bald and ugly'.[45]

In Melbourne on 12 October Scott received the now famous terse telegram from Roald Amundsen, 'Beg leave to inform you *Fram* [his ship] proceeding Antarctic'. The race to the Pole was about to begin although Scott did not at first realise that the Pole was Amundsen's intended target.[46] Roald Amundsen (1872–1928), a Norwegian, had planned and schemed to be a polar explorer from his early years. He was already famous. He had made the first navigation through the Northwest Passage and had travelled to the Antarctic in 1897, though not to its interior. He had sailed from Norway in 1910 on *Fram* with the professed intention of heading to the Arctic basin and the North Pole. But this was a feint (though he kept the truth from his financial backers as well as those on board). Months before, when he heard that two Americans, Frederick A. Cook and Robert E. Peary, had both claimed independently to have reached the North Pole, he understood immediately that this dealt the death blow to his own enterprise and ambition. As *Fram* was about to leave Madeira he summoned the crew and told his astonished listeners that he was sailing for the Antarctic and that their destination was the Bay of Whales. This was a bay on the Barrier that had been discovered by Shackleton in 1908, situated a few hundred miles along the coast from Scott's destination on McMurdo Sound. For Amundsen, the Pole and back was a race with the British from the start. He expected to beat Scott by two or three weeks.[47]

Terra Nova sailed to New Zealand to take her final supply of coal. Here, for the first time, when Scott was in Wellington on more fund-raising efforts, rumours of a 'Challenge for South Pole' reached him when he was eagerly interviewed by local newspaper reporters. Scott now clearly understood that Amundsen could snatch his prize from him. On reflection he decided that it was too late to change the plans that had been widely publicised in his fund-raising campaign, and which could explain the timing of Amundsen's announcement. He decided to continue with the scientific and geographical programmes as planned, as well as the Pole attempt.

Wilson thought that the base that Amundsen had chosen on the Barrier was unsafe; it was on sea ice which he thought might break up. But of course the Norwegian group could be fortunate and the dogs a success, in which case Amundsen would reach the Pole first. He could travel faster, with dogs and expert skiers, than the British with their ponies and could also start earlier; the British did not want to expose the ponies to the October temperatures. Oates also rated their chances of success as good. The Norwegians were a very tough lot, 'very good ski runners while the British could only walk'.[48] He wrote to his mother, 'I must say we have made far too much noise about ourselves. All that photographing, cheering, steaming through the fleet etc is rot and if we fail it will only make us look more foolish.'[49]

Terra Nova arrived in New Zealand on 29 October and was welcomed with open arms. Officers and men were told that 'although already separated by thousands of miles from their native land, here in this new land they would find a second home and those who would equally think of them in their absence and welcome them on their return'.[50] Oriana was waiting for her husband. She was staying with Lady Bowen,[51] 'such a real old English home and such a dear old lady'. Wilson loved New Zealand all over again. He thought that there were the people and places he most wanted to be with. *Terra Nova* spent a month being unloaded and reloaded under Bowers capable instruction. She was put in dry-dock where, once again, leaks were plugged, pumps cleaned and bolts tightened. Tourists toured in their hundreds. For Wilson the time was passed in a whirl of business and social engagements as he and Oriana renewed their friendships with local people. The Bowens and their daughter Lily encouraged the Wilsons to use their house as if it was their home.

But in spite of all the bustle, his faith remained central and he chose this last time before departure to enter into discussions with the Bishop of Wellington about the priesthood. Oriana did not support the idea of a fuller commitment to the church. Years later she wrote to Wilson's younger brother Jim, himself ordained, that she thought a man could do so much for others without taking holy orders, especially a scientific man.[52] Although Wilson abandoned ideas of the Church, he continued to insinuate the 'Truth' into each day; this continued the core of his existence.

In New Zealand, *Terra Nova* was loaded with yet more stores, food, equipment, men, dogs and horses. The extra human cargo included the Australian-based contingent: Griffith Taylor; Frank Debenham; Raymond Priestley; Bernard Day, the motor mechanic; and the camera-artist and cinematographer, 41-year-old Herbert Ponting. When *Terra Nova* finally left New Zealand on 29 November Wilson had more than sixty officers, scientists and seamen as fellow-travellers; thirty-two allocated to the Ship Party, thirty-two to the Shore Party. Other additions included nineteen white or dapple-grey Manchurian ponies; ponies of this colour were bought because lighter ponies lived longer on Shackleton's expedition.[53] The purchase of ponies was helped by donations from schools all over the country, (as were many things including sleeping bags, sledges and tents), they were housed in stables just above the sailors' quarters, so that the animals' urine was intermittently and unceremoniously sprayed onto the sailors' bunks. Also on deck and also bought with help from schools, were thirty-three Siberian dogs, snarling, howling and fouling the decks, each dog chained at a safe distance from the next and so all over the deck. Presumably inflaming the predatory dogs to their limits, were a cat, a kitten, three rabbits, a pigeon, squirrels and a guinea pig. The deck, which looked like a floating farmyard, was further congested, Wilson wrote, by: more than 150 mutton carcasses and two beef carcasses; three deck-houses; all the equipment for the laboratories; an ice house; five boats; sledges; enormous cases with the motor sledges; horse fodder, which Oates had thought was insufficient and bought, at his own expense, two more tons of; and more than 100 cases of petrol, oil and paraffin. Coal was mostly stored in the hold and bunkers but thirty tons were thrown down on the deck wherever there was space. The petrol was stored in cases, which formed a floor to the upper deck.

Not only the dogs and ponies but also their handlers came on board. The choice of the animals had been left to Cecil Meares (1887–1937), the dog expert, who had travelled in Russia, spoke Russian fluently and knew where to purchase dogs in Siberia. His choice of ponies was considered a crucial mistake; Oates thought that they were old, lame and diseased. To get his menagerie back to New Zealand and the ship, Meares hired two Russians: the jockey Anton Lukich Omelchenko (1883–1932) and a dog driver, 22-year-old Demitri Gerof (1888–?1932). They were accompanied by one of Kathleen Scott's brothers, Wilfred Bruce (1874–1953), a Royal Naval lieutenant. The whole troop travelled from Vladivostok to Melbourne and then to Lyttleton.

The time in New Zealand was not without incident; Kathleen Scott and Hilda Evans did not get on. Bowers attributed this to mutual jealousy, though he adored Hilda Evans.[54] This developed eventually to a 'magnificent battle'; Oates said he had been told that it was a draw after fifteen rounds. He said that Oriana flung herself into the fight after the tenth round and there was more blood and hair flying about the hotel than you would see in a Chicago slaughterhouse in a month. The husbands got a bit of the backlash and there is a certain amount of coolness which I hope they won't bring into the hut with them.[55] But before the ship sailed, Kathleen gave conciliatory tea to Hilda and Oriana on the ship. Two of them would never see their husbands again.

On Wilson and Oriana's last day, they bid a sad goodbye to Lady Bowen and Lily and travelled to Christchurch. Friends came to see them off; Wilson was especially pleased with a bouquet of flowers for his Oriana from an old lady who had travelled miles to present it. (Wilson took the verbena out of the bouquet, dried it and took it with him on his travels).[56] Then they travelled to Dunedin for the final send-off. Even there they had to go to a dinner and dance in honour of the officers. After a few hours Oriana and Wilson 'went back to the hotel and there we were very happy

for the last evening together for some time – poor dear'.[57] When
Terra Nova cast off on 29 November Oriana stayed on board for
as long as possible before leaving on a tug. Wilson wrote:

> I saw her disappear out of sight waving happily, a goodbye that
> will be with me till the day I see her again in this world or the next
> – I think it will be in this world and some time in 1912. We had
> excellent weather for a start and a sunny day for a send-off.[58]

He asked Dr Fraser, his friend from St George's, to look after
Oriana when she got back to England and he remembered his
godson; he hoped that he would grow up as honest as his father
'and then he isn't far wrong'.[59]

They were dogged with problems from the start. When *Terra
Nova* was three days out of Port Lyttelton the expedition was hit
by disaster. The winds rose, seas poured over both sides of the
ship filling her waist with water and tearing everything adrift.
Terra Nova was dangerously overladen, and with laboratories,
boats, ice house, sheep carcasses, motor sledges, stables, dogs,
horses, petrol cases and more on the upper deck, she 'wallowed
in the water like a thing without life'.[60] A force-ten wind howled
and shrieked through the rigging. The water gradually dislodged
the petrol cases roped onto the deck and the forage food and
hurled bags of coal around the deck like battering rams. Wilson
wrote that when they plunged into the drowned waist of the
ship to grab a broken case they often got caught by a wave 'and
the green sea would sweep along the deck, over one's shoulders
while the cases beneath all floated up anyhow, jamming one's
seaboots and themselves in every possible direction and forcing
one often to drop everything and cling to the rail'.[61] They had
to throw coal sacks overboard so that they could tie the petrol
cases down again. The ship's violent movements opened up the
deck seams and water poured below, washing quantities of coal
dust into the bilges. This dust combined with oil in the bilges to
form hard balls, which choked the pumps' suction.

The dogs, whose on-board existence was awful at the best of
times, were thrown around, held on board by their neck chains.

One died. The ponies too began to fall: first one, then another, then another. Oates and Atkinson had to work desperately to try to keep them standing. In spite of their efforts one pony died. All hands laboured in the waist of the ship to bail water out of the boiler room, often submerged as they worked. As the night wore on and the wind got higher, the ship plunged up and down even more distractedly. The pumps were clogged, waves of filthy water washed to and fro in the engine rooms, the fires had to be put out and the engines stopped. The ship was at the mercy of the storm. It seemed that unless the pumps could be repaired the expedition would end before it got near the Antarctic. A 'bucket group' bailed water continuously for twelve hours in sweltering heat. It was impossible to get at the pumps through the hatch, so to get at them a hole had to be made in the engine room bulk-head, coal dug out from the next compartment and another hole cut into the suction well where the main handpump was located. Lieutenant Evans and Bowers squeezed into the pump shaft and, sometimes submerging completely in filthy oily water, passed back buckets and buckets of balls of the coal and oil sludge that had been blocking the pump. At last 'to the joy of all, a good stream of water came from the pump for the first time'.[62] Throughout, and in spite of, apparent impending disaster, the crew's courage remained high. Officers and men kept their spirits up by singing sea shanties. Wilson in particular was undismayed:

> I must say I enjoyed it all from beginning to end, and as one bunk became untenable after another, owing to the wet, and com-ments became more and more to the point, as people searched out dry spots here and there to finish the night, in oilskins and great coats on the cabin or wardroom floors, I thought that things were becoming interesting.[63]

When the pumps failed he wrote:

> It was a weird night's work with the howling gale and the darkness and the immense sea running over the ship every few minutes and no engines and no sail and we all in the engine room

black as ink with engine room oil and bilge water, singing shanties as we passed up slopping buckets full of bilge, each man
above slopping a little over the heads of us all below him, wet
through to the skin, so much so that some of the party worked
altogether naked.[64]

He did not get seasick, though some men had to vomit and bail
alternately, but he must have been a calming influence; the men
who worked beside him realised that he had no fear and had
a faith that could interpret a rainbow that he saw fleetingly at
the height of the storm as the hope, or indeed the confirmation,
that all would be well.[65] In two days the nightmare was over.
The fires were relit and the ship was pumped dry. Scott heaped
praise on his crew.

As they pushed southwards using sail and steam they sang the
hymn, 'Eternal Father Strong to Save'. But the hymns were no
talisman; they had to face more problems. On 9 December they
entered the pack ice to the north of the Ross Sea. This year the ice
stretched further north than it had in 1901. Hopes to get through
it quickly, as had happened on *Discovery*, were doomed.

For Cherry-Garrard the slow transit through the ice was a revelation. He wrote, 'No one of us whose privilege it was to be there
will forget our first sight of penguins, our first meal of seal meat,
or the first big berg along which we coasted close in order that
London might see it on film.' He liked the little Adéle penguins
hurrying to meet them, 'Great Scott, they seemed to say, what's
this? "Aark, aark" they said and full of wonder and curiosity and
perhaps a little out of breath, they stopped every now and then to
express their feelings'.[66] Wilson thought the penguins as attractive
as ever. The birds liked the sound of the men singing and would
gather round admiringly as the crew bellowed out 'She's got bells
on her fingers and rings on her toes'. Meares' voice though, singing 'God Save the King', always sent them scurrying into the
water. He sang flat, perhaps that was why.[67]

Terra Nova did not escape from the pack until 29 December,
twenty days after entering (*Discovery* had taken four). Sometimes
she moved so slowly that skiing lessons went on alongside her.

Extra water was harvested. Fresh water, as opposed to seawater, was essential so gangs of sailors, singing sea shanties as they worked, cut great chunks of ice out of old salt-free floes. Wilson occupied himself with drawing, reading, skinning penguins (wanted for eating) and cleaning skulls and skeletons. He taught his assistant zoologist how to kill the birds by the humane method of 'pithing' them with a long needle driven through the back of the head and into the brain, so the birds died straight away. Cherry-Garrard, his enthusiasm and interest thoroughly aroused, wrote that he had never imagined anything as good as the life they were having with its fellowship, novelty, interest, colour and animal life. He wrote that words could not describe the beauty of the scene: the sun-kissed bergs, the brilliant blue sky fading into green and pink on the horizon, pink floes floating in the deep blue sea and ice that shaded from burnished copper to salmon pink.[68] Scott had hoped to be in clear water south of the pack by Christmas Day; this was impossible and he wrote that the scene from the ship on 25 December was 'altogether too Christmassy'. Morale was maintained with a mess decorated with flags and banners, a Christmas service and a special dinner of tomato soup, penguin breast, roast beef, plum pudding, mince pies, asparagus, champagne, port and liqueurs, accompanied by untalented singing till 1a.m.[69] Wilson hung up his flag from Caius College (made by the Master's wife and still in the college) along with a Union Jack, a New Zealand flag and his sledging flag made by Oriana. A rabbit, a New Zealand gift, added her bit to the celebrations by producing seventeen babies. Overall, in spite of the slow progress, there was little bickering or back-stabbing. The men on board had been brought up in a tradition of self-control. Scott thought that they showed tolerance and good humour and was impressed that they could live under such conditions of hardship, monotony and danger in such an atmosphere of good companionship and wrote, 'I have not heard a harsh word or seen a black look. A spirit of tolerance and good humour pervades the whole community'.[70] He thought that such a combination of knowledge, experience, ability and enthusiasm must achieve something.[71] Wilson used the time to study penguins, whales, microscopic crustaceans and 'the wonderful stillness and beauty of the whole fairy-like scene' where daylight lasted for twenty-four hours.[72] He often sat in the crow's nest, which he used as his private chapel, alone, with thoughts of God and of Oriana. By contrast Scott, who was not meditative or resigned, found the delay almost intolerable. He began to think they would have to winter in the pack; he worried about the coal supply. He remembered the days in the pack as days of unceasing struggle.

Finally they were in the open sea. Scott thought he could 'breathe again' though he was conscious of the amount of coal that had been consumed by the fight to get through the pack.[73] Gradually the Antarctic came into view: the Admiralty Range, Mount Erebus. *Terra Nova* steered towards Cape Crozier, the home of the emperor penguins where it was hoped to winter. New Year's Day was celebrated in the mess with a Westal plum pudding filled with shillings, pennies and buttons. Wilson got a button; this little talisman was to have a long life. Wilson took it south with him and it was later sent to his parent's cook, Mrs Hart, in Cheltenham. Over ninety years later it was taken back to the Antarctic by the polar traveller Geoff Somers on his cross-Antarctic journey.[74]

Terra Nova reached Cape Crozier on 3 January. The emperor penguin rookery was in full view, but landing was made impossible by a heavy sea swell. This was a major disappointment for Wilson; one of his reasons for joining Scott's second expedition was to further investigate the birds. But since landing was out of the question, *Terra Nova* returned along the west coast of Ross Island to McMurdo Sound. Here their base was on a small promontory, the Skuary, about twelve miles north of Hut Point. (Hut Point itself was avoided because of the problems there had been in releasing *Discovery*). The base allowed good access to the Barrier across the sea ice and was named 'Cape Evans' in honour of Lieutenant Evans. Wilson wrote, 'the peace of God which passes all understanding reigns here in these days. One only wishes one could bring a glimpse away with one with all its unimaginable beauty'.[75]

They landed on 4 January. Work began on unloading immediately. As in 1902 it was important to get land-based at the
earliest opportunity because at any moment the weather could
deteriorate, forcing *Terra Nova* to move into open water. They
were also already behind schedule. Two motor sledges were
hoisted out looking 'as fresh and clean as if they had been just
packed'. The motors were running by the afternoon.[76] Then
came the ponies, all thin, but seventeen still alive and soon rolling and kicking on the floe with joy; then the dogs which were
soon running light loads to and fro from ship to shore. The
prefabricated hut that was to house them through the winter
was unloaded in bits. All activities had an eager audience; the
penguins were curious and keen to join the fun; they waddled
around, poking their heads from side to side and trying to get
the killer dogs to play. All too often their enticements ended
with a 'spring, a squawk and a horrid red patch on the snow'.[77]
In three days, working round the clock, all the provisions
were on the shore. The ponies pulled loads of between 600 to
1,000 lbs. Men could pull 200 lbs, each dog 100 lbs.

By the time the third motor sledge was taken off the ship
the ice had thawed and the sledge plunged through it. 'R.I.P.'
wrote Wilson. The loss of one of these vehicles, which it was
hoped would transform Antarctic travel, was a blow. In fact the
other two did not get far; one broke down after a few miles,
the second after fifty miles. Scott wrote that there was nothing
wrong with the idea and correctly predicted a future for traction
engines in Canada and other places. Oates disagreed; he thought
they were a waste of money and wrote grumpily, 'motors £100
each, ponies £5 each, dogs ten shillings each'.[78] Another accident was just averted when camera-artist Ponting went onto an
ice floe to photograph killer whales. As he set up his camera, he
and the floe were heaved up as the whales rose in a coordinated
attack, banging against the floe and splitting it into fragments
around him. Somehow Ponting escaped, scrambling from floe
to floe, just ahead of the whales' hungry jaws; an event sadly
not recorded on camera. He later said that the whales' pent-up
breath was like a blast from an air-compressor.[79] He remarked

afterwards that he was perspiring very freely. The crew was impressed with the whales' cunning and orchestrated attack. It was clear that whales were very intelligent, an intelligence that they would treat with every respect.

Terra Nova was to return to New Zealand after she had sailed around the coast to offload an exploratory party. She was to carry the mail. Scott wrote glowingly to Oriana about her husband:

> He is wonderful, at every turn his advice is asked, his sound commonsense and judgement is required for every decision of importance and his remarkable personality seems to stamp itself upon the whole enterprise. The most extraordinary fact of all is the quiet unobtrusive way in which his guidance of events is exerted. He is content to act in the background and as a consequence is wholly beloved as well as esteemed by everyone.[80]

Scott called Wilson to his cabin to show him, unusually, a letter to go on *Terra Nova* expressing his appreciation of all the crew's work. He also revealed his plans for the depot journey to deposit supplies for the following year. Wilson was to be a dog-driver along with Scott, Meares and Teddy Evans.[81] Wilson was pleased; he thought at the time that the dogs could probably get to the top of the Beardmore Glacier, 'and the dog drivers are therefore the people who will have the best chance of doing the top piece of the ice cap to the Pole'. He hoped to be chosen, but 'with so many bloods in the hey-day of youth and strength beyond my own I feel there will be a most difficult task in making choices towards the end'.[82] He also wrote about life in Antarctica, vis-à-vis his eventual return, 'Don't be anxious if we don't come back, remember that here we could live indefinitely without any supplies at all, for with seals, penguin, skuas and a boat with whaling gear we could live for years and years on food and blubber fires'.[83]

By 18 January the hut, fifty feet long and twenty-five feet wide, was ready for occupation. It gave an uninterrupted view across McMurdo Sound to the trans-Antarctic Mountains. The grey-white hut is there still, a living memento of this great period of exploration. Photographs taken in 2003 show the hut and the interior: the picks, hooks, shovels, sledges and skis are still neatly stored along with Griffith Taylor's bicycle.[84] The huts are protected by international treaty and are the focus of international financial support to prevent further deterioration. In 1911 the hut's floor was covered with quilting, felt, boarding and linoleum, its interior divided into an 'officers' and 'lower deck' section by packing cases filled with wine or glass. The interior was warm, the gramophone played, the men were snug and happy.[85] Life was hardly dull. Outside the noise was like a farmyard: howling dogs, horses neighing, skuas fighting with each other and penguins. Inside were cats, kittens, rabbits, squirrels and men. Wilson's cabin was small but he had no complaints. In the first few weeks after landing, only a few men were in the hut anyway. Scott had organised sorties; four parties were to leave Cape Evans before the beginning of the Antarctic winter. They were to go to the Barrier to lay depots for the next year's attempt at the Pole, to the west, to the east and to Cape Royds. Wilson was with the Barrier group.

Wilson's group left for Cape Evans on the depot-laying journey on 24 January 1911, sent off with much excitement and photographing. They were to lay a series of depots starting at the edge of the barrier and stretching south for 140 miles. The final and biggest depot was to be called 'One Ton Depot'. Eight ponies and two dog teams pulling 5,300 lbs (sufficient food and fuel for fourteen weeks) were led by thirteen men who knew that Scott would make his final selection for the Pole attempt in the Antarctic spring from amongst them. They were only allowed to take twelve lbs of personal kit. This included everything that they were not actually wearing: socks, shirts, tobacco, notebook, needles, thread, buttons, safety pins and sleeping boots.[86] On the journey Wilson used his medical skills to remove pus from Atkinson's (the doctor) infected heel. He drove a team of eleven dogs led by 'Stareek' (Russian for 'Old Man'). He was by now relatively experienced with dog teams and could instruct them in their local dialect (Ki Ki for right, Ghui for left). He got to understand the dogs better and Stareek, a 'ridiculous old man' and 'and quite the nicest quietest cleverest old dog', never forgot his voice and always went to him after the trip. The dog teams were driven crazy by the sight and smell of seals. Wilson said that he managed never to get left behind when they rushed off, but on occasion he was dragged full length until the team got tired of running. Only then could he struggle to his feet.[87]

The expedition reached the Barrier in three days, having gone to Hut Point which Wilson said had been left 'in a perfectly filthy condition'[88] after being used by the Shackleton expedition, though he was relieved that it could be used if necessary by his expedition on its return. Old familiar landmarks, Terror and Erebus, were welcome sights. The dogs pulled well and the men kept up on skis, now using two ski sticks, rather than the single stick of *Discovery* days. But the ponies found the Barrier snow surface very heavy going. They moved at a snail's pace and one or two were lame. Only one pair of snow shoes had been brought for the ponies but Wilson and Meares (the dog handler) could not get back to Cape Evans for more. On 30 January Scott called a halt a few miles in from the Barrier edge, Camp 111, Safety Camp (so called because it was built on old Barrier ice and thought to be safe under any circumstances).[89] When the ponies had rested the expedition went on, at first eastward to avoid a crevassed area immediately in the south. Here the men laid another depot they named Corner Camp. After this they were safe to turn south, along 169° E.[90]

Thirty miles from Hut Point, the novice Cherry-Garrard had his first taste of Antarctic blizzards when the wind drove the falling snow:

fight your way a few steps away from the tent and it will be gone. Loose your sense of direction and there is nothing to guide you back. Expose your face and hands to the wind and they will very soon be frostbitten. And this is midsummer. Imagine the added cold of spring and autumn: the cold and darkness of winter.[91]

The blizzard lasted three days. When it abated they continued south. The party was split into two and three men returned with the weakest ponies. In ordering this, Scott ignored advice to slaughter them and store their carcasses as food for the following year. Wilson and Meares remained in charge of the dogs. Scott, Cherry-Garrard, Oates, Gran (the pony handler) and Bowers were in charge of the remaining ponies. Progress was slow as the ponies sank deep into the snow. The dogs got out of hand and 'turned into wolves' and attacked one.[92] The ponies were worn out, hungry and hardly able to pull, in contrast to Wilson's dogs which pulled 100 lbs of horse fodder, 200 lbs of dog biscuits, a tent, floor cloth, poles, sleeping bag, the boatswain's bag, rope and a tank full of provisions – about 50 lbs per dog.[93]

On 15 February temperatures fell to minus 15°F. The ponies were 'dreadfully hungry' and Wilson thought that their compressed fodder was not sufficient food for them (they ate ropes and picketing lines and one ate a cloth puttee).[94] Scott abandoned plans to go further south. He wanted to save the ponies for the big trek later in the year. On 17 February final camp was made, One Ton, thirty-one miles north of the planned site (at 79.29° S rather than 80° S). The depot was marked with a flagstaff and a black flag, biscuit boxes and tea tins attached to sledges acted as reflectors, and stacked with more than 2,000 lbs of fuel, food and equipment. Although Wilson makes no record in his diary of any difference of opinion, Oates profoundly disagreed with the decision, arguing for continuing south, killing the ponies as they failed. Scott's decision was to have important repercussions on his next expedition south. Oates said with some prescience, 'Sir, I am afraid that you will come to regret not taking my advice'.[95]

The return brought many problems. The dog section, Wilson and Meares, set off with Scott and Cherry-Garrard as their passengers. They left Oates, Bowers and Gran to follow with the five exhausted ponies. The journey was eventful. The men pushed the dogs hard and ran beside the sledges in turns, covering twenty-three miles on the first day, then twenty-five, then thirty-three.[96] Near Corner Camp, they were aware that they were surrounded by crevasses. On 21 February, as the two sledges sped along, running parallel, Wilson watched helplessly as most of Meares' dog team disappeared into a crevasse, disappearing one after another through the snow and looking exactly like rats running down a hole.[97] Somehow the front dog, the sledge and rear dogs were still on the surface; ten dogs dangled in the abyss. When Wilson peered into the chasm, eight terrified animals dangled helplessly in their harnesses, the other two had slipped out of their restrainers, fallen forty feet onto a ledge and fallen asleep. The men managed to haul up the harnessed dogs but Scott insisted on rescuing the two further down also. His descent was accompanied by a cacophony of snarling and barking as the surface dogs enjoyed a furious fight. Only after the battle had been sorted out could a freezing Scott and the dogs be hauled up.[98]

They caught up with Evans at Safety Camp on 22 February. By now two of the weakest ponies had died. But this setback paled into insignificance by comparison with the momentous news in the mailbag. Dr Atkinson, left behind on the outward journey because of his foot infection, had returned to Hut Point and had picked up mail left by the navigator of the *Terra Nova*. This contained the unwanted information that *Fram* and Amundsen's expedition had landed on the Bay of Whales[99] across the Barrier, relatively close to Scott's party but sixty miles south of it.[100] Amundsen was not, as the British had imagined, trying to reach the Pole from the other side of the Antarctic. *Terra Nova* had found the Norwegians when she was returning from a failed attempt to drop a party on King Edward VII Land. Returning via the Bay of Whales, named by Shackleton three years earlier, they found Amundsen's camp. The British were impressed by Amundsen's arrangements, which included a sauna and a library as well as quarters for more than a hundred dogs. *Fram* had sailed straight from Madeira, crossed the pack ice in four days, and reached the Bay of Whales on 14 January. Scott's frustration was palpable. But again he stuck to his prearranged plans and Wilson supported this. Scott wrote:

One thing fixes itself definitely in my mind. The proper, as well as the wiser, course for us is to proceed exactly as if this had not happened. To go forward and do our best for the honour of the country without fear or panic. There is no doubt that Amundsen's plan is a very serious menace to ours. He has a shorter distance to the Pole by 60 miles – I never thought he could have got so many dogs safely to the ice. His plan for running them seems excellent. But above and beyond all, he can start his journey early in the season – an impossible condition with ponies.[101]

The ponies could not leave until about three weeks after the dogs and the death of the ponies underlined the inescapable fact that the British attempt at the Pole would have to wait for warmer conditions in the spring.

Meanwhile the men needed to get to the comparative safety and shelter of Hut Point. They started out with dog and pony teams travelling independently, since dogs could go so much faster than ponies. Meares and Wilson were with dog teams; Bowers, Cherry-Garrard and Petty-Officer Crean followed with the remaining ponies. Their loads were light as Oates had thought it would be better for the ponies to do the full march in one stretch and so have a longer rest.[102] Hut Point was only four miles away, but the quickest approach, over sea ice, was risky because the ice could break up. When Wilson was instructed to take his and Meares' dog teams over the sea ice, he said that he thought the route too dangerous and favoured a more difficult route, which meant hauling his sledges over slippery rocks. He set out on 28 February and wrote, 'Then began a remarkable chain of incidents which led to the loss of all the remaining ponies, except one, and very nearly to the loss of three lives', and, incomprehensively, that he 'firmly believed that the whole train of what looked so like a series of petty mistakes and accidents, was a beautifully prearranged plan in which each one of us took exactly the moves and no others that an Almighty hand intended each of us to take'.[103] As he drove his dog sleigh he saw fresh thread-like cracks in the ice caused, he thought, by the sea swell under the ice. He knew that these could open up when the tide turned, so he took his teams back, driving close by

Bowers and the horses, thinking that Bowers would follow him. But Bowers went on over the sea ice under the impression that Wilson had misunderstood the orders. When he too reached the ominous cracks, he moved to firmer ice near the Barrier, which he thought would be safe, and made camp. Early the next morning he was woken by a strange noise. When he climbed out of his tent he found himself in a surrealistic nightmare: he, his tent, his companions and three horses were on a berg in the middle of a floating pack of broken-up ice, heaving up and down with the swell. Long black tongues of water were everywhere. One pony had already disappeared. Crean was sent to get help; he bravely jumped from one piece of ice to another until he reached the Barrier. Wilson said that Crean had had considerable difficulty and ran 'a pretty good risk'.[104] Meanwhile Bowers and Cherry-Garrard forced the ponies towards safe ground, using their sledges and ladders as bridges. The two men and one pony got over the water, two had fallen in. They were bludgeoned to death with pickaxes, apparently a lesser horror than being torn to bits by whales.

When they finally got to Hut Point the men were marooned in the old *Discovery* hut for more than six weeks. No approach to Cape Evans (which now seemed like an oasis to their minds) was possible because the sea ice was still broken up. They slept on the floor on reindeer bags, lived in their sledging outfits and cooked on a blubber stove, killing unfortunate seals at their front door. The monotony and frustration must have been considerable, but no irritation creeps into Wilson's diary; he found a meaning in everything and wrote that the stay with so little to do was a godsend, because colours were at their best and the sunsets were a new challenge every day. Oates thought brandy kept for emergencies might enliven the situation. Told that an epileptic fit would be a definite indication for the need for stimulants he fell into what he hoped was a realistic seizure. Wilson was unmoved and prescribed snow rubbed down his neck.

When the new ice formed, Scott led eight men north to Cape Evans. They arrived on 13 April, just before the beginning of winter. The first man who saw them there did not recognise them.

He thought they were visiting Norwegians. Wilson followed on 21 April. In Cape Evans the men were appreciative of its comfort after their enforced stay at Hut Point: dry clothes, supper and the first wash and change of clothes for three months.

The winter of 1911 was spent with the men continuing their scientific work, zoology, physics, and geology. Wilson's winter routine was: up with the cook, a bath of frozen snow, a walk to read the thermometers before breakfast, at his desk all day in bad weather or in reasonable weather walking around the icebergs in the bay, on the hills or on the glacier. In the evenings he would join in with the discussions. He had overall responsibility for the men's diet and was always on the alert for scurvy; he was called Scorbutic Director or Livery Bill.

He worked up his sketches, helped prepare Ponting's lantern slides and prepared sketches for the first edition of *The South Polar Times*, now edited by Cherry-Garrard and appearing on Midwinter's Day (22 June). This edition included photographs of seals, Erebus (with penguins) and the *Terra Nova* in the pack ice by Ponting. Wilson contributed the frontispiece (the arms of *The South Polar Times*), two paintings, several pictures of sledging flags (Wilson's family motto was *Res non Verba*) and a silhouette of Scott. He also did all the small sketches illustrating the text. He contributed greatly to all three editions and his only poem, 'The Barrier Silence', eighteen lines long and submitted typewritten so that Cherry-Garrard would not be biased in his favour, appeared in a later edition. He produced scientific pictures of ice crystals and parasites. He gave talks on painting and drawing (using Ruskin as his mentor), on the pigmentation of flying birds (he wondered if the absence of pigment increased the feathers' insulating properties) and on penguins. In this lecture he postulated, wrongly, that the birds had branched out at a very early stage of bird life, probably coming directly from the lizard bird in the Jurassic age.[105] In the evenings he drew, listening to records or to the pianola particularly appreciating 'A night hymn at sea' and 'Tis folly to run away from love'. Scott continued to admire him. After he had listened to one of Wilson's lectures he wrote:

There is no member of our party so universally esteemed; only to-night I realise how patiently and consistently he has given time to help the others and so it is all through; he has had a hand in almost every lecture given and has been consulted in almost every effort which has been made towards the solution of the practical or theoretical problems of our Polar world.

He goes on in words as relevant today as then:

The achievement of a great result by patient work is the best possible object lesson for struggling humanity, for the results of genius, however admirable can rarely be instructive. The chief of the Scientific Staff sets an example that is more potent than any other factor in maintaining that bond of good fellowship which is the marked and beneficent characteristic of our community.[106]

In May Wilson recorded his thoughts on Scott's lecture plans for the summer work and the attempt at the Pole. He recognised that if the South Pole party did get back, it would be too late to catch the relief ship. He was mostly concerned that he would not be able to reply to his letters or escape from Antarctica for another year 'however urgent the need may be'.[107] Although this sounds as if he assumed that he would be chosen, he could not be at this stage. He just hoped to be included though 'things always turn out for the best and generally in a different way to what one expects'.[108]

Much of his thoughts and time was spent on the preparation for his return to Cape Crozier, a potentially-suicidal journey when made in the middle of winter and in darkness. He planned to take Bowers and Cherry-Garrard. The expedition was specifically to get newly-hatched emperor penguin eggs and study their embryology. He hoped that he and the *Terra Nova* expedition would make one of the great scientific breakthroughs of the century.

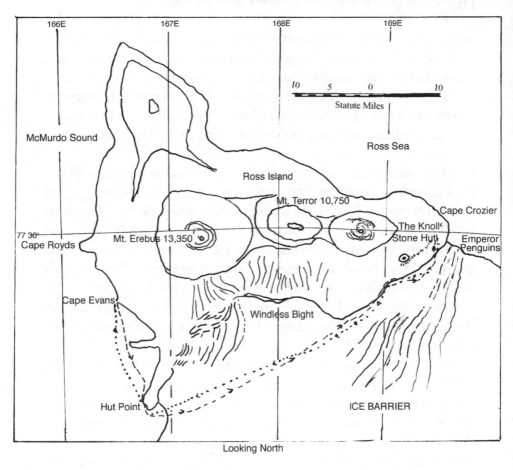

Winter Journey from Cape Evans to Cape Crozier
Bowers, Cherry-Garrard, & Wilson
June 27th to August 1st 1911

166E · 167E · 168E · 169E

10   5   0   10
Statute Miles

McMurdo Sound

Ross Sea

Ross Island

Mt. Terror 10,750

Cape Crozier

The Knoll
Stone Hut

77 30'
Cape Royds

Mt. Erebus 13,350

Emperor
Penguins

Cape Evans

Windless Bight

Hut Point

ICE BARRIER

Looking North

Ross Island Winter Journey

12

The Winter Journey

The House That Cherry Built

The good old Blizzard of local fame,
Compared with which was considered tame,
The best of the bracing South Winds cool,
That blew all day (and the next as a rule),
And cemented the Ice Blocks hard and stout,
That were placed so carefully round about,
But failed to secure the Canvas strong,
That formed a roof about ten feet long,
To cover the Rocks and Boulders Erratic,
Composing the Walls, – with lavas "Basic" –
That stood on the Ridge that topped the Moraine,
And, somewhat collapsed are all that remain
With some fragments of Bamboo Poles dejected,
Of the House of Stone that Cherry erected.

H.R.Bowers
The South Polar Times, Vol. III, Part II (Part of poem)

If it were not for Cherry-Garrard's realistic and graphic account of the horrors of the 1911 winter journey in his book, *The Worst Journey in the World*,[1] they certainly would not have been appreciated from either Wilson's or Bower's descriptions. Wilson described the expedition to Cape Crozier to collect the emperor penguins eggs as 'the weirdest bird nesting expedition that has been or will ever be'. In a letter to Reginald Smith he concentrated on Cherry-Garrard, unfazed about himself. He wrote:

> He really is splendid. I took him on the midwinter journey to Cape Crozier where we had very low temperatures and dreadful weather and had our hut roof and tent blown away and he stuck it like a brick and said nothing. We were none of us the worse for it, but it was a very trying journey, five weeks in the dark practically.[2]

Bowers' brief account to his mother and sisters gave the impression that the experience was just an exciting adventure; he probably did not want to worry them.[3] But Scott was impressed; he wrote lyrically:

> That men should wander forth in the depth of a Polar night to face the most dismal cold and the fiercest gales in darkness is something new; that they should have persisted in this effort in spite of every adversity for full five weeks is heroic. It makes a tale for our generation, which I hope, may not be lost in the telling.[4]

Others disagreed; the expedition has been described as 'a classic example of heroism for heroism's sake' and 'an irrelevance in the context of the expedition'.[5] This might be true if exploration was Wilson's only goal, but it was not. On this expedition he was entirely motivated by the possibility of scientific advance. He hoped to prove a link between dinosaurs and birds. To get emperor penguin eggs at an early stage of their incubation was imperative if this link was to be made. He would have been reassured also that his little group had gathered new meteorological facts about the Barrier in the depth of winter.

The *Discovery* expedition had been a disappointment in relation to the study of penguin embryology. Although the breeding ground was located on Cape Crozier and Wilson now knew that the birds incubated their eggs on the sea ice in winter, he had arrived too late in the penguins' reproductive cycle to obtain early embryos. In 1911 therefore, the journey to Cape Crozier had to be made in the middle of the Antarctic winter.

The emperor 'quest' was an important reason for him joining the expedition.

Scott seems to have promised Wilson that he could take on this potentially-suicidal expedition of more than 100 miles over the Barrier, in darkness and through pressure ridges and crevasses, although, near departure, he does seem to have tried to persuade Wilson against the trip.[6] But Wilson was determined and Scott, who knew that Cape Crozier had been the intended base for *Terra Nova*, would not stop him although he impressed on Wilson the importance of all three returning safely to be ready for the polar attempt.[7] There may have been other insidious attractions for Scott: if the theory of 'development through the ancestors' could be proved, the expedition would have gained an enormous amount of prestige and it was not beyond of the realms of possibility that the connection could have earned the scientists the hugely-influential Darwinian Prize.[8] The expedition was to have other uses: the party were to test the scientific instruments that were to be used by the polar party the following year. The meteorological records that they made were not to be recorded again for seventy years. They experimented with diets to find the best diet to cope with low temperatures, physical work and stress by eating combinations of protein, carbohydrate and fat in their 32 oz daily allowance. They took eiderdown sleeping bags instead of reindeer ones and they took a blubber stove.

Wilson chose two companions, the 'pick of the whole party'.[9] Three meant that there was a 'spare' in case of an accident. He chose the indomitable Birdie Bowers and his protégé, Cherry-Garrard; he presumably felt that Cherry-Garrard's appalling eyesight would hardly matter in the twenty-four hour darkness. His choice was undoubtedly a happy one; both Cherry-Garrard's and Bower's diaries stress their devotion to Wilson. Cherry-Garrard wrote of them both later, 'these two men went through the Winter Journey and lived: later they went through the Polar Journey and died. They were gold, pure, shining, unalloyed. Words cannot express how good their companionship was'.[10]

In 1903 Wilson had seen thousands of emperor chicks at Cape Crozier; he now decided that the eggs must be laid in late June.[11] If he was ever to find vestiges of teeth in early embryos, (which would be evidence towards a connection with dinosaurs), he needed to be on the Cape then. His calculations were not correct. The female emperor actually lays her single egg in May. By the time Wilson left Cape Evans the chicks were already being incubated. Any scientist of the time could have made the same miscalculation. The life cycle of the emperor penguins was a total mystery.

The five-week trek started on 27 June 1911. Ponting used his magnesium flash-powder to take photographs of them in front of the hut. 'Never was there such a collection of apparatus taken on a sledge journey but then also never was anyone before so led to undertake such a journey in midwinter darkness on the Barrier. It is an experimental journey'.[12] The darkness lasted through the twenty-four hours, the temperature dropped many degrees below freezing. They battled against an uneven and often sand-like ice surface, lurking crevasses and permanent fatigue. For Cherry-Garrard the darkness was the worst; day and night ceased to have meaning:

> I don't believe minus seventy temperatures would be bad in daylight, not comparatively bad, when you could see where you were going, where you were stepping, where the sledge straps were, the cooker, the primus, the food; could see your footsteps lately trodden into the soft snow that you might find your way back to the rest of your load; could see the lashings of the food bags; could read a compass without striking three or four boxes to find one dry match; could read your watch to see if the blissful moment of getting out of your bed was come . . . when it would not take you five minutes to lash the door of your tent and five hours to get started in the morning.[13]

They pulled two nine-foot sledges in tandem, 750 lbs of equipment.[14] They went without dogs; dogs they thought would be unable to cope with the winter conditions. At the last moment, realising the enormous weight that they had to haul, they left their skis, aware or their probable limited value in darkness and on uneven surfaces. They pulled their double-lined tent, pick-axes, ropes, eiderdown-lined sleeping bags, provisions and oil for six weeks.

It was obvious immediately that this expedition was even worse than previous ones, however terrible they had been. Although they had hoped that the moon might give them a glimmer of light, this rarely happened, clouds blocked the moon. On 'day' two they passed their old friend, Hut Point, and moved from the sea ice onto the Barrier. This was to be their only 'good' pulling time throughout the round trip. As they got onto the Barrier a steady stream of cold air flowed down it onto the relatively warm sea ice. Wilson recorded the temperature change: minus 26.5°F at Hut Point and minus 47°F a few miles on. Not only did the temperature drop but also the snow surface got worse and worse. It was much more difficult for them to pull.[15]

No one had ever encountered such conditions. Scott wrote that although Amundsen had experienced similar temperatures on a journey to the north magnetic Pole, he had a reasonable amount of light, 'Esquimaux' who could build igloos and he turned home after five days rather than five weeks.[16] These three had a thin canvas tent. All three were affected by the conditions but Cherry-Garrard was particularly bothered. He learnt quickly that he had to get into the right position for pulling just as soon as he left the tent; their clothes froze to iron armour in seconds and did not thaw out again until the next meal. Once, Cherry-Garrard had to pull for hours with his neck arched backwards because he had glanced up at the stars. On another occasion he took off his mitts briefly to pull on a rope to be rewarded with inch-long blisters on his finger-tips that were filled with frozen pus and which only thawed out when he got into the tent and the relative warmth of the primus stove. His glasses fogged up and he could only see anything very close up. All three got excruciating leg cramps. Bowers got stomach cramps, though not badly enough to stop him sleeping and snoring, a remarkable cacophony which interfered with his companions' already fragmented sleep. Wilson got bad foot blisters. They found that cooking was so difficult and slow that they started a daily rota instead of the usual weekly arrangement. The sleeping bags became solid lumps that took about forty-five minutes of tortuous negotiation to force an entry. When they got out of the bags they stuffed clothes into the opening to make a plug that could be pulled out. This helped them slightly when it was time to start the struggle again. Cherry-Garrard's bag was too big, a serious problem because he lay surrounded by cold air shuddering and shaking until his back seemed to break. His breath froze on his skin. He thought that the best time of the twenty-four hours was when they had breakfast, because they would not have to get back into their bags for seventeen hours. Perhaps Dante was right to put circles of ice below circles of fire.

They understood the importance of 'layering'. They wore similar protection to that worn in the *Discovery* days with layers of thick wool jerseys and underwear, gabardine overshirts, trousers and a woollen hood covered with a wind-proof covering. Their faces were covered with a guard. They had three pairs of gloves, three or four pairs of socks and reindeer-skin finesco.[17] As the clothes froze, so they could do less and less and 'climbing up ropes or out of crevasses becomes exceedingly difficult for anyone but an acrobat'.[18] Clothes froze in whatever shape they were in when the blubber stove was put out.

They pulled to the 'Windless Bight', so called because here the Barrier winds are deflected to the Ross Sea in front and McMurdo Sound behind.[19] This did not help; because of the lack of wind, the snow surface changed from being hard and polished (relatively easy to run over) into sand-like crystals impossible to pull on. At low temperatures there is less lubrication; the sledge runners roll the crystals over each other increasing friction so that pulling the sledge is just like pulling through sand.[20] Pulling the two sledges and their 750 lbs of equipment became impossible. The half load was heavier than the whole one had been on the sea ice.[21] They had to start the dreaded process of relaying on 30 June only three days after they had set out. For nine days they relayed wearily. On the first day they covered ten miles to actually advance three and a quarter.[22] Sometimes they used a naked candle to find the second sledge. Whenever the planet Jupiter could be seen through the clouds they steered by his friendly faint light, 'and I never see him now without recalling his friendship in those days'.[23] The temperatures were lower than any recorded on *Discovery* days. On 6 July the temperature was virtually always below minus 70°F. Wilson wrote that the lowest temperature they recorded on that day was minus 77°F, i.e. 109 degrees below freezing. He thought this was a record.[24]

Anxiety about frostbite was ever present. Wilson was frightened 'beyond all else' of any one of the trio getting damaged feet and he had to keep a careful watch on all three pairs. If there was any fear of frostbite, the remedy was clear: stop and stamp around until the circulation improved, if this was unsuccessful, camp and drink hot water. The problem was how to make a clinical decision with companions who announced that their feet had been cold but were now most comfortable. Cherry-Garrard suffered badly and not only with his feet; his heart beat slowly at the end of the day and he wrote 'it was difficult not to howl'. To keep going he repeated a little mantra, 'you've got it in the neck – stick it, stick it, you've got it in the neck'.[25] But he never complained; it would have been difficult to do so in the company of the selfless older men. In general the three talked little, but discussions about whether they were having particularly bad conditions or whether they were experiencing the normal for the area, lasted about a week.[26] They discussed whether to turn back, but decided to struggle on, dividing their day into three: seven hours for resting, nine hours for camp work, and eight hours for marching.

The auroras were remarkable features that they discussed and described. These brilliant lights in the sky appear near the magnetic poles. In the south they are called 'aurora australis'. They appear sixty miles up when charged particles streaming from the sun hit low-density holes around the sun and are pulled towards the north and south magnetic poles by the earth's magnetic fields. In 1911, the sky absolutely blazed with 'long swaying curtains, shaken by the breeze',[27] and brilliant swathes and whirls of pale orange, yellow, emerald green and pink whirling into vortices or opening like vast mushrooms, or darting into beams like searchlights. All three lay on their backs to see them. Bowers and Wilson marvelled; Cherry-Garrard saw a blur.

When George Simpson later analysed their recordings he wrote that Bowers' meteorological record was a masterpiece. These records were, to say the least, a trial to prepare. Water vapour from their breath condensed on the paper and covered it with a film of ice that the pencil could not bite through. Sir George wrote:

> Throughout the journey that lasted for thirty-six days in the depth of winter; when for days at a time the temperature was below −50°F, frequently below −60 and on one day −76, when every observation had to be made by candlelight, the meteorological log is practically complete with three observations per day.[28]

Simpson observed that the coldest month on the Barrier was about twenty-five degrees lower than at Cape Evans. When the temperature was at its lowest even Bowers wrote, 'I was beginning to think I could stand most things but then I didn't want to ask for any more'.[29] Because of the conditions they could only pull a few miles each day. Cherry-Garrard decided that they hadn't a ghost of a chance of getting as far as the penguins. Then, on 4 July, a new problem: snow. The temperature rose to minus 27°F, visibility was so bad that they lay in their tents all day. Their clothes became saturated and as soon as they got out of the tent, the clothes froze stiffly, like tin mail.[30]

Some days they could not even relay: snow covered their footprints, fog blocked visibility and they could not get back to the sledge they had left behind. Most days they relayed determinedly until, after nine days the snow surface improved enough for them to pull the sledges together. Their main concerns were to avoid both crevasses and huge pressure ridges (undulating masses of compressed ice gradually flowing towards the sea). One day they fell foul to both, getting lost in the ridges and falling into crevasses each one dangling in a crevasse in his sledging harnesses until the other two managed to pull him out. Wilson could not decide whether their difficulties with pulling were due to the slopes of the pressure ridges or to the bad snow surface; it was too dark to see.[31] They learnt to judge the surface of the snow by listening to their footsteps. On deeper (and safer) snow their footsteps made a lower note and when their feet made a higher sound, they knew they were in danger of running into cracks.[32] At night they could hear the ice groaning and creaking sounding like a giant banging an empty tank. Cherry-Garrard wrote:

> I for one had come to that point of suffering at which I did not care if only I could die without much pain. They talk of the heroism of dying – they little know – it would be easy to die, a dose of morphia, a friendly crevasse, and blissful sleep. The trouble is to go on.[33]

After nineteen days they reached Cape Crozier. Wilson had planned to camp on the beach but this was impossible and he decided to pitch their tent 800 feet above the cape on the slopes of Mount Terror. In addition he wanted to build a stone shelter, a makeshift laboratory, in which he could cut out the embryos before the eggs froze. He hoped to get a series of embryos at various stages of development. So the three men climbed up to a ridge below the top of the Knoll (a hill), a site that they thought would be protected from the wind. Here they spent precious time building a stone igloo. In retrospect this was unrealistic. The conditions were simply too ghastly for careful scientific work. Wilson would have been better off simply collecting eggs and returning with them to Cape Evans. If he had done this there would have been a slight danger of moisture and bacteria getting into the egg, although the likelihood of this happening is probably slight,[34] and a definite possibility of the eggs cracking as they cooled (as did happen). But they would have had more time and energy to concentrate on the actual business of collecting numbers of eggs, rather than the one visit of a few hours that they eventually managed. As it was, it took them three days to dig out frozen rocks for the walls of their igloo, which Wilson called 'Oriana Hut', and bank it with snow blocks which they had to chip out of the solid snow. They used a sledge as a ridge beam and canvas weighted down with stones, as the roof. They looked out in the dim moonlight, on huge pressure ridges running to the Barrier edge and beyond the edge, the frozen Ross Sea. In 1957 Sir Edmund Hillary and four companions retraced Wilson's journey in the Antarctic summer, travelling by tractor rather than on foot. Remarkably, they found the remains of the stone walls, a sledge, test tubes, unexposed film and Wilson's pencils.

By now low oil reserves had become a big concern. Only one of the six cans they had brought was left. They had been keeping the stove going after supper to keep warm. It was imperative to get to the rookery and the eggs. They made an attempt on 19 July, leaving in gloom and knowing that they would have to return in darkness. Wilson's knowledge of the area dated back ten years, when his visit had been made in relatively good visibility. He found that the pressure ridges had moved since 1903 and the trio got lost in a deep valley between the ridges. 'Quite exciting work but it grew very much more exciting as the light got worse and worse'.[35] They could not get down to the rookery and had to retreat, having the irritation of hearing the birds squawking only a quarter of a mile below them.

The following day, playing a sort of 'blind man's buff', they found a perilous new route over huge pressure ridges and down steep slopes. They struggled for hours, having to make steps in the ice with their pickaxes and crossing crevasses by using their sledges as bridges, finally getting to ten feet above the penguins.

After indescribable effort and hardship we were witnessing a marvel of the natural world and we were the first and only men who had ever done so; so we had within our grasp material which might be of the utmost importance to science; we were turning theories into facts with every observation we made.[36]

Wilson and Bowers climbed down to the ice where the emperors were huddling, trumpeting in their curious metallic way, shuffling around with their eggs balanced on their feet and pressed against the bald patch under their breasts. Wilson was surprised at the numbers, only about a hundred rather than the thousands he had seen on his previous visit a decade before. But the visit was a scientific first. They collected only five eggs because it was important to get back to their base as soon as possible (they had difficulty in finding Cherry-Garrard in the conditions) and they killed three penguins to provide blubber for the stove. The journey back to their hut was awful. Cherry-Garrard's sight was so bad he could not even see the footholds that they had made on the way down. He had to kick and kick at the icy surface to get some form of toehold. He just let himself go and trusted to luck. Wilson muttered patiently, 'Cherry, you *must* learn how to use an ice axe'.[37] He had been given two eggs to carry and these smashed when he fell, leaving only three to show for the Herculean efforts. They almost missed the way to the hut and as Cherry-Garrard wrote:

> such extremity of suffering cannot be measured. Madness or death may give relief. But this I know, on this journey we were already beginning to think of death as a relief. As we groped our way back that night, sleepless, icy and dog-tired in the dark and the wind and the drift, a crevasse seemed almost a friendly gift.[38]

More was to come: they slept in the hut and when the stove was lit, a blob of rendered penguin fat spat into Wilson's eye causing such pain and swelling that he thought he would loose the vision in one eye. His stifled groans kept the other two awake. Next morning Wilson said, 'Things must improve. I think we hit bedrock last night'.[39] They hadn't by a long way.

That night a blizzard raged. The hut site, carefully chosen, proved disastrous. They had far better have built it in the open.

The wind was deflected from the top of the Knoll onto the hut in furious whirling gusts and strained and tore at the canvas roof. They hoisted more slabs of ice onto the roof to try to secure it and brought the tent up and pitched it close to the hut; it was easier to warm than the hut and they could dry their mitts and socks in it. On the next day, 22 July, with the wind blowing 'as though the world was having a fit of hysterics',[40] Birdie looked out of the igloo and found that the tent had blown away. This was the most major catastrophe: they were three weeks from base, temperatures were minus 30 or 40°F. Without tent, food or oil it would be virtually impossible to get back to base. Fortune had only relented in one way: although the wind had snatched the tent up like a folding umbrella many of the contents were left scattered on the snow. Meanwhile the storm continued unrelenting. The wind blew snow through every crack and crevice on the little hut covering everything inside in snowdrift and fine black dust. It sucked the canvas roof up, creating a vacuum effect and so sucking in even more snow. The ice slabs on the roof were blown off, the stove did not work and they lay in their sleeping bags listening to the canvas roof straining and snapping.

On 23 July, Wilson's birthday and 'quite the funniest I had ever spent',[41] the roof ripped 'into hundreds of little fragments in fewer seconds than it takes to read this',[42] dislodging the sledge and rocks and leaving the men lying open to the raging elements. They lay mummified in snow, in the darkness and with no food or drink. They were like this for forty-eight hours. Wilson and Birdie sang songs and hymns: 'He who would valiant be'. Cherry-Gerard joined in. They slaked their thirst by sucking small pieces of snow, Wilson prayed and intermittently Birdie thumped him; if he still moved he knew he was still alive. Now Wilson's steady character came to the fore, his courage never left him:

> we had to think out a plan for getting home again without our tent and without the canvas roof of the hut. We still had the floor cloth of the tent and this we were lying on so it couldn't

blow away. We could build a snow hut every night on the way home and put this on the top or we could always build a burrow in the Barrier big enough for all three of us and make a very good roof with the canvas flush with the surface. We had no doubt of getting back so long as this blizzard did not last till we were all stiffened with the cold in our bags.[43]

The effort that this would have required is almost indescribable, certainly Cherry-Garrard had long since given up all hope: 'Without the tent we were dead men'.[44] He reflected that his life had been a bit wasted, 'the road to Hell might be paved with good intentions: the road to Heaven is paved with lost opportunities'.[45] He decided he was going to try to die. He was not going to try to keep warm. He thought he might be able to get hold of some of Wilson's morphine.[46] Meanwhile the indomitable Bowers made a note of the wind speed, it was force twelve on the Beaufort scale. This was the only time when his meteorological observations fell to just one recording in the day.[47]

On 24 July they managed to get the primus lamp working and eat pemmican and drink tea. They sat on their bags with the floor cloth above them to protect the primus. Never was a meal, choked with hair, feathers and dust, so delicious. With a lull in the blizzard they were able to explore around the hut. Miraculously they found the tent had only blown for a quarter of a mile. It had been snapped shut by the wind on its careering ride but was relatively unharmed and definitely usable. Bowers 'thanked God in his mercy'.[48] Their lives 'had been taken away and given back to us'.[49] They moved the tent reverently and solemnly to a new position lower down the slope and put their equipment into it. Birdie tied his sleeping bag to the tent; anywhere the tent was going, he was going too.

By now Wilson's priority was to get back to Cape Evans. He was responsible for Bowers and Cherry-Garrard and he knew that they still faced deadly conditions on the return journey. They had only one can of oil left.[50] Characteristically Birdie was prepared to go back to the rookery, but by now Wilson had abandoned all thoughts of dissecting embryos at their different stages of development. Cherry-Garrard, weak from lack of sleep, accepted the offer of Bowers' eiderdown lining. The first few nights he spent in it were wonderful, but then the new liner began to ice up like the old one. Wilson's bag had been splitting badly for days. They could not roll the bags but laid them out on the sledge 'like three squashed coffins'.[51] Bowers' balaclava helmet became so frozen that his head was in a solid ice block and to look down he had to bend his whole body. All their socks and finesco and mitts were frozen; when put into the men's breast pockets or inside their vests at night they did not even thaw out, let alone dry.[52] Even Bowers wrote, 'We had really reached the pit'.[53]

The return journey took seven days. They went too far east and got onto a crevasse field. Bowers fell in one and dangled in his harness until the others managed to haul him out with blistered hands, an effort that caused non-stop pain because of the raw sores on their fingers.

On the slopes of Mount Terror the temperature dropped from minus 21 to 46°F. They moved forward cautiously listening to the sound of the snow and its feel under their feet. The Windless Bight gave them a better surface on the return journey and they managed several miles each day instead of the dismal one and a half they had on the way out. Cherry-Garrard's teeth split in the cold, and he drifted in and out of sleep as he walked, waking up as he bumped into his companions. Finally they reached Hut Point, the *Discovery* base. By now the light was a little better and Cherry-Garrard wrote that he could not describe the relief that that gave him. They found that the relative warmth in The Hut affected their feet; they walked around 'like cats on hot bricks' and could only get relief by making their feet cold again when the pain wore off. Their hands were very painful. They finally reached base on 1 August, wearily climbed out of their frozen clothes, had a good meal, a haircut, a shave and lots of sleep. The journey was over.

The expedition lived vividly in Cherry-Garrard's memory. He wrote that the journey had beggared belief, 'no words could express its horror'.[54] Wilson appreciated his colleagues. As they packed for the last time he said, 'I want to thank you two for what you have done. I couldn't have found two better companions and what is more I never shall'.[55] Cherry-Garrard was proud of that.

Scott wrote that they looked more weatherworn than anyone he had ever seen, with wrinkled and scarred faces, dull eyes and their hands whitened and creased.[56] Cherry-Garrard 'looked like nothing human. He had on a big nose guard covering all but his eyes and huge icicles and frost stuck out like duck's bills from his lips. Ponting said he had seen the same look on some half-starved Russian prisoners' faces'.[57] When they warmed up, their feet, hands, noses and mouths swelled and tingled.

What could Wilson claim they had achieved? The meteorological data was to be of use and importance. Experimentation with different proportions of fat, protein and carbohydrate in the diet was of use; although this could have been done without a journey to Cape Crozier, it did give a unique experience of the most extreme conditions and Scott and Wilson and Bowers were able to formulate different rations for the next expedition. On the expedition all three had 32 oz of food. Bowers had had 12 oz of pemmican and 20 oz of biscuit; the other two eventually had had fat in their diet although Cherry-Garrard started on the same amounts of pemmican and biscuit. When Wilson could not manage his allocated 8 oz of butter, he and Cherry-Garrard settled on a butter (4 oz), biscuit (16 oz) and pemmican (12 oz) combination. It was thought that the inclusion of fat made this the best diet, as has been confirmed subsequently.[58] Information about the increase in weight of the equipment in the course of the journey was of interest; the bags weighed in total 52 lbs at the start of the expedition and 118 lbs at the end and the tent had increased by 25 lbs in weight mostly due to ice collecting on the inside.[59] But on the question of the connection between primitive birds, as represented by penguins, and reptiles, no conclusion could be made. The embryos Wilson collected were more advanced than he had thought; they were too developed to test Haeckel's theory.

There were no teeth, scales or feathers to connect the birds with reptiles. More importantly, though Wilson could not know this at the time, the premise on which he was working was wrong. Penguins are not, as he thought and wrote, 'the most primitive and behindhand birds in existence',[60] they are in fact quite far down the avian evolutionary tree. Flightless birds have evolved from birds with flight rather than the other way around. Penguins have specialised and adapted to life in the Antarctic from their more primitive flying ancestors over millions of years. If there was a connection between birds and dinosaurs, penguins were the wrong breed of bird to study. But Sarah Wheeler in her biography of Cherry-Garrard writes how his reward was an affirmation of the value of dignity and the abnegation of the self.[61] Although the timing of the expedition has been criticised, Wilson would have remained serene. Although it could be classified as a failure, he would have seen God's purpose in the expedition.

Facts about the emperor's lifecycle were not discovered for years. If Wilson could have anticipated the appalling problems they encountered and impossibility of proving a connection between dinosaurs and birds, the journey would have been lunacy. But he could not; every explorer, adventurer and trailblazer must take risks, either to be rewarded with huge success or nothing. Wilson hoped for great achievements with this journey and his determination to push through with it rings loud and clear.

He took some time to recover. His fingers remained numb and his hands were painful for weeks; it was not so easy to restart work on his sketches and his journal. He wrote that the winter, his last alive, was quiet as judged by the regularity of the horse exercising and the lack of incident to report in his journal.[62] The Winter Journey was recorded tongue-in-cheek in *The South Polar Times* by Bowers who wrote a four-page poem (some lines recorded at the beginning of this chapter). Cherry-Garrard, in his editorial, merely stated, 'The Cape Crozier Party left on June 27th and returned on August 1st.[63] Wilson, constitutionally busy, got up early and woke Bowers at

6a.m. and the cook, sweeper and stable man at 7a.m. He also woke Simpson with a cup of tea, so that he could start work for an hour before breakfast; before 8a.m. was the only quiet time in the day. Dr Atkinson lectured on scurvy. But important preparations continued for the summer programme. The mess table was piled with rations to be weighed and bagged for the great journey to the Pole. The plans were for sixteen men to set out: four with motors, ten with ponies and two with dogs. Only the chosen few would attempt the Pole. Lieutenant Evans wrote, 'Dr Wilson, our Chief of Scientific Staff helped us all. To 'Uncle Bill' we all went for sound practical advice. Wilson was a friend and companion to Captain Scott and to all the expedition'.[64] Scott also heaped praise on Wilson, writing in his journal in October:

> Words must always fail me when I talk of Bill Wilson. I believe he really is the finest character I ever met – the closer one gets to him the more there is to admire. Every quality is so solid and dependable; cannot you imagine how that counts down here? Whatever the matter one knows that Bill will be sound, shrewdly practical, intensely loyal and quite unselfish. Add to this a wider knowledge of persons and things than is first guessable, a quiet vein of humour and really consummate tact, and you have some idea of his values. I think he is the most popular member of the party and that is saying much.[65]

By August the twilight hours increased until at last Wilson saw the sun again on 26 October. It was glorious to stand bathed in it; they all felt very young and sang and cheered. There were celebrations and champagne. Scott, having decided that Amundsen would not push him into changing his plans, wrote in October that he did not know what to think of Amundsen's chances; he thought that if Amundsen got to the Pole it would be due to the dogs. But his anxieties must have been many. He knew that Amundsen's base was sixty miles closer to the Pole; he would have been more anxious if he had known that Amundsen was to start on 22 October.

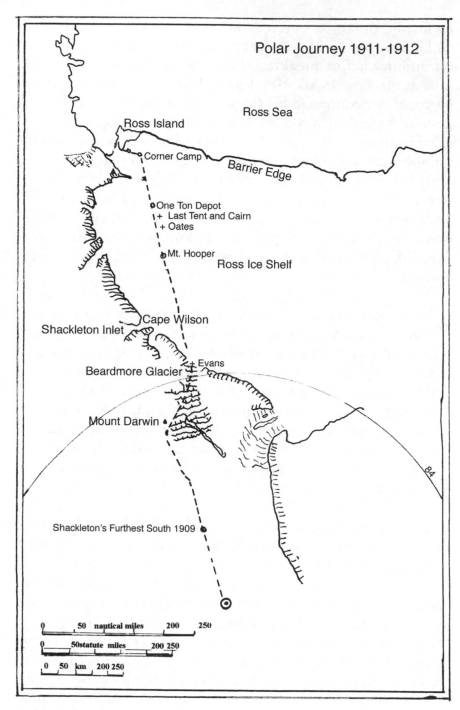

Polar Journey 1911

13

Death in the Antarctic

By October the party for the main southern journey had been selected; Wilson was amongst them and each member of the party knew that the men to be picked for the final assault on the Pole would come from this group. He wrote in his Journal:

> I don't see any other course than to carry through the job I came here for, which was, in the main, this sledge journey to the Pole. 'L'homme propose, mais le bon Dieu dispose' is an honest creed, and in this case, l'homme hasn't decided to do anything from first to last that he wasn't convinced would be approved by his infinitely better half and Le Bon Dieu will do the rest. . . . Whatever happens, even if it's worse than anything one can bring oneself to imagine, there is no more to be said or done than this.[1]

Right up until the expedition's departure he continued painting, adding picture after picture to his portfolio, painting on wet paper and working quickly. As always, he aimed at accuracy; if the result was only attractive but not exact, he threw it away. He hoped that the paintings would be exhibited along with Ponting's photographs in London and so keep things Antarctic, and Antarctic exploration, in the public consciousness. Ponting was returning to England in 1912, so the exhibition would be before Wilson's planned return. Generously he gave permission for his sketches to be shown before they had been completely worked up.[2] In addition, as Chief of Scientific Staff he had prepared his report for the Royal Society. It was to go into the press telegram returning with the ship in March[3] and was to be published in *The Times* in May. It describes the scientific objectives of the expedition (illustrating the essential difference between British and Norwegian expeditions) and Wilson recorded details of Antarctic pressures, temperatures and wind velocity, the investigation of the high atmosphere using small balloons, the weekly magnetic observations and work on the glacier fronts. He reported his own expedition to Cape Crozier and said that he had got three chicks at different stages of development, which he hoped would be scientifically interesting. He wrote to Oriana also:

> Be assured I am content to feel that I was really wanted here after all, as you assured me I was and would be when we parted. . . . Whether we reach the Pole or not I really care very little as long as we feel we have done all we could. I feel I am here for a better purpose than to merely get to the Pole. . . . God comfort you my own dear wife.[4]

He was realistic about British chances, 'we are not as cocksure about it as we were',[5] and realised that if he was on the final Polar party, he would not get back to base before the ship had to leave for New Zealand. This had implications for publicity. 'Amundsen may reach the Pole and get his news back in 1912. We may not'.[6] He was only unhappy when he thought of Oriana's disappointment when *Terra Nova* got back to New Zealand in 1912 without him, 'Help Ory, dear Mr and Mrs Smith'.[7]

The influence he wielded remained noticed. Scott, writing to Reginald Smith, said:

> Wilson has been all that you expected of him. I find myself wondering at his energy, his tact and his unselfishness: such qualities have made him beloved by all and in return he wields the power of an oracle. . . . I hold him mainly responsible for the extraordinary amicable relations which have existed amongst us; it is really a fact that there have been no quarrels or other social

troubles since the expedition started. To sum up he has proved himself a greater treasure than even I expected to find.[8]

The much-heralded Pole assault began in a low-key fashion. The dog teams with Meares and Dimitri in charge, left on 21 October to lay depots and advance loads.[9] On 24 October the two motor tractors, each pulling three laden sledges, spluttered into life and pulled slowly away from Cape Evans, recorded on film by Ponting. Scott, in his heart of hearts, thought that the tractors would not be very useful on this expedition,[10] but he was eager that they should succeed enough to show their possibilities which, he thought, might revolutionise Polar travel.[11] He was right in both thoughts: the motors stuttered and often broke down, the track chains skidded on the hard sea ice and the mechanics' work, on cold metal, at temperatures below minus 30°F, was exasperating and painful. One machine lasted six days, the other eight, after which they were abandoned. After the final breakdown, the motor party, led by Lieutenant Teddy Evans, packed all the supplies on the sledges and man-hauled. But Scott was also correct about their possibilities; they were to be developed further and may be considered precursors of the tanks used in France in the First World War.

On the same day that the tractors were abandoned, the pony caravan started out. Wilson was one of ten pony leaders who followed Lieutenant Evans' trail south. The plan was that the ponies would go over the Barrier sea ice and then cross onto the Beardmore Glacier (named after William Beardmore, Shackleton's sponsor) nearly 400 miles south and discovered by Shackleton as being the route onto the high Arctic plateau and thence to the Pole. Scott knew that it was unlikely that he would be able to take the ponies further than the first stage of the Beardmore Glacier.[12] He planned to sacrifice them there and store the meat to be eaten later. The dog teams would also turn back at the glacier. Shackleton, on his expedition, had concluded that dogs were unsuited to the glacier, and could slow the expedition down.[13] Scott planned that when the men reached the plateau they would man-haul southwards towards the Pole, along 160° E, laying food and fuel depots along the route, a distance of less than 300 miles. Each depot was to be marked with black flags flying on bamboos (Amundsen had a system of markers stretching out at mile intervals from each depot) and each was to contain enough rations to take the party to the next depot, assuming progress of fourteen geographical miles per day.[14]

The ponies took just over four hours to get from Cape Evans to Hut Point, their departure also recorded on film by Ponting. At Hut Point someone remembered that the Union Jack, presented by Queen Alexandra to plant at the Pole, had been left behind. It was unthinkable to go without it, so Scott used the landline telephone (installed in the winter) to instruct Gran to ski over to Hut Point with it. A Norwegian therefore carried the British flag for the first few miles of the expedition. The ponies departed in order: weakest first, then the stronger ones followed by the dog teams. They marched at night when the snow surfaces were harder, though temperatures colder, and the men experienced the predictable problems of getting reasonably synchronised arrivals from convoys travelling at strikingly different speeds. Sometimes the dog teams had to wait for hours before leaving. But the first real setback for the pony party was a blizzard on 7 November, which trapped the men in their tents and left the ponies suffering behind protective snow walls. Meanwhile, the dogs raced into camp, hardly affected by the atrocious conditions. Scott said that it showed that the dogs ought to be able to help them a good deal.

Their progress to the Beardmore Glacier (more than 300 miles between Corner Camp and the Lower Glacier Camp) was calculated to take the heart out of men and beasts. The snow surface was 'abominable'.[15] Soft snow built up inch by inch and Scott wrote that a worse set of conditions for the ponies could scarcely be imagined; the crock (ponies) had had enough at nine and a half miles.[16] They would have been more disheartened if they had known that by 13 November Amundsen's men were ascending onto the plateau via a steep route up a glacier, the Axel Heiberg Glacier, which they had found by sheer good fortune south of the Bay of Whales. The glacier was sixty miles south of the Beardmore. The Norwegians had left twelve days in front of the British party and were now some 300 miles further south.[17]

The British reached One Ton Depot, on the Barrier and 150 statute miles from Cape Evans, on 15 November. Here they rested and lightened the pony loads, dropping off bundles of seal liver to eat on the return trip. On 21 November, Wilson's party caught up with Lieutenant Evans' motor party at a prearranged rendezvous. Teddy Evans and his three companions had pulled so hard after abandoning their motor sledges that they had arrived six days earlier and passed the time by building a fifteen-foot cairn and, says Wilson, reading *Pickwick* through.[18] They were very hungry, demonstrating, if this was needed, that rations sufficient for men leading ponies are insufficient for men doing hard pulling work.

They left the depot in five little groups: first the man-haulers, then the three pony groups, then the dogs. Scott's aim was to keep pace with Shackleton's 1908 progress. If he could do this, he felt, there was a chance of success. But they were soon several days behind schedule. The ponies were needed for a last 'push' at the glacier but they were failing in spite of 10 lbs of oats and 3 lbs of oil cake per day. Wilson wrote that they did not plan to shoot any pony until they had passed the distance that Shackleton's first horse had been shot. When they passed this milestone on 24 November, Oates dispatched the first pony, Jehu; the dogs devoured the fresh meat eagerly. Jehu made four days' rations for twenty dogs.[19]

On the same day the first two men turned back as arranged, leaving three parties of four men to go on. Wilson was in a group with Scott, Cherry-Garrard and Chief Stoker Lashly. He sent his letter to Ory with the men going back. He said that the teams were getting on well, everyone was fit and that he hoped to be chosen to go to the Pole, 'just for your sake'.[20] When they set off the three teams pushed on grimly through a blank white expanse of fog but Wilson also recorded a fine solar corona, a series of coloured rings around the sun, formed by the low fog. They moved on from Mid Barrier Depot on 26 November towards the foot of the Beardmore Glacier passing, finally in glorious sunshine, on 30 November, the 'best south' set by Wilson, Scott and Shackleton in 1902. Wilson wrote that he could see Cape Wilson, the snow-covered rocky cape that had been named after him in 1902, from time to time. Now they only had Shackleton's record ahead of them, but they were behind his schedule and the going was hard. The horses were tiring rapidly; as each failed it was shot and made into good, sweet 'pony hoosh'. The meat would have contained next to nothing in the way of vitamin C,[21] although raisins in the hoosh would have had a little. Eventually the Beardmore Glacier loomed in front of them, spilling onto the Barrier in heavily-crevassed waves and Wilson made a series of beautiful pencil sketches of the scene. To get onto the glacier the men needed to follow Shackleton's approach of 1908, called 'the Gateway'. This required good visibility; a huge chasm separated the Barrier from the mountains. But they could not go on. On 3 December they woke to a blizzard, thick drift and heavy snowfall. Scott thought that their luck with the weather was 'preposterous' and Birdie Bowers wrote that he was glad that Wilson was in a tent with Scott, 'there is something so reassuring about Bill – he comes out best in adversity'.[22] The gale, their fifth, was to last for four days and to hold them up at an important time. It raged 'such as one might expect to be driven at us by all the powers of darkness'[23] at a time when only one more march would have got them onto the Beardmore itself. The unlooked-for delay meant that they had to start on their summit rations. As they camped with no visibility, the living ponies buried in snowdrift and dug out periodically, the temperature rose to above freezing. The men lay in their sleeping bags encased in slushy snow, rather than ice. Wilson writes that everything was soaking wet: the sleeping bags were sodden, the tent dripping, clothes sopping wet and their tobacco juice running in a brown stream out of the gear bag.[24] He read Tennyson and his pocket Testament and Prayer Book, 'What a perfect piece of faith and hope and religion it is, makes me feel that if the end comes to me here or hereabouts there will be no great time for O. to sorrow. All will be as it was meant to be'.[25] He did not seek death, but his trust in God was such that he did not fear death either, if this was God's will. The surprising feature is that he did not seem to worry unduly about Oriana's future; he imagined that she would be sustained by the same convictions as him and feel that all would be for the best if it were left in God's hands.

The teams finally got on the move on 9 December and crossed the Gateway ramp. The man-hauling party went first to make a track in the deep soft snow for the ponies, which had to be flogged on as they floundered, belly-deep in snow. They had now completed their duties and Wilson's pony, Nobby, after 'a mere apology for a ration', was shot along with all the other ponies that night. Wilson 'thanked God that the horses were done with and they could begin the heavier work themselves'.[26] He had given his pony his own supper biscuits as a parting gift. With no apparent soul-searching he then spent several hours at his butcher's work, cutting and skinning the ponies up for food. Afterwards he 'slept like a log'.[27] They called the site 'Shambles Camp'.

They made a cache, the Lower Glacier Depot, at the base of the glacier and at the top of the Gateway's snow ramp. They raised a cairn on it with a black flag and black bunting. Here, Meares and Dimitri took the (fit) dog teams back on 11 December carrying another letter from Wilson:

All is well with us and as for me I was never stronger or fitter in my life . . . I am as fit as can be and I just thrive on it. We shall have another party returning in ten or twelve day's time reducing us then to eight. I expect to be one of the eight at any rate: but whether I shall have the good fortune to be considered strong enough to be one of the final 4 or not – why, I don't know. No one knows yet who they will be – but I do hope to be one of them for your dear sake . . .[28]

The twelve men looked up with awe at the fearsome glacier they had to climb: an ascent of more than 120 crevasse-ridden miles, to the plateau at 9,000 feet. Each party of four were man-hauling 600 lbs over ice ridges of nearly thirty feet. Sometimes they could use their skis, sometimes they could not. Slowly they toiled up, making depots at mid-glacier on 17 December and upper glacier on 21 December. Wilson wrote that their ascent was very difficult; they had to pull their sledges through soft, heavy snow in contrast to Shackleton's ice and they gasped for breath as they sunk knee-deep in the snow or took ten or more desperate jerks to get the sledge even started. When the sledge ran they had to strain 'every muscle and fibre' to keep it going. Scott felt nothing could replace the four days lost in the blizzard. On the ascent, Wilson made a further panoramic series of sketches of the glorious surroundings, the sketches unfolding page after page. He did this in spite of his inflamed, painful eyes which streamed continuously, marginally helped by repeated zinc sulphate eye drops, but preventing any hope of sleep. As the team struggled up the glacier, still more than 300 miles from the Pole, Amundsen reached it with his four companions on 14 December. He later reported that the approach to the Pole had been in fine sunny weather, across a vast and apparently endless plain.

At the Upper Glacier Depot Scott made his selection of the eight men who were to continue southwards and the four who were to return. He chose Wilson, Bowers, Petty Officer Edgar Evans, Oates, Lieutenant Evans, Seaman Crean and Seaman Lashly to go on. Dr Atkinson, Cherry-Garrard, Wright and the third seaman, Keohane, were to return. Wilson sent back letters at every opportunity. Now he wrote to Oriana 'from Upper Glacier Depot by Mount Darwin', saying that they were less than 300 miles from the Pole and well in hand for time. He wondered if his grouse work had been well received (or slated), but said that come what may, it was the best piece of work that he could have produced.[29] He wrote to Reginald Smith saying that they should reach the Pole but if they did not then he and Cherry-Garrard would probably remain in the Antarctic and make another attempt between October 1912 and March 1913. If, however, they reached the Pole in 1911–12 and Scott went home, Wilson and Cherry-Garrard would return with him.[30]

Christmas Day was, 'a real good and happy one,' only marred by the ever-present menace of crevasses. Seaman Lashly tumbled into one fifty-footer, dropping down the whole length of his harness. He wrote in his diary that the crevasse was 'rather a ghastly sight while dangling in one's harness'.[31] The men celebrated with 'a magnificent lunch: three biscuits, one and a half pannikins (containers) of tea, a spoonful of raisins, a whack of butter, and a stick of chocolate. For supper, an amazing mess of extra pemmican (horse meat, onion, curry powder and biscuit), a pannikin of cocoa and sugar and a large slice of plum pudding followed by caramel, ginger pieces and a biscuit.'[32]

By the last day of December they had caught up with Shackleton's dates. Scott laid the first plateau cache, Three Degree Depot. They were now at 10,000 feet and 180 miles from the Pole. From here speed and light loads were essential. In the interests of greater speed, Petty-Officers Crean and Evans were ordered to dismantle the twelve-foot sledges and refashion them as ten-footers. As they did the work, Scott described Petty-Officer Evans as a most valuable asset,[33] but in fact the alterations were to have important consequences. Edgar Evans cut his hand as he worked and this injury was to cause an ongoing problem, though it was probably only minor initially and Evans did not mention it. He was strong. Like all of them he hoped to be chosen for the Pole assault. At a time when things were going comparatively well, they all dreamed of success. Being a member of the first group to reach the Pole would bring Evans national fame. In relation to the weights on the sledges, to keep these at a minimum Wilson wrote that although he, Oates, Petty Officer Evans and Scott were to continue with skis, sticks and shoes,[34] the other men were to leave their skis behind and go forward on foot.

On 3 January, within 150 miles of the Pole, Scott announced his final plans. Lieutenant Evans and Seamen Lashly and Crean were to be sent back. Scott had decided unexpectedly to take a five-man party south. Lieutenant Evans later said that Scott had come into his tent and said that he had decided that five men would be best to reach the Pole. He asked Evans if he was prepared to make the return journey short-handed and 'of course [Evans later recorded in his lecture in the Albert Hall] we consented'.[35] Scott merely says that he had decided to reorganise.[36] Bowers moved into the now five-man tent with Wilson, Scott, Oates and Seaman Evans. It has been suggested that the five-man option had been planned for some time. One of Wilson's watercolours, given to his godson, illustrates five men, all on skis, hauling a loaded sledge,[37] and Wilson is renowned for his accurate representations. However the expedition's supplies, equipment, food and oil had all been planned around teams of four, as had the food depots for the returning men. Also, Bowers' skis had been left at Three Degree Depot and he was on foot. Wilson does not comment on this change of plan. He merely wrote:

To-morrow . . . the last supporting party returns to the winter quarters and they will take this note home, arriving probably in time to catch the ship. I am one of the five to go on to the Pole. So this may be the last you hear from me for another whole year . . . only I am glad for your sake I am one of the five . . . all fit and strong and well and only 148 more miles to go. . . . It seems too good to be true that this long journey to the Pole should be realising itself – we ought to be there in less than a fortnight now . . .

He continues:

you know my love for you – it's just myself, and all I do and all I pray for is your good. Be strong in hope and in faith if you hear no more of me after this till next year. . . I believe firmly that we have a lot to do together when we meet again . . .[38]

As the last supporting party prepared for the long march home, they gave three huge cheers for the polar party group disappearing into a tiny black speck on the southern horizon. The little group, marching into legend, were never to be seen alive again. Initially, they made good marches over the plateau; Scott and Wilson pulled in front, Oates and Petty Officer Evans behind, Bowers on foot between the four. But the surfaces were variable and when he was confronted by 'a sea of fish-hook waves' Wilson wrote that they left the skis behind 'as the surface is too much cut up for them and we think it continues so'. After a few miles, when the surface improved, they returned to pick up them up again losing more than an hour.[39]

By 9 January, Scott could write 'RECORD' in his diary. They were beyond Shackleton's furthest south at 88.25°, 'All is new ahead'.[40] But Wilson does not even mention this; he knew they were still ninety-five miles from the Pole. Retrospectively, by this date, their attempt was beginning to unravel for several unrelated reasons. Their haul up the Beardmore Glacier had taken its toll; Scott wrote, 'It's going to be a stiff pull *both ways* apparently' and 'none of us ever had such hard work before'.[41] Cooking caused unexpected problems. They had food for a month for five men, but to do the cooking took an extra half hour each day. They felt the cold badly at this stage, though the temperatures were not really low (minus 7°F at midday, minus 3°F later). Camping conditions were worse with five; the teepee-shaped tent made it difficult for more than one person to stand at a time and the floor-covering (not fixed to the tent) left the two on the outside lying partially on snow when they crawled into their sleeping bags. Apart from problems with cold, sleeplessness, weakness and hunger, they were to be at an altitude of 10,000 feet for seven weeks. This level can cause altitude sickness. Ranulph Fiennes states that virtually every year, one scientist based at the south polar station has to be evacuated back to sea level because of altitude problems. Severe cases can get cerebral oedema (swelling of the brain).[42] On the plateau in 1912 the men were regularly to experience temperatures in the minus-twenty range. This extreme cold reduces the barometric pressure which exaggerates the effects of altitude and means that the men were experiencing the physiological effects that they would have experienced at much higher altitudes on equatorial mountains, such as the Andes.[43] The men would have had to hyperventilate in the dry conditions to maintain an adequate oxygen level in the 'thinner' dry air. This causes dehydration. Every movement would have been an effort; jerking the sledges to start the run and pulling them over the uneven surface was a daily endurance test.

It is now known that their problems were increased by poor nutrition. Their summit rations, consisting of butter, pemmican, biscuit, cocoa, sugar and tea[44] provided approximately 4,500 calories per day though this eventually became less on the return journey because of failing supplies. Even this large intake was not nearly sufficient for man-hauling, which can use up more than 7,000 calories per day.[45] Over the weeks they would have built up a big calorie deficit. In addition the diet was deficient in the vitamin B complex[46] and ascorbic acid (vitamin C). These deficiencies would result in loss of muscle as well as insulating body fat. The men were voraciously hungry. The slow marches with extra halts, the muscle loss, the dehydration, their increased susceptibility to cold and consequent poor coordination for performing the simplest actions, would have compounded their exhaustion.

They had hard and heavy marches and were held up by a summit blizzard on 8 January, but by the 14 January they were just over forty miles from the Pole, and on the next day, twelve miles less.

It is wonderful to think that two long marches would land us at the Pole. We left our depot to day with nine days provisions, so that it ought to be a certain thing now and the only appalling possibility the sight of the Norwegian flag forestalling ours. . . . Only twenty-seven miles from the Pole. We *ought* to do it now.[47]

On 16 January they started off in high spirits. They were sure they had a good chance of 'bagging the Pole' first. Then, 'The worst has happened, or nearly the worst'.[48] On the afternoon march the sharp-eyed Bowers saw a black speck in the distance. As they struggled towards it, it took the shape of a ragged black flag, near the remains of a camp with sledge, ski and dog tracks. This told them the whole story. They had been beaten. The flag was frayed at the edges and the British estimated it had been there for several weeks.[49] Wilson wrote simply, 'The Norwegians came up evidently by another glacier'.[50] He made no further comment in his diary. Scott wrote, 'The Norwegians have forestalled us and are first at the Pole. It is a terrible disappointment and I am very sorry for my loyal companions'.[51] Oates commented in his usual laconic fashion, 'We are not a very happy party tonight'.[52] Bowers wrote to his mother:

> Well, here I really am and very glad to be here too. It is a bleak spot – what a place to strive so hard to reach. . . . It is sad that we have been forestalled by the Norwegians, but I am glad we have done it by good British man-haulage. That is the traditional British sledging method and this is the greatest journey done by man since we left our transport at the foot of the glacier.[53]

The following day the British made their own line for the Pole, marching in cutting winds of over force four and temperatures of minus 30°F, 'the coldest march I ever remember'.[54] They camped on what Wilson wrote was the Pole itself on Wednesday 17 January at 6.30p.m. and tried to console themselves with a double hoosh, some last bits of chocolate and some cigarettes given by Wilson's brother Bernard, 'a queer taste'.[55] The following day, after careful measurements, they decided that they were three and a half miles away from the Pole and marched to their calculated spot. Here they built a cairn and took photographs of themselves with the Queen Mother's Union Jack and all their other flags. As expected, Wilson looks drawn in the photographs. The British accepted Amundsen's claim to the Pole. They had arrived, but in very different circumstances to those that they had hoped for and expected. Rarely has such endeavour been met by such an anticlimax. They were frostbitten, they were cold and Scott already wondered if they would make it back.[56] 'Great God! this is an awful place and terrible enough for us to have laboured to it without the reward of priority'.[57] But Wilson's inner voice and convictions held. He barely comments on the disappointment, but wrote that they (the British), had done what they had come for and as their programme had dictated. Amundsen had beaten them in so far as he had made a race of it. 'We have done what we came for all the same and as our programme was made out'.[58] This was enough for him.

At the Norwegians' most southerly camp, *Polheim* (Pole-base), they found a small tent with Norwegian and *Fram* flags flying, discarded gear and a note to say that five Norwegians had arrived a month earlier, Scott thought 15 December, and had spent some days determining the Pole's precise location. There was another note for Scott to forward to the Norwegian king, King Haakon. Wilson made pencil sketches of the tent and a nearby black flag attached to a sledge runner which he found had a note attached saying that this was the Norwegians' final Pole position. He took some silk strips from the tent seams, the black flag, the note with Amundsen's signature and a piece of the sledge-runner as souvenirs.[59] Although he and Bowers were sanguine (Bowers wrote to his mother about them being a most congenial party and five being a pleasant little crowd),[60] Scott wrote 'Well, we have turned our back on the goal of our ambition and must face our 800 miles of solid slogging and good-bye to most of the day dreams'.[61] Had they got home, they would have been feted, but then probably lost from popular interest as the unfolding drama of the First World War progressed. As it was they marched to death and posterity.

They had to start by pulling up a rise. The Pole is lower than the highest part of the plateau, which had to be climbed before the descent to the Beardmore Glacier. The snow surface around the Pole was uneven. Snow blew in snow-drifts, which covered their tracks from the southbound journey. Visibility was bad enough to make the picking up of the cairns difficult. Evans' fingertips were badly blistered.[62] Scott wrote that Wilson had discovered that Evans' nose was also frostbitten and that Evans was very annoyed with himself. Scott thought that this was a bad sign.

On 29 January Wilson wrote that he had a nasty bruise on his shin, in his *tibialis anterior* muscle, after more than nineteen miles of difficult skiing. The front of his left leg was swollen and tight, the skin red. It was initially so painful that he could not ski and gave his skis to Bowers. Scott was worried that he would hold up the party. The pain grew less after three days, though the shin was still badly swollen and he could not ski for more than a week.[63] Wilson's description of the injury is considered to be the first record of a condition known as a 'compartment syndrome'. This syndrome is due to a compromised blood supply to the shin muscle. This causes swelling in the muscle and raises the pressure within the rigid bony-fibrous compartment that surrounds it, so causing more pain. The injury can follow strenuous activity or injury and is now a well-recognised phenomenon occurring in high-performance athletes.[64, 65]

On 31 January they reached Three Degree, the last depot on the Plateau. They picked up a note from Lieutenant Evans, Bowers' skis and a week's provisions. They plodded on north. Wilson wrote that Edgar Evan's fingers were in a very bad state, his cut hand a festering mess and both hands raw, the fingernails falling off leaving suppurating sores. Evans was losing heart. Wilson dressed the fingers with boric vaseline and on 4 February wrote that they were 'still sweet' (not gangrenous).[66] On that day Evans and Scott fell into a crevasse (Scott said it was the second fall for Evans). Evans fell in to his waist, but it is possible that he jerked his head. He was deteriorating rapidly from his usual self-confident extrovert self to a mumbling incoherent wreck, unable to help with camp work. Because he was deteriorating so badly the men scaled down the distances to be covered each day. Scott wrote, 'the party is not improving in condition, especially Evans who is becoming rather dull and incapable. Thank the Lord we have good food at each meal but we get hungrier in spite of it'. They were all weakening. Scott was worried about the easy way that Oates, as well as Evans, got frostbitten; about a shoulder injury he himself had had after a fall; and about Wilson's painful leg, which was better but which 'might easily get bad again'. 'Three out of five injured'.[67] The polar party had been going for more than ninety days and would have lost much of the body fat they needed for insulation.[68] They were fatigued. They were famished. Evans, the man who had been chosen for his strength was now holding up the marches. But in spite of his deterioration they still managed thirteen miles and some-times more and they got down the Beardmore Glacier in a day less than they had taken to get up. They would have needed all their strength for this; they had to control the sledge on the icy slopes and avoid crevasses. Above all was the lurking fear that they would miss their next depot. (Wilson, to their immense relief, spotted the flag on 13 February). But even under these circumstances Wilson's serenity did not desert him. He carefully studied the geology and took samples from the Upper Glacier Depot and recorded his findings: he found sandstone, dolorite and quartz boulders.[69]

On 16 February, Edgar Evans collapsed with sickness and giddiness. He could not walk and camp was made early. Scott wrote that Evans had stopped the march on some trivial excuse.[70] On 17 February, 'a very terrible day', Evans had difficulty keeping his ski shoes on. Possibly he could not tie his laces with his infected hands; possibly he was in an unrec-ognised confused state. Whatever the reason, he could not pull effectively. He was ordered to unhitch, to sort himself out and rejoin, but he trailed well behind his companions. After their lunch they went back for him; he was dishevelled, on his knees, unable to stand. He was comatose by the time he was carried to the tent. He died at 10p.m. They left his body at the base of the Beardmore Glacier. His companions did not show much understanding of Evans' deterioration. In discussion with his religious mother Wilson had accepted the concept of 'the healing power of sickness', taking the view that the lack of previous suffering made a patient less able to withstand illness. As late as 16 February, he wrote that Evans' collapse had 'much to with the fact that he had never been sick in his life and is now helpless with his hands frostbitten',[71] implying, with no evidence, a psychosomatic cause for Evans' collapse. These uncharacteristically unsympathetic comments were made at a time when he himself was greatly debilitated. The fact that Evans struggled to cooperate (he said, as he always did, that he was well when the group started out) up to the day he died makes depression and withdrawal unlikely.

When the four survivors went over Evans' problems they thought that he had begun to deteriorate well before they reached the Pole, but they also thought, reasonably, that his downward path had been accelerated by his frostbitten fingers and falls. The latter, they thought, could have caused an injury to the brain. While this may be so, Evans' death was clearly due partially to the compounding general problems common to them all: malnutrition with loss of fat reserves, vitamin deficiency, dehydration and the effects of altitude and fatigue. In addition, he had problems specific to himself; for example, infection could have played a significant part in his death. Staphylococcus aureus is a bacterium present on the skin and in the nose. It is not eliminated by Antarctic temperatures[72] and is a likely cause of his hand becoming infected. Abscess formation occurs typically seven days after a wound infection with this organism, as happened to Evans. By February his frostbitten fingers were suppurating and his nose was very bad and rotten looking. A possible sequence is: nasal carriage resulting in wound infection and following this, invasion of the blood stream, probably repeated.[73] There need have been no signs in the arm; the bacteraemia could have silently gained ascendancy. The final picture can be interpreted as collapse due to low blood pressure caused by infection. Another explanation for his odd behaviour and collapse is that the staphylococci could have gained direct entry to Evans' brain from his 'rotten-looking' nose resulting in a brain abscess or an infected thrombus extending into the brain. Others have discounted a brain abscess but it remains a possibility.[74] Dehydration would increase this risk.

A repeated suggestion has been brain damage following a minor head injury when Evans fell into the crevasse, related particularly to vitamin C deficiency. Although by this time the men's diet had been deficient in vitamin C for more than fourteen weeks, this seems unlikely. It is accepted that the earliest signs of scurvy (which caused Lieutenant Teddy Evans to collapse when he returned from the plateau with his two companions) are skin thickening and small skin haemorrhages from capillary leaks, which appear after about four months of deficiency and which precede other signs. Problems with bleeding, such as cuts not healing, come later.[75] Wilson, a careful observer and well versed in the early signs of scurvy, reported no early signs in Evans. This makes it less likely that Evans' death, some days after minor trauma, was due to blood leaking around the brain secondary to a low vitamin C level.[76]

The remaining four struggled on probably hoping and believing that they would get on better without Evans. Their chances of survival critically depended on them doing a minimum distance each day. Although the depots contained, Bowers calculated, sufficient food and fuel to last them to the next one, they were by now hugely deficient in their total calorie intake. They knew, all too well, that their chances would be seriously prejudiced if any of them could not keep going. Hunger was always with them, but they were buoyed up by the knowledge that the string of depots stretching out in front of them had food for five men in each of them. In Shambles Camp on 18 February they split Evans' rations and had 'a fine supper' with plenty of horsemeat. 'New life seems to come with greater food almost immediately'.[77] But the odds were against them; the Barrier surface was very bad, the sun was shining on it so its covering of soft loose snow was like sand to pull through. The men pulled wearily on the sledge tracks stretching for miles behind them, like ploughed furrows. Progress was erratic, sometimes pitifully below what was needed: fourteen miles with ski and sail on 15 February, but five and a half miles on 19 February. In spite of apparent good meals, excellent 'pony hoosh', they would be getting weaker daily. Having lost so much insulation they were completely vulnerable to the temperatures. Wilson frequently could not see to sketch or track-find.[78] His fingers were raw. At the end of February, instead of a southerly wind which would have allowed them to use a sail, they pulled against no wind or winds from the north. The temperature was minus 37°F.

As the situation became desperate Wilson continued to man-haul, to cook and sketch when his eyes allowed, to help his colleagues. But clearly something was seriously amiss. He, who had kept up his dairy for most of his life, stopped making entries. His last entry was on 27 February, three weeks before Scott's and just over three weeks after Bowers. There is no hint of anxiety, no hint that he would not continue, 'Overcast all forenoon and cleared to splendid clear afternoon. Good march on 12.2m ski. Some fair breeze. Turned in at -37.'[79]

Misfortunes multiplied: at Mid Barrier on 2 March their fuel was found to have evaporated leaving insufficient to get to the next depot. This meant that they could not melt their drinking water. The weather turned worse, the temperature was again minus 40°F. And here Oates showed his companions his frostbitten, black, gangrenous feet. They may not have been his only problem. The thigh wound that he had suffered in the Boer War could also have been breaking down secondary to low vitamin C (and other vitamin) levels. Old wounds can break down even in the absence of overt signs of scurvy.[80] Wilson could do precious little but his energies would have been concentrated on helping Oates. All of them would know that the gangrene was likely to spread up the leg and that that there was no hope of recovery. They knew also that they had not only lost Evans' pulling power but that now Oates' input would lessen. Scott, Wilson and Bowers, barely able to pull the sledge themselves, faced the likelihood of their burden being increased by their having to pull Oates too. By the time Oates revealed his problems his condition was well advanced. He had mentioned his black toe in his diary more than six weeks before and Wilson had commented on Oates' black toe and yellow nose and cheeks more than three weeks previously.[81] Hopes of survival for any of them were irredeemably compromised. They were more than 100 miles from One Ton Depot, and more than seventy from their small depot at Mount Hooper.

Wilson would never abandon a sickening colleague. This would be against his entire ethos. He would make it his business to help and comfort as best he might, though with few practical options. He dressed Oates' feet and he was his companion, probably sacrificing any residual strength to do so; Scott wrote of Wilson's 'self-sacrificing devotion'. Oates, lying helpless and suffering, must have thought bitterly about his disagreement with Scott the previous year when Scott had decided to save the ponies and deposit One Ton Camp short of the original plans. Scott wrote, 'We are in a very queer street since there is no doubt we cannot do the extra marches and feel the cold horribly'.[82] He wrote on 3 March, 'Amongst ourselves we are unendingly cheerful, but what each man feels in his heart I can only guess'.[83]

By now each day was increasingly dangerous. They could not melt much snow for fluid. It took them over an hour to put on their boots. They managed variable distances: ten miles on 2 March, just over four on 3 March in spite of a now strong wind and full sail, but with a snow surface covered in woolly crystals. But in spite of these misfortunes they did not retreat into sullen, hopeless resentment even though Scott wrote, 'God help us indeed. We are in a very bad way'.[84] Though the crisis for Oates was approaching he never complained but grew more and more silent. Wilson's feet were also giving trouble, but they still remained cheerful.

By 6 March Oates sat on the sledge, his black feet hugely swollen and his enfeebled, famished colleagues hoisted him slowly and painfully over the icy surface. Scott, who managed entries in his diary until 29 March wrote, 'If we were all fit I should have hopes of getting through, but the poor Soldier [Oates] has become a terrible hindrance, though he does his utmost and suffers much I fear'.[85] Four days later

Oates asked Wilson if there was any chance that he could pull through, and Wilson, avoiding the truth, replied that he did not know. There was in fact, no hope and by now Oates took so long to get going in the morning that he was vitally prejudicing any hope for his companions' survival.[86] Scott ordered Wilson, who was strongly against suicide, to give each of them enough tablets to allow each man to make an end of his suffering. Under protest Wilson gave thirty opium tablets to Oates (who probably could not have put them in his mouth himself because of his frostbitten hands), Scott and Bowers, and kept a vial of morphine for himself. On 16 March, Oates hoped he would die in his sleep. When death was not merciful and he woke on 17 March he said, 'I am just going outside and may be some time'.[87] He crawled out of the tent, whose flaps must have been opened, into a blizzard and temperatures of minus 40°F. He would have lapsed into unconsciousness quickly. He died on his thirty-second birthday, near the spot where One Ton Depot had originally been planned the year before.

Oates' sacrifice was not unexpected. The moral issues of holding up colleagues had been discussed repeatedly. Lieutenant Teddy Evans wrote after the expedition that he had suffered so badly with scurvy on his return to base, that he told his two companions to leave him in his sleeping bag and go on without him. He said afterwards that it was the only occasion in his naval career that he had been disobeyed.[88] In allowing Oates to crawl out, Wilson would not have worried about his own survival, but he must have decided that if Oates continued with them then Bowers and Scott would definitely die. If Oates sacrificed himself, the slightest chance still remained for his companions.

Wilson, Scott and Bowers grimly continued to trudge northwards but Scott's right foot was now gangrenous. On 19 March they had food for two days but scarcely any fuel. In the face of apparent common sense, they clung to the rock specimens from the Beardmore Glacier. This decision has been criticised, but all of the three and particularly Wilson, were passionately involved in the advancement of science and this was one small advance that might be salvaged from the disaster. In fact the rocks were of immense scientific interest. They contained traces of fossils and vegetation that proved conclusively that Antarctica had once been part of a warmer environment.

The doomed trio continued for a few more days. On 21 March they pitched their tent only eleven miles short of One Ton Camp. Here they faced death calmly though Wilson and Bowers had fleeting hopes that they might still get to One Ton Depot and get fuel and food. Whilst they were planning this Wilson wrote his farewell to his wife. He wrote, 'To-day may be the last effort. Birdie and I are going to try and reach the Depot 11 miles north of us and return to this tent where Captain Scott is lying with a frozen foot'. He continued, saying that if he did not make it

> I shall simply fall and go to sleep in the snow and I have your little books, (the testament and prayer book) with me in my breast pocket. . . . Don't be unhappy – all is for the best. We are playing a good part in the great scheme arranged by God himself and all is well . . . I am only sorry I couldn't have seen your loving letters and Mother's and Dad's and the Smiths' and all the happy news I had hoped to see – but all these things are easily seen later, I expect . . . God be with you – my love is as living for you as ever . . . we will all meet after death and death had no terrors . . . my own dear wife, good-bye for the present . . . I do not cease to pray for you, – to the very last . . .[89]

They did not even try to get to the depot. A blizzard pinned them in their tent. Wilson could not know if he or his letters would be found but he could hope. He wrote to the Smiths saying again that he had no fear of death, only sorrow for Oriana and his family and he said they would meet in the hereafter.[90] He wrote to his parents that he had loved them and loved to think of them all. 'My own time is fulfilled'.[91] He wrote again to Oriana:

I leave this life in absolute faith and happy belief that if God wishes you to wait long without me it will be to some good purpose. All is for the best to those that love God and oh, my Ory, we have both loved Him with all our lives. All is well. . . . All the things I had hoped to do with you after the expedition are as nothing now, but there are greater things for us to do in the world to come. . . . One of my notes will surely reach you. . . . All is well.[92]

They lay together in their little tent, the Barrier blizzard howling around them. Here they slowly perished and here they lay for eight months. They had been due back early in 1912 and for weeks the party at Cape Evans continued to hope. Sometimes they were misled by a party of seals, sometimes by a mirage. Sometimes the sledge dogs would howl in greeting and the men would rush out, shouting to the cook to get things moving, whilst the national anthem was played on the gramophone. But when the winter began all hope was extinguished.

The search party set out in October. On 12 November, they saw the tip of the tent. It was some time before they could steel themselves to enter; Dr Atkinson went in first. Scott lay between Wilson and Bowers, his arm flung out over Wilson. One of the discovery party wrote:

Dr Wilson was sitting in a half reclining position with his back against the inside of the tent facing us as we entered. On his features were traces of a sweet smile and he looked exactly as if he were about to wake from a sound sleep. I had often seen the same look on his face in the morning as he awakened as he was of the most cheerful disposition. The look struck us to the heart and we all stood silent in the presence of death.[93]

The rescue party collapsed the tent and left it with its bodies inside. They built a cairn surmounted with a cross on the spot. Scott's skis were planted in a small pile of frozen snow nearby. A twelve-foot cross was erected on Observation Hill, above Hut Point. This was made of an Australian hard wood, jarrah, and stands there today. The five names are inscribed on it and below is the last line of Tennyson's 'Ulysses': *To strive, to seek, to find and not to yield.*

Their relatives felt that the bodies should be left undisturbed 'amid the eternal snows, the scene of their great achievement and beneath the cairn which the loving hearts and hands of their comrades have erected in their memory. Requiescant in pace'.[94]

Epilogue

Oriana was in New Zealand waiting for Wilson. By the time she got the terrible news she had been a widow for nearly a year. Her husband, never a seeker of personal fame, had become a public hero, a courageous explorer who had died at the height of his achievements, a man who had risked and finally given his life in the quest for knowledge about the earth's last great frontier.

In 1912 British confidence was faltering. Old certainties were being challenged: Women's Suffrage and the Irish Home Rule Bill had divided Parliament and the country. Winston Churchill was agitating for ships to be built in line with Germany. *Titanic*, the huge, new (and thought to be unsinkable) liner, had sunk on her maiden voyage, with the loss of 1,500 lives. The First World War was looming. The country needed reassurance and men to admire. In this setting, Antarctic exploration with its values of courage, cheerfulness, persistence, loyalty and self-sacrifice struck an inspiring note. Wilson was the personification of these values. His loyalty to Scott was absolute. His scientific and artistic output was huge; he was modest, supportive and tough.

The news of the men's deaths caused a national outpouring of grief. A memorial service was held in London's St Paul's Cathedral in the presence of King George V. More than 10,000 people, unable to get in to offer their respects, stood outside. Services were held throughout the country. The deaths gripped the national imagination and fixed the events in the national consciousness in a way that was probably not to be felt again until the death of Diana, Princess of Wales.

The family was devastated; Wilson's father wrote, 'No words can express what our dear Ted meant to us all and to our dear, good Ory, vainly awaiting his return in New Zealand'.[1] Oriana was on a train, making her way back to Christchurch, when she heard newspaper hawkers shouting the news of her husband's death.[2] She was looked after by friends until she could make her sorrowful journey home. She treasured Wilson's last letter, stained by the icy film of his dying breath, until she herself died. The two had been tightly bound by their faith. The letters that he wrote to her when he knew his situation was hopeless must have both helped her and spared her from the anguish of gnawing resentment, but they could not assuage her suffering. After her return she lived for a time in Cheltenham with the Wilson family before returning to Bushey. She never remarried; she had lost a man who had cherished and needed her, a powerful combination. For the rest of her life she treasured the memory of the precious years she had shared with Wilson. When she was in Cheltenham many expedition members visited Westal; Debenham and Cherry-Garrard frequently. A statue of Wilson, carved by Kathleen Scott, was unveiled, with full civic pageantry, on the town's promenade in July 1914. It remains there, overlooking the bustle of modern Cheltenham life.

Wilson would have felt that his life was fulfilled. His faith, the essence of his character, enabled him to put his life into his maker's hands with confidence and serenity. Comments that he had not fulfilled his potential are wide of the mark.[3] He believed in the importance of individual action in the scheme of things, the importance of putting others before himself. He always wanted to commit himself totally to anything he undertook and when he died he had done this. He was content, 'All is well'.

How should he be remembered? For his paintings, his scientific work, his work on grouse, as well as for his character: his loyalty, his ability to 'bind and bond'. As a child he was wilful and temperamental but gradually, under the imprint of his faith, all his energies became channelled into doing his best at whatever occupation he was at, doing everything, however small, as if for his maker.

His paintings and drawings are a rich and vibrant inheritance. As a follower of Ruskin his works accurately reflected their subjects; interpretative work was secondary. His drawings of the coastlines, mountains and interior of the Antarctic, made even when he was sledging in terrible conditions, were an important record. Complementing his journal, accurate and beautiful, they were the first documentation of the topography and geology of the interior of the unknown continent. They stimulated, and still stimulate, enthusiasm and appreciation. They are more than pictorial records; his love of nature, his faith and his painstaking determination to find the truth in everything are integral to his works. His drawings of birds and animals also ranked him amongst the great nature artists of his day.

His fascination with emperor penguins was an overriding scientific interest and he was pivotal in discovering facts about those extraordinary birds and one of the first to get to their breeding grounds to study their peculiar life cycle. Before *Discovery* it was thought impossible that any bird could survive, let alone breed, in the Antarctic winter. From 1903 this was known to be a scientific fact as were other new details about the birds: how the eggs were carried, descriptions of the chicks in their grey fluffy coats, details of their thick tufted feathering. Though his hope to find a link between bird and dinosaurs was based on a false premise, many years later, in the 1990s, the link was made.[4] His winter journey was the earliest in a long line of investigations undertaken in a thirst for accurate knowledge on the subject.

After the *Discovery* expedition his work with birds continued with the Grouse Commission report, published when he had already left for the Antarctic on *Terra Nova*. He was credited with saving the red grouse. Wilson confirmed the parasite that caused grouse disease, charted its life cycle and was able to make suggestions for control, such as rotational burning of heather and limiting the number of birds to the food available, which contributed hugely to well-maintained moorland. His work took years and his self-discipline; attention to detail; and his careful, undramatic, patient observation and determination to push the project through reflected his strengths and his lifelong belief that the effort put into any project was of paramount importance. The fight against *strongylosis* continues; worms were at a low level in England and at a moderate level in Scotland in 2006.[5]

He has invisibly touched many fields of Antarctic science through his work as chief of scientific staff on the *Terra Nova* expedition. In addition there were the much-criticised geological specimens, collected and kept against all odds on the doomed return from the Pole. He was right to keep them. They were found to contain fossil specimens of a genus *Glossopteris* that has also been found in South America, Australia and India. It is an extinct seed plant, which dates back to the Palaeozoic Era of 245 million years ago. *Glossopteris'* presence in Antarctica proved that the continent had once had a warm climate and provided a link to other continents in the southern hemisphere.

The wooden huts that he and his colleagues lived in are still there, frozen and silent legacies to the endurance and heroism of the early Antarctic explorers. An international Antarctic Treaty governs the continent. Wilson would have approved of the fact that the Antarctic wastes, of which he is now a permanent part, are protected to ensure peaceful scientific research and international cooperation.

Notes on Sources

Prologue

1   Scott, R.F. *Scott's Last Expedition*. Vol.1. John Murray, London, 1935. p. 473.
2   *Daily Mirror*. 6 November 1913. p. 3.
3   Wilson, E.T. *E.A. Wilson: Memoir by his father*. The Wilson Collection, Cheltenham Art Gallery and Museum, 1955, 550.36. p. 120.
4   Cherry-Garrard, A. *The Worst Journey in the World*. Picador, London, 2001. p. 207.
5   Wilson, E.A. *Letters to Apsley Cherry-Garrard*, 1909–1910, SPRI. MS. 841/10.

Chapter 1

1   Cheltenham Census 1871. Cheltenham Museum and Library.
2   Cheltenham Census 1881. Cheltenham Museum and Library.
3   Blake, S. *Cheltenham: A pictorial history*. Phillimore, Chichester, 1996. p. xi.
4   *Ibid*. p. xiii.
5   *Ibid*. p. xiii.
6   *Ibid*. p. xvii.
7   *Ibid*. p. xix.
8   Wilson, D.M. and Elder, D.B. *Cheltenham in Antarctica: The Life of Edward Wilson*. Reardon Publishing, Cheltenham, 2000. p. 6.

9 The Wilson Collection, Cheltenham Art Gallery and Museum, 1995, 550.41.
10 Ida Wilson's scrapbook. SPRI. MS. 715/5/BJ.
11 Munk's Roll. *The Lives of the Fellows of the Royal College of Physicians of London.* Compiled, Brown, G.H. 1955.
12 *The Illustrated London News,* March 1895.
13 Munk's Roll. *The Lives of the Fellows.* Brown, 1955.
14 Annual Report of the Sanitary Condition of the Borough of Cheltenham for the year 1894 by J.H. Garrett. M.D M.O.H.
15 Personal communication. Dr David M. Wilson.
16 Ida Wilson's scrapbook.
17 Darwin, C. *Origin of the Species by means of Natural Selection.* John Murray, London, 1859.
18 Cadbury, D. *The Dinosaur Hunters.* Fourth Estate, London, 2001. p. 305.
19 *Ibid.* p. 305.
20 *The Independent,* 5 August 2005.
21 Wilson, E.A. *On the nature of God compared with the luminiferous ether.* Cheltenham Art Gallery and Museum, 1995, 550.178.
22 Wilson, M.A. *The ABC Poultry Book.* Cassell Petter Galpin, London, 1880. [Held by the Wellcome Trust Library, London].
23 Wilson, E.T. *E.A. Wilson: Memoir by his Father.* Cheltenham Art Gallery and Museum, 1995, 550.36, p. 1.
24 *Ibid.* p. 2.
25 Cheltenham Census 1881. Cheltenham Museum and Library.
26 *British Medical Journal Advertiser,* 1884. The income for a Medical Practitioner of about twenty years' experience in an area like Cheltenham would be approximately £900 net. Medical income varied widely according to experience and the area of work. Cheltenham would be a good area (though not as prestigious as London). In the 1880s the *British Medical Journal Advertiser* was offering practices from £400 per annum to more than £1,000, with one outstanding offer to work in Canada of £2,000.
27 Wilson. *E.A. Wilson: Memoir by his Father.* p. 5.
28 *Ibid.* p. 4.
29 *Ibid.*
30 Certified copy of entry of death. Jessica Frances Wilson, Cheltenham. HD013712.
31 Annual Report of the Sanitary Condition of the Borough of Cheltenham for the year 1894 by J.H. Garrett. M.D M.O.H.

32 *Ibid.*

33 Wilson. *E.A. Wilson: Memoir by his Father,* p. 12.

34 *Ibid.* p. 8.

35 Wilson and Elder. *Cheltenham in Antarctica.* p. 11.

36 Wilson. *E.A. Wilson: Memoir by his Father*, p. 14.

37 *Ibid.* p. 18.

38 Strachey, L. *Eminent Victorians.* The Folio Society, London,1967. p. 179.

39 Wilson. *E.A. Wilson: Memoir by his Father.* pp. 23, 29.

40 *Ibid.* p. 14.

41 *Ibid.* p. 31.

42 Gonville and Caius Library, Cambridge.

43 St George's Hospital Medical School. Session 1892–3. St George's Hospital Library. Tooting, London. The subjects were: English language, Latin and mathematics, and a paper of choice from French, German, Italian, any other foreign language, logic, botany, zoology or elementary chemistry.

Chapter 2

1 Certificate of registration for entry to medical course at Gonville and Caius College, Cambridge. SPRI. MS. 715/3/BJ.

2 Hodgkinson, R.G. (ed. A. Rook). 'Cambridge and its Contribution to Medicine', in *Proceedings of the 7th British Conference on the History of Medicine.* September 1968. Medical Education in Cambridge in the nineteenth century. 1971. p. 95.

3 *Ibid.* p. 80.

4 *Ibid.* p. 95.

5 Wilson, E.T. *E.A. Wilson: Memoir by his Father.* The Wilson Collection, Cheltenham Art Gallery and Museum, 1995, 550.36, p. 41.

6 Wilson. *E.A. Wilson: Memoir by his Father.* p. 46.

7 U.A. Graduati 25. Cambridge University Archives.

8 Seaver, G. *Edward Wilson of the Antarctic.* John Murray, London, 1950. p. 22.

9 Wilson. *E.A. Wilson: Memoir by his Father.* p. 49.

10 Seaver. *Edward Wilson of the Antarctic.* p. 24.

11 U.A. Graduati 25. Cambridge University Archives.

[12] Students in Medicine. General Regulations. Cambridge University. 1883.

[13] U.A. Graduati 25. Cambridge University Archives.

[14] Wilson, D.M. and Elder, D.B. *Cheltenham in Antarctica: The Life of Edward Wilson*. Reardon Publishing, Cheltenham, 2000. p. 24.

[15] *Ibid*. p. 26.

[16] Seaver. *Edward Wilson of the Antarctic*. p. 101.

[17] *Biographical History of Gonville and Caius College*. Vol.2 (1713–1897). Cambridge University Press. pp. 518–19, 526.

[18] Wilson. *E.A. Wilson: Memoir by his Father*. p. 36.

[19] A first-year student.

[20] The Wilson Collection, Cheltenham Art Gallery and Museum, 1995, 550.107-122.

[21] Wilson and Elder. *Cheltenham in Antarctica*. p. 29.

[22] Seaver. *Edward Wilson of the Antarctic*. p. 14.

[23] The Caian. 1900–1. Vol. 10.

[24] Seaver. *Edward Wilson of the Antarctic*. p. 19.

[25] Wilson. *E.A. Wilson: Memoir by his Father*. p. 40.

[26] Wilson and Elder. *Cheltenham in Antarctica*. p. 25.

[27] Seaver. *Edward Wilson of the Antarctic*. p. 21.

[28] *Ibid*. p. 21.

[29] The Caian. 1892–3. Vol. 2.

[30] The Caian. 1895–6. Vol. 5.

[31] The Wilson Collection. pp. 107–22.

[32] Wilson. *E.A. Wilson: Memoir by his Father*. p. 48.

[33] Wilson, E.T. *The life of Gwladys by her father*. The Wilson Collection, Cheltenham Art Gallery and Museum, 1995, 550.37.

[34] Certified copy of entry of death. Gwladys Elizabeth Wilson, Cheltenham. HD013737.

[35] Wilson. *The life of Gwladys*.

[36] Wilson. *E.A. Wilson: Memoir by his Father*. p. 53.

[37] U.A. Graduati 25. Cambridge University Archives.

Chapter 3

[1] Wilson, E.T. *E.A. Wilson: Memoir by his father*. The Wilson Collection, Cheltenham Art Gallery and Museum, 1955, 550.36. p. 47.

2   Prospectus for St George's Hospital Medical School. Session 1892–3. St George's University of London.

3   *Ibid.*

4   A guinea is one pound and one shilling.

5   Blomfield, J. *St George's Hospital 1733–1933*. Published for St George's Hospital by the Medici Society, London, 1933. p. 86.

6   *Ibid.* p. 89.

7   Prospectus for St George's Hospital Medical School. Session 1892–3. p. 6.

8   *Ibid.* p. 5.

9   *Ibid.* p. 2.

10 *Ibid.* p. 6.

11 *Ibid.* p. 7.

12 Seaver, G. *Edward Wilson of the Antarctic*. John Murray, London, 1950. p. 26.

13 Fellow of the Royal College of Surgeons of England.

14 Wilson. *E. A. Wilson: Memoir by his father*. p. 55.

15 Hilton, T. *The Pre-Raphaelites*. Thames and Hudson, London, 1979. p. 11.

16 Herbert, R.L. (ed.). *The Art Criticism of John Ruskin*. Doubleday & Co., Garden City, 1964. p. 30.

17 *Ibid.* p. 31.

18 Dr John Henry Pearson Fraser (1872–1949). His son was Wilson's godson.

19 Wilson, D.M. and Elder, D.B. *Cheltenham in Antarctica: The Life of Edward Wilson*. Reardon Publishing, Cheltenham, 2000. p. 37.

20 Wilson. *E.A. Wilson: Memoir by his father*. p. 58.

21 Seaver, G. *The Faith of Edward Wilson of the Antarctic*. John Murray, London, 1949. p. 12.

22 Wilson. *E.A. Wilson: Memoir by his father*. p. 56.

23 Seaver. *Edward Wilson of the Antarctic*. p. 28.

24 Wilson. *E.A. Wilson: Memoir by his father*. p. 60.

25 Wilson, E.T. *The life of Gwladys by her father*. The Wilson Collection, Cheltenham Art Gallery and Museum, 1995, 550.37. p. 37.

26 Seaver. *Edward Wilson of the Antarctic*. p. 29.

27 Wilson. *E.A. Wilson: Memoir by his father*. p. 59.

28 *Ibid.* p. 61.

29 Seaver. *Edward Wilson of the Antarctic*. p. 29.

30 *Ibid.* p. 31.

31 Wilson. *E.A. Wilson: Memoir by his father*. p. 68.

32 *Ibid.*
33 *Ibid.* p. 69.
34 Obituary. *The Church Times.* 1 August 1941.
35 Seaver. *Edward Wilson of the Antarctic.* p. 31.
36 Wilson. *E.A. Wilson: Memoir by his father.* p. 61.
37 *Ibid.*
38 *Ibid.* p. 62.
39 *Ibid.* p. 64.
40 U.A. Graduati 25. Cambridge University Archives.
41 Letter to Ida Wilson. 26 May 1897. SPRI. MS. 861/D.
42 Seaver. *Edward Wilson of the Antarctic.* p. 34.
43 Wilson. *E.A. Wilson: Memoir by his father.* p. 70.
44 Seaver. *Edward Wilson of the Antarctic.* p. 44.
45 Wilson. *E.A. Wilson: Memoir by his father.* p. 84.
46 *Ibid.* p. 85.
47 Keers, R.A. *Pulmonary Tuberculosis: A Journey Down the Centuries.* Ballier Tindall, London, 1978. p. vii.
48 There are pathogenic bacteria that cause disease and non-pathogenic bacteria that may not. The absolute diagnosis depends on the cultural characteristics of the mycobacterium which would have taken weeks to grow. There is no record of a culture in Wilson's case.
49 Williams, I. *Edward Wilson: Medical aspects of his life and career.* Polar Record. 44, (228) 2008. p. 77.
50 Non-pathogenic saprophitic mycobacterium, found in dust and water, were often found in scrapings from metal cold water taps and could have been present as contaminants.
51 Brown, L. *The Story of Clinical Pulmonary Tuberculosis.* Williams and Wilkins, London, 1941. p. 76.
52 Wilson. *E.A. Wilson: Memoir by his father.* p. 86.
53 Mann, T. *The Magic Mountain.* Vintage, London, 1999.
54 Prospectus for St George's Hospital Medical School. Session 1898–9. St George's University of London. p. 21.
55 Seaver. *Edward Wilson of the Antarctic.* p. 48.
56 Wilson. *E.A. Wilson: Memoir by his father.* p. 87.
57 Seaver. *Edward Wilson of the Antarctic.* p. 49.
58 *Ibid.* p. 50.
59 Wilson. *E.A. Wilson: Memoir by his father.* p. 95.
60 Seaver. *Edward Wilson of the Antarctic.* p. 51.
61 Wilson. *E.A. Wilson: Memoir by his father.* p. 95.
62 *Ibid.* p. 54.

63 *Ibid.* p. 96.
64 Seaver. *Edward Wilson of the Antarctic.* p. 56.
65 Wilson. *E.A. Wilson: Memoir by his father.* p. 97.
66 Seaver. *Edward Wilson of the Antarctic.* p. 57.
67 U.A. Graduati 25. Cambridge University Archives.
68 Seaver. *Edward Wilson of the Antarctic.* p. 64.

Chapter 4

1   Wilson, E.T. *E.A. Wilson: Memoir by his father.* The Wilson
    Collection, Cheltenham Art Gallery and Museum, 1995, 550.36,
    p. 108.
2   Cheltenham Census 1901.
3   A journal which promoted country matters and interests and
    which was, in the 1890s, a rival publication to *The Field*, which
    continues to be popular.
4   An international weekly medical journal.
5   Seaver, G. *Edward Wilson of the Antarctic*, John Murray,
    London, 1950. p. 65.
6   *Ibid.* p. 65.
7   A scented hair dressing.
8   A reference book.
9   Seaver. *Edward Wilson of the Antarctic.* p. 67.
10 Wilson. *E.A. Wilson: Memoir by his father.* p. 106.
11 *Ibid.*
12 Seaver. *Edward Wilson of the Antarctic.* p. 67.
13 Huntford, R. *Scott and Amundsen.* Hodder and Stoughton,
    London, 1979. p. 144.
14 St George's Medical School Student Records. St George's
    University of London.
15 A hospital specialising in obstetrics and gynaecology.
16 Wilson. *E.A. Wilson: Memoir by his father.* p. 105.
17 *Ibid.* p. 108.
18 Savours, Ann (ed.) *Edward Wilson: Diary of the Discovery
    Expedition to the Antarctic Regions 1901–1904.* Blandford
    Press, London, 1966. p. 23.
19 Seaver. *Edward Wilson of the Antarctic.* p. 72.
20 Ida Wilson's scrapbook. SPRI. MS. 715/5/BJ.
21 Savours. *Edward Wilson: Diary of the Discovery Expedition.* p. 23.

22 A town in Natal besieged by the Boers between 2 November 1899 and 28 February 1900. Relieved by Sir Henry Buller. Named after the Spanish wife of the governor of Cape Town.

23 Wilson, D.M. and Elder, D.B. *Cheltenham in Antarctica: The Life of Edward Wilson*. Reardon Publishing, Cheltenham, 2000. p. 48.

24 Wilson, B. *Letters from the Boer War*. The Wilson Collection, Cheltenham Art Gallery and Museum, 1995, 550.74.

25 Churchill, W. *My Early Life*. Eland, London, 2002. p. 227.

26 Seaver. *Edward Wilson of the Antarctic*. p. 68.

27 *Ibid.* p. 70

28 *Ibid.* p. 71

29 Wilson. *E.A. Wilson: Memoir by his father*. p. 108.

30 Scott, R.F. *Scott's Voyage of the Discovery*. John Murray, London, 1929. p. 51.

31 Wilson. *E.A. Wilson: Memoir by his father*. p. 108.

32 *Ibid.* p. 110.

33 Seaver. *Edward Wilson of the Antarctic*. p. 75.

34 Savours. *Edward Wilson: Diary of the Discovery Expedition*. p. 25.

35 *Ibid.* p. 26.

36 Wilson. *E.A. Wilson: Memoir by his father*. p. 113.

37 Seaver. *Edward Wilson of the Antarctic*. p. 75.

38 *Ibid.* p. 76.

39 A club for gentlemen in central London. Women members now admitted.

40 Savours. *Edward Wilson: Diary of the Discovery Expedition*. p. 26.

41 Wilson and Elder. *Cheltenham in Antarctica*. p. 53.

42 A Discussion between David Wilson and Evelyn Forbes. 25 August 1995. Recorded by Dr David Wilson.

43 Wilson. *E.A. Wilson: Memoir by his father*. p. 114.

44 Markham, C. (ed. C. Holland) *Antarctic Obsession. The BNAE. 1901-4*. Erskine Press, Alburgh, Norfolk, 1986. p. x.

45 Fiennes, R. *Captain Scott*. Hodder and Stoughton, London, 2003. p. 7.

46 Markham. *Antarctic Obsession*. p. xii.

47 *Ibid.* p. x.

48 *Ibid.*

49 Report of the 7th International Geographical Congress. London, 1895.

50 Baughman, T.H. *Pilgrims on the Ice*. University of Nebraska Press, Lincoln and London, 1999. p. 18.

51 Armitage, A.B. *Cadet to Commodore*. Cassell, London, 1925. p. 145.
52 Markham, C. *Letters to Robert Falcon Scott. Papers of the British National Antarctic Expedition, 1901–1904*. SPRI. MS. 366/15/25-64/BJ.
53 *Ibid*. p. 16.

Chapter 5

1   Huntford, R. *Scott and Amundsen*. Hodder and Stoughton, London, 1979. p. 147.
2   Markham, C. (ed. C. Holland) *Antarctic Obsession. The BNAE. 1901–4*. Erskine Press, Alburgh, Norfolk, 1986. p. 86.
3   Scott, G. Journal, SPRI. MS. 1485/D.
4   Wilson, E.T. *E.A. Wilson: Memoir by his father*. The Wilson Collection, Cheltenham Art Gallery and Museum, 1995, 550.36, p. 114.
5   Savours, Ann (ed.) *Edward Wilson: Diary of the Discovery Expedition to the Antarctic Regions 1901–1904*. Blandford Press, London, 1966. p. 30.
6   *Ibid*.
7   Skelton, Judy (ed.) *The Antarctic Journals of Reginald Skelton*. Reardon Publishing, Cheltenham, 2004. p. 18.
8   Scott, G. Journal, SPRI. MS. 1485/D.
9   Savours. *Edward Wilson: Diary of the Discovery Expedition*. p. 30.
10 Hodgson, T.V. Journal. BNAE 1901–1904. SPRI. MS. 595/I/MJ
11 Savours. *Edward Wilson: Diary of the Discovery Expedition*. p. 31.
12 *Ibid*.
13 Scott, R.F. *Scott's Voyage of the Discovery*. John Murray, London, 1929. p. 31.
14 Baughman, T.H. *Pilgrims on the Ice*. University of Nebraska Press, Lincoln and London, 1999. p. 77.
15 Skelton, J.V. and Wilson, D.M. *Discovery Illustrated*. Reardon Publishing, Cheltenham, 2001. p. 21.
16 Scott. *Scott's Voyage of the Discovery*. p. 38.
17 *Ibid*. p. 44.
18 Skelton. *The Antarctic Journals of Reginald Skelton*. p. 15.

19 Scott. *Scott's Voyage of the Discovery*. p. 27.
20 *Ibid*. p. 51.
21 Wilson, E.A. *Lecture to St George's*, 1904. Archives Manuscript Collection. St George's University of London.
22 Scott, G. Journal, SPRI. MS. 1485/D.
23 Savours. *Edward Wilson: Diary of the Discovery Expedition*. p. 62.
24 Wilson. *E.A. Wilson: Memoir by his father*. p. 114
25 *Virtue's Household Physician*. Virtue, London, 1926. p. 530.
26 Koettlitz, R. 'Scurvy and Antiscorbutics', *Guy's Hospital Gazette*, 30 March 1900. p. 152.
27 Wilson. *E.A. Wilson: Memoir by his father*. p. 114.
28 Scott. *Scott's Voyage of the Discovery*. p. 24.
29 Papers of the BNAE 1901–1904. SPRI. MS. 366/15/BJ.
30 Markham. *Antarctic Obsession*. p. 25.
31 Baughman. *Pilgrims on the Ice*. p. 108.
32 Markham. *Antarctic Obsession*. p. 13.
33 *Ibid*. p. 15.
34 Savours. *Edward Wilson: Diary of the Discovery Expedition*. p. 49.
35 Markham. *Antarctic Obsession*. p. 15.
36 Baughman. *Pilgrims on the Ice*. p. 32.
37 Wilson. *E.A. Wilson: Memoir by his father*. p. 112.
38 Markham. *Antarctic Obsession*. p. 15.
39 *Ibid*. p. 16
40 Baughman. *Pilgrims on the Ice*. p. 54.
41 One of the most eminent scientists in the land, Sir Almoth Wright of St Mary's Hospital London, continued with this opinion until an assistant in his own laboratory, L.C. Holt, demonstrated years later that pure ascorbic acid cured the condition in experimental animals. Holt, L.C. University of London MSc Thesis. Quoted in Lewis, H.E. Proc. Royal Soc. Med. 1972. 65. p. 39.
42 Koettlitz. 'Scurvy and Antiscorbutics'. p. 152.
43 Markham. *Antarctic Obsession*. p. 82.
44 *Ibid*. p. 87.
45 *Ibid*. p. 91.
46 Wilson, D.M. and Elder, D.B. *Cheltenham in Antarctica: The Life of Edward Wilson*. Reardon Publishing, Cheltenham, 2000, p. 54.
47 Baughman. *Pilgrims on the Ice*. p. 66.
48 Seaver G. *Edward Wilson of the Antarctic*, John Murray, London, 1950, p. 78.

[49] Wilson *E.A. Wilson: Memoir by his father*. p. 112

[50] Savours. *Edward Wilson: Diary of the Discovery Expedition*. p. 36.

Chapter 6

[1] Wilson, D.M. and Elder, D.B. *Cheltenham in Antarctica: The Life of Edward Wilson*. Reardon Publishing, Cheltenham, 2000. p. 55.

[2] Seaver G. *Edward Wilson of the Antarctic*. John Murray, London, 1950, p. 79.

[3] Wilson, E.T. *E.A. Wilson: Memoir by his father*. The Wilson Collection, Cheltenham Art Gallery and Museum, 1995, 550.36, p. 116.

[4] Yelverton, D.E. *Antarctica Unveiled*. University Press of Colorado, Boulder, CO, 2000. p. 77.

[5] Savours, Ann (ed.) *Edward Wilson: Diary of the Discovery Expedition to the Antarctic Regions 1901–1904*. Blandford Press, London, 1966. p. 44.

[6] Scott, R.F. Journal, BNAE 1901–04, SPRI. MS. 352/1/1/BJ.

[7] Yelverton. *Antarctica Unveiled*. p. 77.

[8] Savours. *Edward Wilson: Diary of the Discovery Expedition*. p. 44.

[9] Scott, R.F. *Scott's Voyage of the Discovery*. John Murray, London, 1929. p. 69.

[10] Savours. *Edward Wilson: Diary of the Discovery Expedition*. p. 50.

[11] Seaver. *Edward Wilson of the Antarctic*. p. 81.

[12] Wilson. *E.A. Wilson: Memoir by his father*. p. 120.

[13] Seaver. *Edward Wilson of the Antarctic*. p. 81.

[14] Savours. *Edward Wilson: Diary of the Discovery Expedition*. p. 56.

[15] Baughman, T.H. *Pilgrims on the Ice*. University of Nebraska Press, Lincoln and London, 1999. p. 74.

[16] Scott, G. Journal, SPRI. MS. 1485/D.

[17] Scott. *Scott's Voyage of the Discovery*. p. 73.

[18] Scott, G. Journal.

[19] Skelton, Judy (ed.) *The Antarctic Journals of Reginald Skelton*. Reardon Publishing, Cheltenham, 2004. p. 21.

[20] Wilson. *E.A. Wilson: Memoir by his father.* p. 115.
[21] Scott. *Scott's Voyage of the Discovery.* p. 73.
[22] Scott, R.F. Journal, BNAE 1901–04. SPRI. MS. 352/1/1/BJ.
[23] Winds.
[24] Yelverton. *Antarctica Unveiled.* p. 83.
[25] Scott. *Scott's Voyage of the Discovery.* p. 73.
[26] *Ibid.* p. 74.
[27] Wilson. *E.A. Wilson: Memoir by his father.* p. 118.
[28] *Ibid.* p. 120.
[29] Seaver. *Edward Wilson of the Antarctic.* p. 68.
[30] Yearly fireworks celebration commemorating an English Catholic's attempt to blow up the Houses of Parliament in 1604.
[31] Baughman. *Pilgrims on the Ice.* p. 79.
[32] Savours. *Edward Wilson: Diary of the Discovery Expedition.* p. 73.
[33] Wilson. *E.A. Wilson: Memoir by his father.* p. 122.
[34] Scott. *Scott's Voyage of the Discovery.* p. 76.
[35] Savours. *Edward Wilson: Diary of the Discovery Expedition.* p. 74
[36] *Ibid.* p. 76.
[37] *Ibid.* p. 77.
[38] *Ibid.* p. 78.
[39] Baughman. *Pilgrims on the Ice.* p. 79.
[40] Savours. *Edward Wilson: Diary of the Discovery Expedition.* p. 72.
[41] Seaver. *Edward Wilson of the Antarctic.* p. 84.
[42] Scott. *Scott's Voyage of the Discovery.* p. 82.
[43] Baughman. *Pilgrims on the Ice.* p. 84.
[44] Wilson. *E.A. Wilson: Memoir by his father.* p. 122.
[45] *Ibid.* p. 121.
[46] Personal correspondence. Dr David Wilson.
[47] Baughman. *Pilgrims on the Ice.* p. 85.
[48] *Ibid.* p. 87.
[49] Savours. *Edward Wilson: Diary of the Discovery Expedition.* p. 85.
[50] Scott. *Scott's Voyage of the Discovery.* p. 83.
[51] Baughman. *Pilgrims on the Ice.* p. 88.
[52] Scott, G. Journal. SPRI. MS. 1485/D.
[53] *Ibid.* 19 December 1901.
[54] Skelton. *The Antarctic Journals of Reginald Skelton.* p. 33.
[55] Scott. *Scott's Voyage of the Discovery.* p. 85.

56 Savours. *Edward Wilson: Diary of the Discovery Expedition.* p. 87.
57 Skelton. *The Antarctic Journals of Reginald Skelton.* p. 33.
58 Scott. *Scott's Voyage of the Discovery.* p. 97.
59 Savours. *Edward Wilson: Diary of the Discovery Expedition.* p. 89.
60 Scott. *Scott's Voyage of the Discovery.* p. 87.
61 *Ibid.* p. 89.
62 Skelton. *The Antarctic Journals of Reginald Skelton.* p. 37.
63 Scott, G. Journal. SPRI. MS. 1485/D.
64 Savours. *Edward Wilson: Diary of the Discovery Expedition.* p. 91.
65 *Ibid.* p. 92

Chapter 7

1   Savours, Ann (ed.) *Edward Wilson: Diary of the Discovery Expedition to the Antarctic Regions 1901–1904.* Blandford Press, London, 1966. p. 93.
2   Seaver, G. *Edward Wilson of the Antarctic.* John Murray, London, 1946. p. 87.
3   Scott, R.F. *Scott's Voyage of the Discovery.* John Murray, London, 1929. p. 102.
4   Savours. *Edward Wilson: Diary of the Discovery* Expedition. p. 93.
5   Scott. *Scott's Voyage of Discovery.* p. 100.
6   *Ibid.* p. 102.
7   Scott, G. Journal. SPRI. MS. 1485/D.
8   Savours. *Edward Wilson: Diary of the Discovery Expedition.* p. 98.
9   *Ibid.* p. 109.
10 *Ibid.* p. 100.
11 *Ibid.*
12 *Ibid.* p. 101.
13 *Ibid.* p. 104.
14 *Ibid.* p. 105.
15 Scott, G. Journal. SPRI. MS. 1485/D.
16 Savours. *Edward Wilson: Diary of the Discovery Expedition.* p. 107.
17 *Ibid.*

18 Skelton, Judy (ed.) *The Antarctic Journals of Reginald Skelton*. Reardon Publishing, Cheltenham, 2004. p. 48.
19 Royds, C.W.R. *Letter to Admiral Pelham Aldrich*. SPRI. MS. 582/1/D.
20 Scott. *Scott's Voyage of Discovery*. p. 131.
21 *Ibid*. p. 132.
22 Savours. *Edward Wilson: Diary of the Discovery Expedition*. p. 109.
23 Scott. *Scott's Voyage of Discovery*. p. 135.
24 Savours. *Edward Wilson: Diary of the Discovery Expedition*. p. 111.
25 *Ibid*.
26 Scott. *Scott's Voyage of Discovery*. p. 148.
27 Savours. *Edward Wilson: Diary of the Discovery Expedition*. p. 112.
28 *Ibid*. p.113.
29 Fiennes, R. *Captain Scott*. Hodder and Stoughton, London, 2003. p. 66.
30 Markham, C. (ed. C. Holland) *Antarctic Obsession. The BNAE. 1901–4*. Erskine Press, Alburgh, Norfolk, 1986. p. 65.
31 Savours. *Edward Wilson: Diary of the Discovery Expedition*. p. 115.
32 Frostbite happens when, in extreme cold, blood normally flowing to the surface skin is deflected to deeper, essential organs such as the heart, kidneys or liver. The skin is relatively poorly supplied and goes white and eventually dies.
33 Wilson, E.A. *Notes on the pressure ridges at Cape Crozier*. SPRI. MS. 366/14/15/ER.
34 A calorific mixture of meat and fat.
35 Wilson, E.T. *E.A. Wilson: Memoir by his father*. The Wilson Collection, Cheltenham Art Gallery and Museum, 1955, 550.36. p. 131.
36 Savours. *Edward Wilson: Diary of the Discovery Expedition*. p. 116.
37 Wilson. *E.A. Wilson: Memoir by his father*. p. 131.
38 *Ibid*. p. 132.
39 Fiennes. *Captain Scott*. p. 66.
40 *Ibid*. p. 69.
41 *Ibid*. p. 67.
42 Skelton. *The Antarctic Journals of Reginald Skelton*. p. 110.
43 *Ibid*. p. 110.
44 *Ibid*. p. 56.

45 Seaver. *Edward Wilson of the Antarctic.* p. 95.

46 Scott. *Scott's Voyage of Discovery.* p. 170.

47 Savours. *Edward Wilson: Diary of the Discovery Expedition.* p. 120.

48 *Ibid.* p. 125.

49 Scott. *Scott's Voyage of Discovery.* p. 186.

50 Savours. *Edward Wilson: Diary of the Discovery Expedition.* p. 125.

51 Royd, C.W.R. *Report on Sledge Expedition.* SPRI. MS. 366/12/9/ER.

52 Savours. *Edward Wilson: Diary of the Discovery Expedition.* p. 129.

53 *Ibid.* p. 130.

54 Wilson, E.A. Lecture to St George's, 1904. Archives Manuscript Collection. St George's University of London.

55 Bartholomew, M. *James Lind's Treatise of the Scurvy (1753),* Postgraduate Medical Journal, 2002, 78. pp. 695–6.

56 Lloyd, C and Coulter, J. *Medicine and the Navy, 1200–1900.* Vol. 3 (1815–1900) Livingstone, Edinburgh and London, 1963. p. 120.

57 Carpenter, K.J. *The History of Scurvy and Vitamin C.* Cambridge University Press, 1986.

58 Skelton. *The Antarctic Journals of Reginald Skelton.* p. 130.

59 Fiennes. *Captain Scott.* p. 77.

60 Savours. *Edward Wilson: Diary of the Discovery Expedition.* p. 135.

61 Lines of verse or arrangements of words in which certain letters from each line, such as the first and the last, when taken in order spell out a word or motto.

62 'Notes on Penguins', in *The South Polar Times.* Vol.1, part 4.

63 Savours. *Edward Wilson: Diary of the Discovery Expedition.* p. 135.

64 Just over a pound.

65 Seaver. *Edward Wilson of the Antarctic.* p. 97.

66 Savours. *Edward Wilson: Diary of the Discovery Expedition.* p. 151.

67 Seaver. *Edward Wilson of the Antarctic.* p. 98.

68 *Ibid.* p. 101.

69 Savours. *Edward Wilson: Diary of the Discovery Expedition.* p. 163.

70 *Ibid.* p. 136.

71 *Ibid.* p. 138.

72 *Ibid.* p. 147.

73 Gilbert Scott's Journal. SPRI. MS 1485; D (19 May 1902).

74 Seaver. *Edward Wilson of the Antarctic.* p. 100.

75 Savours. p.155.

76 Scott, G. Journal. SPRI. MS. 1485/D.

77 Scott. *Scott's Voyage of Discovery.* p. 254.

78 Skelton. *The Antarctic Journals of Reginald Skelton*. p. 130.
79 Savours. *Edward Wilson: Diary of the Discovery Expedition*. p. 164.
80 Seaver. *Edward Wilson of the Antarctic*. p. 103.
81 Savours. *Edward Wilson: Diary of the Discovery Expedition*. p. 175.
82 Wilson. *E.A. Wilson: Memoir by his father*. p. 133.
83 *Ibid*. p. 134.

Chapter 8

1 Savours, Ann (ed.) *Edward Wilson: Diary of the Discovery Expedition to the Antarctic Regions 1901–1904*. Blandford Press, London, 1966. p. 179.
2 *Ibid*. p. 182
3 They called the islets Tortoise Rock and Erebus Islet.
4 *Ibid*. p. 184.
5 Yelverton, D.E. *Antarctica Unveiled*. University Press of Colorado, Colorado, 2000. p. 165.
6 Armitage, A.B. *Letters to H.R. Mill*. 1898–1939. SPRI. MS. 100/11/1–8.
7 Savours. *Edward Wilson: Diary of the Discovery Expedition*. p. 192.
8 Scott, R.F. *Scott's Voyage of the Discovery*. John Murray, London, 1929. p. 398.
9 Wilson, E.A. Lecture to St George's. 1904. Archives Manuscript Collection. St George's University of London.
10 Yelverton. *Antarctica Unveiled*. p. 168.
12 Scott. *Scott's Voyage of the Discovery*. p.399.
13 Personal Communication. Professor Jeffrey Wood, Professor of Food and Animal Science, Bristol University.
14 Baughman, T.H. *Pilgrims on the Ice*. University of Nebraska Press, Lincoln and London, 1999. p. 166.
15 Crandon, J.H., Lund, C.C. and Dill, D.B. *Experimental Human Scurvy*, New England Journal of Medicine. 1940, 223. p. 353.
16 Scott. *Scott's Voyage of the Discovery*. p. 405.
17 Savours. *Edward Wilson: Diary of the Discovery Expedition*. p. 201.
18 *Ibid*. p. 193.
19 *Ibid*. p. 206.
20 Skelton, Judy (ed.) *The Antarctic Journals of Reginald Skelton*. Reardon Publishing, Cheltenham, 2004. p. 119.

21 Personal communication. Rob Thomas, Curator and Conservator, Edinburgh Zoo.
22 Savours. *Edward Wilson: Diary of the Discovery Expedition.* p. 207.
23 *Ibid.* p. 199.
24 *Ibid.*
25 Scott. *Scott's Voyage of the Discovery.* p. 386.
26 Savours. *Edward Wilson: Diary of the Discovery Expedition.* p. 195.
27 Yelverton. *Antarctica Unveiled.* p. 176.
28 Seaver, G. *Edward Wilson of the Antarctic,* John Murray, London, 1950. p. 107.
29 Savours. *Edward Wilson: Diary of the Discovery Expedition.* p. 209.
30 *The South Polar Times.* Vol. 2, part 7, June 1903. p. 4.
31 Scott. *Scott's Voyage of the Discovery.* p. 417.
32 Savours. *Edward Wilson: Diary of the Discovery Expedition.* p. 208.
33 *Ibid.* p. 209.
34 Huntford, R. *Scott and Amundsen.* Hodder and Stoughton, London, 1979. p. 161.
35 Scott. *Scott's Voyage of the Discovery.* p. 435.
36 Savours. *Edward Wilson: Diary of the Discovery Expedition.* p. 210.
37 Yelverton. *Antarctica Unveiled.* p. 178.
38 Savours. *Edward Wilson: Diary of the Discovery Expedition.* p. 212.
39 *Ibid.* p. 213.
40 Yelverton. *Antarctica Unveiled.* p. 181.
41 *Ibid.* p. 181
42 Savours. *Edward Wilson: Diary of the Discovery Expedition.* p. 214.
43 *Ibid.* p. 215
44 *Ibid.*
45 *Ibid.* p. 225.
46 *Ibid.* p. 215.
47 Scott. *Scott's Voyage of the Discovery.* p. 429.
48 Savours. *Edward Wilson: Diary of the Discovery Expedition.* p. 216.
49 Scott. *Scott's Voyage of the Discovery.* p. 431.
50 *The South Polar Times.* Vol. 2, part 7, June 1903. p. 7.
51 Savours. *Edward Wilson: Diary of the Discovery Expedition.* p. 216.
52 *Ibid.* p. 217.
53 *Ibid.*
54 Fiennes, R. *Captain Scott.* Hodder and Stoughton, London, 2003. p. 92.
55 *The South Polar Times.* Vol. 2, part 7, June 1903. p. 5.
56 *Ibid.* p. 218.

57 Fiennes. *Captain Scott*. p. 285.
58 Hammond, K.A. and Diamond, J. *Maximum Sustained Energy Budgets in Humans and Animals*, Nature, 1997, 386. p. 457.
59 Savours. *Edward Wilson: Diary of the Discovery Expedition*. p. 217.
60 Swelling in the front part of the eye that causes intense pain and interferes with vision.
61 Savours. *Edward Wilson: Diary of the Discovery Expedition*. p. 217.
62 *Ibid*. p. 218.
63 Scott. *Scott's Voyage of the Discovery*. p. 434.
64 Savours. *Edward Wilson: Diary of the Discovery Expedition*. p. 218.
65 Yelverton. *Antarctica Unveiled*. p. 191.
67 *Ibid*.
68 Savours. *Edward Wilson: Diary of the Discovery Expedition*. p. 220.
69 *Ibid*. p. 221.
70 Cherry-Garrard, A. *Diaries*. 1912. SPRI. MS. 559/18/2/BJ, p. 277.
71 Savours. *Edward Wilson: Diary of the Discovery Expedition*. p. 223.
72 *Ibid*.
73 *Ibid*. p. 224.
74 Scott. *Scott's Voyage of the Discovery*. p. 454.
75 Savours. *Edward Wilson: Diary of the Discovery Expedition*. p. 224.
76 Scott. *Scott's Voyage of the Discovery*. p. 455.
77 As weight reduces, a hormone, leptin, which lowers appetite, is decreased.
78 *The South Polar Times*. Vol. 2, part 7, June 1903. p. 11.
79 Scott. *Scott's Voyage of the Discovery*. p. 450.
80 British Pharmaceutical Codex. Published by the Pharmaceutical Society of Great Britain, London, 1907. p. 183.
81 Martindale, M. and Wescott, W.W. *The Extra Pharmacopoeia*. 10th ed. (ed. Lewis, H.K.) London, 1901. p. 102.
82 Information from the Royal Pharmaceutical Society of Great Britain.
83 *Ibid*.
84 British Pharmaceutical Codex. Published by the Pharmaceutical Society of Great Britain, London, 1907. p. 1,042.
85 Martindale and Wescott. *The Extra Pharmacopoeia*. p. 103.
86 *Ibid*. p. 133.
87 Information from the Royal Pharmaceutical Society of Great Britain.
88 Martindale and Wescott. *The Extra Pharmacopoeia*. p. 137.
89 Savours. *Edward Wilson: Diary of the Discovery Expedition*. p. 227.
90 Yelverton. *Antarctica Unveiled*. p. 193.

[91] Savours. *Edward Wilson: Diary of the Discovery Expedition.* p. 228.
[92] *The South Polar Times.* Vol. 2, part 7, June 1903. p. 10.
[93] Crandon, Lund and Dill. *Experimental Human Scurvy.* p. 353.
[94] Later named Mount Christmas.
[95] Savours. *Edward Wilson: Diary of the Discovery Expedition.* p. 227.
[96] *Ibid.* p. 228.
[97] Scott. *Scott's Voyage of the Discovery.* p. 458.
[98] Savours. *Edward Wilson: Diary of the Discovery Expedition.* p. 229.
[99] Yelverton. *Antarctica Unveiled.* p. 195.
[100] *Ibid.*
[101] Savours. *Edward Wilson: Diary of the Discovery Expedition.* p. 230.
[102] *Ibid.*
[103] *Ibid.*
[104] *Ibid.*
[105] *Ibid.* p. 232.
[106] Baughman. *Pilgrims on the Ice.* p. 188.
[107] Cherry-Garrard. *Diaries.* p. 277
[108] Scott. *Scott's Voyage of the Discovery.* p. 484.
[109] *Ibid.* p. 485.
[110] Savours. *Edward Wilson: Diary of the Discovery Expedition.* p. 238.
[111] Scott. *Scott's Voyage of the Discovery.* p. 487.
[112] Savours. *Edward Wilson: Diary of the Discovery Expedition.* p. 238.
[113] *Ibid.* p. 240.
[114] *Ibid.* p. 241
[115] Scott. *Scott's Voyage of the Discovery.* p. 495.
[116] Savours. *Edward Wilson: Diary of the Discovery Expedition.* p. 242.
[117] *The South Polar Times.* Vol. 2, part 7, June 1903. p. 27.
[118] Savours. *Edward Wilson: Diary of the Discovery Expedition.* p. 243.
[119] Scott. *Scott's Voyage of the Discovery.* p. 499.
[120] Savours. *Edward Wilson: Diary of the Discovery Expedition.* p. 238.
[121] *Ibid.* p. 244.
[122] *Ibid.*
[123] Fiennes. *Captain Scott.* p. 107.
[124] Savours. *Edward Wilson: Diary of the Discovery Expedition.* p. 245.

Chapter 9

[1] Seaver, G. *Edward Wilson of the Antarctic*, John Murray, London, 1950. p. 117.

2   Wilson, E.T. *E.A. Wilson: Memoir by his father*. The Wilson
    Collection, Cheltenham Art Gallery and Museum, 1955,
    550.36. p. 139.
3   Savours, Ann (ed.) *Edward Wilson: Diary of the Discovery
    Expedition to the Antarctic Regions 1901–1904*. Blandford
    Press, London, 1966. p. 250.
4   Wilson. *E.A. Wilson: Memoir by his father*. p. 140.
5   Seaver. *Edward Wilson of the Antarctic*. p. 117.
6   Wilson. *E.A. Wilson: Memoir by his father*. pp. 134–5.
7   Auroras are phenomena related to the sun because of its emission
    of electric particles. Protons and electrons originating in the sun
    are caught by terrestrial magnetic fields. When these electrical
    particles meet the ionised gases of the higher layers of the atmos-
    phere, a light is produced in the sky. Auroras vary depending on
    solar activity and the phenomenon takes place between 100 and
    1,000 km, most frequently in a large circle around the magnetic
    pole. Antarctic auroras are seen in South America as well as the
    Antarctic. They are easily seen on clear nights, but when solar
    activity is intense they can be seen in broad daylight.
8   Cherry-Garrard, A. *The Worst Journey in the World*. Picador,
    London, 2001. (First published in 1922 by Constable and Co.)
9   Seaver. *Edward Wilson of the Antarctic*. p. 118.
10 *Ibid.*
11 Wilson. *E.A. Wilson: Memoir by his father*. p. 140.
12 *Ibid.* p. 141.
13 *Ibid.* p. 136.
14 *Ibid.*
15 *Ibid.* p. 137
16 Seaver. *Edward Wilson of the Antarctic*. p. 124.
17 *Ibid.* p. 123.
18 *Ibid.* p. 125.
19 Wilson. *E.A. Wilson: Memoir by his father*. p. 138.
20 Baughman, T.H. *Pilgrims on the Ice*. University of Nebraska
    Press, Lincoln and London, 1999. p. 220.
21 Savours. *Edward Wilson: Diary of the Discovery* Expedition. p. 271.
22 *Ibid.* p. 288
23 *Ibid.* p. 289.
24 *Ibid.* p. 294.
25 *Ibid.* p. 295.
26 Seaver. *Edward Wilson of the Antarctic*. p. 129.
27 Savours. *Edward Wilson: Diary of the Discovery Expedition*. p. 298.

28   *Ibid.* p. 306.
29   *Ibid.* p. 307.
30   Seaver. *Edward Wilson of the Antarctic.* p. 130.
31   Savours. *Edward Wilson: Diary of the Discovery Expedition.* p. 310.
32   *Ibid.*
33   *Ibid.* p. 312.
34   Seaver. *Edward Wilson of the Antarctic.* p. 132.
35   Wilson, E.A. *Notes on the pressure ridges at Cape Crozier.* SPRI.
     MS. 366/14/15/ER.
36   Savours. *Edward Wilson: Diary of the Discovery Expedition.* p. 316.
37   Seaver. *Edward Wilson of the Antarctic.* p. 133.
38   Savours. *Edward Wilson: Diary of the Discovery Expedition.* p. 318.
39   *Ibid.* p. 328.
40   *Ibid.* p. 331.
41   Baughman. *Pilgrims on the Ice.* p. 233.
42   Scott, R.F. Journal, BNAE, 1901–1904, 4 SPRI. MS. 352/1/3/BJ.
43   Savours. *Edward Wilson: Diary of the Discovery Expedition.* p. 332.
44   *Ibid.*
45   Scott, R.F. Journal, BNAE, 1901–1904, 4 SPRI. MS. 352/1/3/BJ.
46   Armitage, A.B. *Two Years in the Antarctic.* Paradigm Press,
     London, 1984. p. 283.
47   Savours. *Edward Wilson: Diary of the Discovery Expedition.* p. 334.
48   *Ibid.*
49   Savours. *Edward Wilson: Diary of the Discovery Expedition.* p. 338.
50   *Ibid.* p. 339.
51   *Ibid.* p. 340.
52   *Ibid.* p. 354.
53   *Ibid.* p. 346.
53   *Ibid.* p. 348.
54   *Ibid.* p. 357
55   Seaver. *Edward Wilson of the Antarctic.* p. 141.
56   Savours. *Edward Wilson: Diary of the Discovery Expedition.* p. 357.
57   Armitage, A.B. *Letters to H.R. Mill, 1898–1939.* SPRI. MS.
     100/11/1–8/D.
58   Savours. *Edward Wilson: Diary of the Discovery Expedition.* p. 357
59   Seaver. *Edward Wilson of the Antarctic.* p. 142.
60   Wilson, E.A. *Letter to J.J. Kinsey,* Sir Joseph James' papers. Ms-
     Papers-0022-23. Alexander Turnbull Library, New Zealand.
61   Seaver. *Edward Wilson of the Antarctic.* p. 143.
62   Wilson. *E.A. Wilson: Memoir by his father.* p. 143.
63   Seaver. *Edward Wilson of the Antarctic.* p. 144.

64 *Ibid*. p. 145.
65 Wilson, C. *Letters*. The Wilson Collection, Cheltenham Art Gallery and Museum, 13804, 1995, 550.89. (v).

Chapter 10

1   Wilson, E.T. *E.A. Wilson: Memoir by his father*. The Wilson Collection, Cheltenham Art Gallery and Museum, 1955, 550.36. p. 145.
2   *Ibid*.
3   *Ibid*. p. 147
4   *Ibid*. p. 148.
5   Wilson. *E.A. Wilson: Memoir by his father*. p. 151.
6   A guinea is just over one pound.
7   Royal Geographical Society. RGS/LMS/W21.
8   Wilson. *E.A. Wilson: Memoir by his father*. p. 150.
9   *Ibid*.
10 *Ibid*. p. 152.
11 Seaver, G. *Edward Wilson of the Antarctic*, John Murray, London, 1950. p. 149.
12 Hubert von Herkomer, CVO. RA. RI.
13 Seaver, G. *Edward Wilson: Nature Lover*. John Murray, London, 1947. p. 170.
14 The original deathbed scene is the property of HRM the Queen. A photographic reproduction is in the Bushey Museum and Art Gallery. Queen Victoria lies surrounded by tulle and lilies, a royal Ophelia.
15 Seaver. *Edward Wilson: Nature* Lover. p. 169.
16 Seaver. *Edward Wilson of the Antarctic*. p. 150.
17 *Ibid*.
18 *Ibid*.
19 Wheeler, S. *Cherry: A life of Apsley Cherry-Garrard*. Jonathan Cape, London, 2001. p. 45.
20 *Ibid*.
21 Wilson, E.A. *Letter to Mr and Mrs Reginald Smith*. SPRI. MS. 559/142/4/D.
22 Simon Joseph Frazer, 14th Lord Lovat and 3rd Baron Lovat.
23 Committee of Enquiry on Grouse Disease. *The Grouse in Health and Disease*. Smith, Elder, and Co., London, 1911. p. 498.

24 Seaver. *Edward Wilson: Nature Lover.* p. 169.
25 Wilson. *E.A. Wilson: Memoir by his father.* p. 153.
26 *The Grouse in Health and in Disease.* p. 498.
27 Bachelor of Medicine. Fellow of the Zoological Society. Member of the British Ornithological Society.
28 *The Grouse in Health and in Disease.* p. xviii.
29 Wilson. *E.A. Wilson: Memoir by his father.* p. 154.
30 Oldfield, T. *British Mammals*, 15, London, 1914.
31 Seaver. *Edward Wilson of the Antarctic.* p. 168.
32 Wilson, D.M. and Elder., D.B. *Cheltenham in Antarctica: The Life of Edward Wilson.* Reardon Publishing, Cheltenham, 2000. p. 77.
33 Wilson. *E.A. Wilson: Memoir by his father.* p. 155.
34 Seaver. *Edward Wilson of the Antarctic.* p. 154.
35 A Government Department.
36 *The Grouse in Health and in Disease.* p. 201.
37 *Ibid.* p. 199.
38 *Ibid.*
39 *Ibid.* p. 201.
40 Wilson and Elder. *Cheltenham in Antarctica.* p. 76.
41 Seaver. *Edward Wilson of the Antarctic.* p. 160.
42 *Ibid.* p. 175.
43 *Ibid.* p. 176.
44 *Ibid.*
45 Wilson and Elder. *Cheltenham in Antarctica.* p. 78.
46 Seaver. *Edward Wilson of the Antarctic.* p. 177.
47 Scott, R.F. *Letters to Ernest Henry Shackleton.* SPRI. MS. 1537/2/14/8-9/D.
48 *Ibid.*
49 Seaver. *Edward Wilson of the Antarctic.* p. 178.
50 Wilson,E.A. *Letters to Ernest Henry Shackleton.* SPRI. MS. 1537/2/14/15/D.
51 Seaver. *Edward Wilson of the Antarctic.* p.178
52 Wilson. *E. A.Wilson: Memoir by his father.* p. 163.
53 Seaver. *Edward Wilson of the Antarctic.* p. 161.
54 *The Grouse in Health and in Disease.* p. xvi.
55 Review. Report of the activities of the Game Conservancy Trust, 2006. p. 18.
56 Wilson, E. A. *Letters to Cherry-Garrard.* SPRI. MS. 841/10/3/D.
57 Wheeler. *Cherry: A life of Apsley Cherry-Garrard.* p. 60.
58 Wilson, E. A. *Letters to Cherry-Garrard.* SPRI. MS. 841/10/4/D.

[59] Cherry-Garrard, A. *The Worst Journey in the World*. Picador, London, 2001.

[60] *Evening Standard* (London). 6 December 1922.

[61] Sir John Everett Millais (1829–1896). One of the three principle members of the Pre-Raphaelite Brotherhood formed in 1848 with the aim of pursuing truth and seriousness in art. The group reacted against the artificial and idealising tendencies that they considered had stemmed from the great Renaissance master Raphael.

[62] Wilson. *E.A. Wilson: Memoir by his father*. p. 159.

[63] Seaver. *Edward Wilson of the Antarctic*. p. 169.

[64] Wilson E.A. *Letters to James William Dell*, 20th March 1909, pp. 19–20, in Dell papers, held in Mitchell Library, State Library of New South Wales, ML MSS 1723.

[65] Crane, D. *Scott of the Antarctic*. Harper Collins, London, 2005. p. 350.

[66] William Beardmore (1856–1936), a Glasgow industrialist. He was created a baronet in 1914 and in 1921 he was granted a peerage and became Lord Invernarn.

[67] Wilson, E.A. *Letter to Ernest Shackleton*. SPRI. MS. 1537/2/14/1-3/D.

[68] Seaver. *Edward Wilson of the Antarctic*. p. 182.

[69] Wilson. *E.A. Wilson: Memoir by his father*. p. 166.

[70] Seaver. *Edward Wilson of the Antarctic*. p. 182.

[71] Wilson. *E.A. Wilson: Memoir by his father*. p. 173.

[72] Richards R.I. *Caedmon of Whitby*, Whitby, 1985. p. 106

[73] *Ibid*. p. 177.

[74] Seaver. *Edward Wilson of the Antarctic*. p. 189.

[75] *Ibid*. p. 190.

[76] *Ibid*.

[77] *Ibid*. p. 194

[78] *Ibid*. p. 195.

[79] Wilson. *E.A. Wilson: Memoir by his father*. p. 170.

[80] *Ibid*. p. 196.

Chapter 11

[1] Ponting, H. *With Scott to the Pole*. Bloomsbury, London, 2004. p. 24.

2   Wilson, E.T. *Letter to Bernard Wilson*. SPRI. MS. 963/4/D.
3   *The Geographical Journal*. Vol. xxxvi, July 1910. p. 13.
4   King, H.G.R. (ed.) *Edward Wilson: Diary of the 'Terra Nova' Expedition to the Antarctic 1910–1912*. Blandford Press, London, 1972. p. 12.
5   Wilson, E.T. *Letter to Bernard Wilson*.1910. SPRI. MS. 963/4/D.
6   Wilson, D.M. and Elder, D.B. *Cheltenham in Antarctica: The Life of Edward Wilson*. Reardon Publishing, Cheltenham, 2000. p. 84.
7   *The Geographical Journal*. Vol. xxxvi, July 1910. p. 11.
8   *Ibid*. p. 12.
9   *Ibid*. p. 22.
10 Scott, R.F. *Scott's Last Expedition*. Vol.1. John Murray, London, 1935. p. xxv.
11 King. *Edward Wilson: Diary of the 'Terra Nova'*. p. 13.
12 *Ibid*. p. 251.
13 Wilson, E.T. *E.A. Wilson: Memoir by his father*. The Wilson Collection, Cheltenham Art Gallery and Museum, 1955, 550.36. p. 172.
14 *Ibid*. p. 18. *The Manchester Guardian* was a national newspaper, now *The Guardian*.
15 Fiennes, R. *Captain Scott*. Hodder and Stoughton, London, 2003. p. 170.
16 Seaver, G. *Edward Wilson of the Antarctic*, John Murray, London, 1950. p. 201.
17 Fiennes. *Captain Scott*. p. 169.
18 A marking on ships' sides showing the limit of legal submersion.
19 Eton is a well-known English public school.
20 Seaver, G. *'Birdie' Bowers of the Antarctic*. John Murray, London, 1947. p. 15.
21 A distinguished Irish Regiment raised in 1690 from around Enniskillen in Northern Ireland.
22 Fiennes. *Captain Scott*. p. 172.
23 Scott. *Scott's Last Expedition*. p. 462.
24 Wilson, E.A. *Letter to Reginald Smith*. SPRI. MS. 559/142/9/D.
25 Seaver, G. *Edward Wilson of the Antarctic*. p. 200.
26 *Ibid*. p. 14.
27 Wilson, E.A. *Letters to Sir Clements Markham*, 1910. SPRI. MS. 27/D.
28 Cherry-Garrard, A. *The Worst Journey in the World*. Picador, London, 2001. p. 6.
29 King. *Edward Wilson: Diary of the 'Terra Nova'*. p. 23.

30 Seaver. *Edward Wilson of the Antarctic*. p. 201.
31 Wilson, E.A. *Letter to Sir Clements Markham*, 1910. SPRI. MS. 27/D.
32 Seaver. *'Birdie' Bowers of the Antarctic*. p. 152.
33 Wilson. *E.A. Wilson: Memoir by his father*. p. 184.
34 King. *Edward Wilson: Diary of the 'Terra Nova'*. p. 30.
35 Cherry-Garrard. *The Worst Journey in the World*. p. 15.
36 Wilson, A.E. *Letters to Reginald Smith*. SPRI. MS. 599/142/6/D.
37 Wilson. *E.A. Wilson: Memoir by his father*. p. 185.
38 Wilson, E.A. *Letters to Sir Clements Markham*, 1910. SPRI. MS. 27/D.
39 Wilson, A.E. *Letters to Reginald Smith*. SPRI. MS. 559/142/6/D.
40 Wilson, E.A. *Letter to Sir Clements Markham*, 1910. SPRI. MS. 27/D.
41 Wheeler, S. *Cherry: A life of Apsley Cherry-Garrard*. Jonathan Cape, London, 2001. p. 158.
42 *Ibid*. p. 194.
43 King. *Edward Wilson: Diary of the 'Terra Nova'*. p. 51.
44 Wilson, E.A. *Letter to Sir Clements Markham*, 1910. SPRI. MS. 27/D.
45 King. *Edward Wilson: Diary of the 'Terra Nova'*. p. 54.
46 Huntford, R. *Scott and Amundsen*. Hodder and Stoughton, London, 1979. p. 322.
47 *Ibid*. p. 303.
48 Smith, M. *I Am Just Going Outside*. Spellmont, Staplehurst, 2002. p. 112.
49 *Ibid*. p. 111.
50 Cherry-Garrard. *The Worst Journey in the World*. p. 43.
51 The wife of the Hon. Charles Christopher Bowen (1813–1936), a keen supporter of the New Zealand preparations for the Scott expedition.
52 Wilson Family Collection, Cheltenham Art Gallery and Museum, 1955, 550.106. (19/19/1912).
53 Lyons, H.G. *The British Antarctic Expedition, 1910. Miscellaneous Data*. Harrison and Sons, London, 1924. p. 26.
54 Smith. *I Am Just Going Outside*. p. 118.
55 Fiennes. *Captain Scott*. p. 189.
56 Smith. *I Am Just Going Outside*. p. 119.
57 King. *Edward Wilson: Diary of the 'Terra Nova'*. p. 61.
58 *Ibid*. p. 62.
59 *Ibid*.

60 Seaver. *Edward Wilson of the Antarctic*. p. 205.
60 King. *Edward Wilson: Diary of the 'Terra Nova'*. p. 64.
61 *Ibid*.
62 Scott. *Scott's Last Expedition*. p. 12.
63 King. *Edward Wilson: Diary of the 'Terra Nova'*. p. 65.
64 *Ibid*. p. 67.
65 Seaver. *Edward Wilson of the Antarctic*. p. 209.
66 Cherry-Garrard. *The Worst Journey in the World*. p. 63.
67 *Ibid*. p. 64.
68 *Ibid*. p. 61.
69 Jones, M. (ed.) *Robert Falcon Scott, Journals: Captain Scott's Last Expedition*. Oxford University Press, Oxford, 2005. p. 47.
70 *Ibid*. p. 44.
71 *Ibid*. p. 47.
72 Seaver. *Edward Wilson of the Antarctic*. p. 211.
73 Jones. *Robert Falcon Scott, Journals*. p. 55.
74 Personal communication. Geoff Somers, polar traveller. 2006.
75 King. *Edward Wilson: Diary of the 'Terra Nova'*. p. 92.
76 Cherry-Garrard. *The Worst Journey in the World*. p. 87.
77 Jones. *Robert Falcon Scott, Journals*. p. 72.
78 Preston, D. *A First Rate Tragedy*. Constable, London, 1995. p. 164.
79 Ponting, H.G. *The Great White South*. Duckworth, London, 1932. p. 63.
80 Wilson. *E.A. Wilson: Memoir by his father*. p. 200.
81 King. *Edward Wilson: Diary of the 'Terra Nova'*. p. 95.
82 Wilson. *E.A. Wilson: Memoir by his father*. p. 198.
83 *Ibid*. p. 199.
84 Hoflehner, J. *Frozen History*. Roemerstr, Austria, 2003. pp. 164–275.
85 Cherry-Garrard. *The Worst Journey in the World*. p. 108.
87 King. *Edward Wilson: Diary of the 'Terra Nova'*. p. 100.
88 *Ibid*. p. 99.
89 *Ibid*.
90 *Ibid*. p. 102.
91 Cherry-Garrard. *The Worst Journey in the World*. p. 116.
92 Jones. *Robert Falcon Scott, Journals*. p. 123.
93 King. *Edward Wilson: Diary of the 'Terra Nova'*. p. 103.
94 *Ibid*. p. 104.
95 Smith. *I Am Just Going Outside*. p. 143.
96 King. *Edward Wilson: Diary of the 'Terra Nova'*. p. 105.
97 *Ibid*.

98 *Ibid.* p. 106.
99 A natural harbour in the Barrier about 330 miles east of Cape Crozier.
100 King. *Edward Wilson: Diary of the 'Terra Nova'.* p. 107.
101 Jones. *Robert Falcon Scott, Journals.* p. 135.
102 Seaver. *'Birdie' Bowers of the Antarctic.* p. 177.
103 King. *Edward Wilson: Diary of the 'Terra Nova'.* p 109.
104 *Ibid.* p. 112.
105 Jones. *Robert Falcon Scott, Journals.* p. 194.
106 *Ibid.* p. 209
107 King. *Edward Wilson: Diary of the 'Terra Nova'.* p. 127.
108 *Ibid.* p. 128

Chapter 12

1 Cherry-Garrard, A. *The Worst Journey in the World.* Picador, London, 2001.
2 Wilson, E.A. *Letter to Reginald Smith.* SPRI. MS. 559/142/9/D.
3 Seaver, G. *'Birdie' Bowers of the Antarctic.* John Murray, London, 1947. p. 206.
4 Jones, M. (ed.) *Robert Falcon Scott, Journals: Captain Scott's Last Expedition.* Oxford University Press, Oxford, 2005. p. 259.
5 Huntford, R. *Scott and Amundsen.* Hodder and Stoughton, London, 1979. p. 401.
6 Wilson, D.M. and Elder, D.B. *Cheltenham in Antarctica: The Life of Edward Wilson.* Reardon Publishing, Cheltenham, 2000. p. 89.
7 Wilson, E.T. *E.A. Wilson: Memoir by his father.* The Wilson Collection, Cheltenham Art Gallery and Museum, 1955, 550.36. p. 205.
8 Wheeler, S. *Cherry: A life of Apsley Cherry-Garrard.* Jonathan Cape, London, 2001. p. 109.
9 King, H.G.R. (ed.) *Edward Wilson: Diary of the 'Terra Nova' Expedition to the Antarctic 1910–1912.* Blandford Press, London, 1972. p. 142.
10 Cherry-Garrard. *The Worst Journey in the World.* p. 251.
11 Wilson. *E.A. Wilson: Memoir by his father.* p. 205.
12 *Ibid.*
13 Cherry-Garrard. *The Worst Journey in the World.* p. 242.
14 Jones. *Robert Falcon Scott, Journals.* p. 256.

15 King. *Edward Wilson: Diary of the 'Terra Nova'*. p. 142.
16 Jones. *Robert Falcon Scott, Journals*. p. 256.
17 Wilson. *E.A. Wilson: Memoir by his father*. p. 207.
18 *Ibid*. p. 207.
19 Soloman, S. *The Coldest March*. Yale University Press, New Haven and London, 2001. p. 152.
20 Cherry-Garrard. *The Worst Journey in the World*. p. 245.
21 Jones. *Robert Falcon Scott, Journals*, p. 256.
22 King. *Edward Wilson: Diary of the 'Terra Nova'*. p. 143.
23 Cherry-Garrard. *The Worst Journey in the World*. p. 245
24 King. *Edward Wilson: Diary of the 'Terra Nova'*. p. 146.
25 Cherry-Garrard. *The Worst Journey in the World*. p. 247.
26 *Ibid*. p. 246.
27 Wilson. *E.A. Wilson: Memoir by his father*. p. 206.
28 Seaver. *'Birdie' Bowers of the Antarctic*. p. 209.
29 *Ibid*. p. 207.
30 King. *Edward Wilson: Diary of the 'Terra Nova'*. p. 144.
31 *Ibid*. p. 147.
32 Wilson. *E.A. Wilson: Memoir by his father*. p. 208.
33 Cherry-Garrard. *The Worst Journey in the World*. p. 242.
34 Personal discussion. Dr Robert Thomas, Conservation and Research Manager, Edinburgh Zoo, 2006.
35 *Ibid*.
36 Cherry-Garrard. *The Worst Journey in the World*. p. 274.
37 *Ibid*. p. 277.
38 *Ibid*. p. 278.
39 *Ibid*.
40 *Ibid*. p. 281.
41 King. *Edward Wilson: Diary of the 'Terra Nova'*. p. 156.
42 Cherry-Garrard. *The Worst Journey in the World*. p. 284.
43 King. *Edward Wilson: Diary of the 'Terra Nova'*. p. 157.
44 Cherry-Garrard. *The Worst Journey in the World*. p. 286.
45 *Ibid*.
46 *Ibid*. p. 287.
47 Seaver. *'Birdie' Bowers of the Antarctic*. p. 210.
48 *Ibid*. p. 208.
49 Cherry-Garrard. *The Worst Journey in the World*. p. 289.
50 King. *Edward Wilson: Diary of the 'Terra Nova'*. p. 157.
51 Seaver. *'Birdie' Bowers of the Antarctic*. p. 207.
52 Jones. *Robert Falcon Scott, Journals*. p. 259.
53 Cherry-Garrard. *The Worst Journey in the World*. p. 293.

54 *Ibid*. p. 304.
55 *Ibid*.
56 Jones. *Robert Falcon Scott, Journals*. p. 255.
57 Wheeler. *Cherry: A life of Apsley Cherry-Garrard*. p. 118.
58 They had 4,250 K cal per man per day. Cherry-Garrard lost only 1 lb in weight in spite of his trials, Wilson just over three. They were (wrongly) satisfied with their diets. Apart from any other problem, the lack of vitamin C and the inadequate amounts of vitamins A, B and D were to haunt them later.
59 Jones. *Robert Falcon Scott, Journals*. p. 260.
60 *The South Polar Times*. Vol.4. July 1902. p. 3.
61 Wheeler. *Cherry: A life of Apsley Cherry-Garrard*. p. 119.
62 Wilson. *E.A. Wilson: Memoir by his father*. p. 211.
63 *The South Polar Times*. Vol III, Part II, p. 53.
64 *The Geographical Journal*. Vol. 42, No. 1. p. 15.
65 Jones. *Robert Falcon Scott, Journals*. p. 302.

Chapter 13

1 King, H.G.R. (ed.) *Edward Wilson: Diary of the 'Terra Nova' Expedition to the Antarctic 1910–1912*. Blandford Press, London, 1972. p. 181.
2 After Wilson's death, Oriana arranged for the pictures to be exhibited separately at the Alpine Club, London.
3 King. *Edward Wilson: Diary of the 'Terra Nova'*. p. 182.
4 Seaver, G. *Edward Wilson of the Antarctic*, John Murray, London, 1950. p. 267.
5 Wilson, E.T. *E.A. Wilson: Memoir by his father*. The Wilson Collection, Cheltenham Art Gallery and Museum, 1955, 550.36. p. 219.
6 Wilson, E.A. *Letter to Mr and Mrs Reginald Smith*. SPRI. MS. 599/142/9/D.
7 *Ibid*.
8 Seaver. *Edward Wilson of the Antarctic*. p. 267.
9 King. *Edward Wilson: Diary of the 'Terra Nova'*. p. 183.
10 Scott, R.F. *Scott's Last Expedition*. Vol.1, John Murray, London, 1935. p. 335.
11 *Ibid*. p. 342.

12 *The Geographical Journal.* Vol. xxxvi, July 1910. p. 15.
13 Fiennes, R. *Captain Scott.* Hodder and Stoughton, London, 2003. p. 239.
14 Lyons, H.G. *The British Antarctic Expedition, 1910. Miscellaneous Data.* Harrison and Sons, London, 1924. (One geographical mile = 2,027 yards or 1853 m. One statute mile = 1,760 yards or 1,609 m.)
15 King. *Edward Wilson: Diary of the 'Terra Nova'.* p. 196.
16 Scott. *Scott's Last Expedition.* p. 360.
17 Fiennes. *Captain Scott.* p. 274.
18 King. *Edward Wilson: Diary of the 'Terra Nova'.* p. 203.
19 *Ibid.* p. 206.
20 Seaver. *Edward Wilson of the Antarctic.* p. 271.
21 Personal communication. Professor Jeffrey Woods, Food and Animal Science Department, University of Bristol, 2006.
22 Seaver. *Edward Wilson of the Antarctic.* p. 272.
23 Seaver, G. *'Birdie' Bowers of the Antarctic.* John Murray, London, 1947. p. 239.
24 King. *Edward Wilson: Diary of the 'Terra Nova'.* p. 212.
25 Seaver. *Edward Wilson of the Antarctic.* p. 272.
26 King. *Edward Wilson: Diary of the 'Terra Nova'.* p. 212.
27 *Ibid.* p. 213.
28 Seaver. *Edward Wilson of the Antarctic.* p. 273.
29 *Ibid.* p. 275.
30 Wilson, E.A. *Letters to Mr and Mrs Reginald Smith.* SPRI. MS. 559/142/2/D.
31 Ellis, A.R. (ed.) *Under Scott's Command: Lashly's Antarctic Diaries.* Victor Gollancz, London, 1969. p. 131.
32 King. *Edward Wilson: Diary of the 'Terra Nova'.* p. 220.
33 Scott. *Scott's Last Expedition.* p. 410.
34 King. *Edward Wilson: Diary of the 'Terra Nova'.* p. 221.
35 'The British Antarctic Expedition 1910–1913', *Geographical Journal.* Vol. 42, No. 1. pp. 11–28.
36 Scott. *Scott's Last Expedition.* p. 412.
37 A copy is in the property of Wilson's godson's daughter.
38 Seaver. *Edward Wilson of the Antarctic.* p. 276.
39 King. *Edward Wilson: Diary of the 'Terra Nova'.* p. 230.
40 Scott. *Scott's Last Expedition.* p. 418.
41 Seaver. *Edward Wilson of the Antarctic.* p. 278.
42 Fiennes. *Captain Scott.* p. 322.
43 West, J. 'Acute Mountain Sickness in the South Pole', in *High*

Altitude Medicine and Biology. Vol. 2, No. 4, 2001. p. 559.

44 Cherry-Garrard, A. *The Worst Journey in the World*. Picador, London, 2001. p. 572. (Rations per man per day consisted of 16oz (454g) biscuits; 12oz (336g) pemmican; 2oz (56g) butter; 0.57oz (0.57g) cocoa; 3oz (84g) sugar; and 0.86oz (24.1g) tea. This totalled 34.43oz daily per man and nearly 4,500 calories per day.)

45 Fiennes. *Captain Scott*. p. 285.

46 Vitamin B complex consists of thiamin, riboflavin and nicotinic acid.

47 Jones, M. (ed.) *Robert Falcon Scott, Journals: Captain Scott's Last Expedition*. Oxford University Press, Oxford, 2005. p. 375.

48 *Ibid*. p. 375.

49 King. *Edward Wilson: Diary of the 'Terra Nova'*. p. 231.

50 *Ibid*. p. 232.

51 Jones. *Robert Falcon Scott, Journals*. p. 376.

52 Smith, M. *I Am Just Going Outside*. Spellmount, Staplehurst, 2002. p. 204.

53 Seaver. *'Birdie' Bowers of the Antarctic*. p. 250.

54 King. *Edward Wilson: Diary of the 'Terra Nova'*. p. 232.

55 Scott. *Scott's Last Expedition*. p. 424.

56 *Ibid*.

57 *Ibid*.

58 King. *Edward Wilson: Diary of the 'Terra Nova'*. p. 232.

59 *Ibid*. p. 233.

60 Seaver. *'Birdie' Bowers of the Antarctic*. p. 250.

61 Scott. *Scott's Last Expedition*. p. 426.

62 King. *Edward Wilson: Diary of the 'Terra Nova'*. p. 237.

63 *Ibid*. p. 238.

64 Freedman, B.J. 'Dr Edward Wilson of the Antarctic', in *Proceedings of the Royal Society of Medicine*. Vol. 74, p. 183.

65 Murbarak, S.J. Exertional Compartment Syndrome. SPRI. Held at location Pam 91(08):(*7)(191013Scott).

66 King. *Edward Wilson: Diary of the 'Terra Nova'*. p. 240.

67 Scott. *Scott's Last Expedition*. p. 436.

68 Fiennes. *Captain Scott*. p. 318. When Fiennes and Stroud were manhauling in the Antarctic, Fiennes lost 25 per cent of his body weight and had virtually no body fat for insulation against the cold, after sixty-eight days' travel.

69 King. *Edward Wilson: Diary of the 'Terra Nova'*. p. 242.

70 Scott. *Scott's Last Expedition*. p. 446.

71   King. *Edward Wilson: Diary of the 'Terra Nova'.* p. 243.

72   Nasal carriage of staphylococci in an Antarctic community. Hadley, M.D.M. 'The Staphylococci', in *Proceedings of the Alexander Ogston Centennial Conference.* (eds. A. Macdonald and G. Smith) Aberdeen University Press, 1981.

73   Personal communication. Professor T.H. Pennington, University of Aberdeen. 2006.

74   Williams, I, *Edward Wilson: medical aspects of his life and career.* Polar Record. 44, 2008, 80.

75   Crandon, J.H., Lund, C.C. and Dill, D.B. *Experimental Human Scurvy*, New England Journal of Medicine. 1940, 233. p. 353. In an experiment on human scurvy conducted in 1940, reduced levels of vitamin C in platelets and white cells were recorded at three months, in the absence of clinical signs of scurvy, when a diet with no vitamin C was taken. At this time an experimental wound healed rapidly and normally. Skin dryness with hyperkeratosis developed in four months (the earliest clinical sign) and skin petechiae a month later. At six months a further experimental wound failed to heal. During this experiment it was noted that gum lesions did not occur in the volunteers whose mouths were previously healthy.

76   Williams. *Edward Wilson: medical aspects of his life and career.* Polar Record. 44, 2008 79.

77   Scott. *Scott's Last Expedition.* p. 448.

78   Seaver. *Edward Wlson of the Antarctic.* p. 286.

79   King. *Edward Wilson: Diary of the 'Terra Nova'.* p. 245.

80   Personal communication. Professor Christopher Bates, Honorary Senior Scientist, Medical Research Council, Human Nutrition Research, University of Cambridge. 2006. The protein that makes scars is continually remodelled in health and needs vitamin C as a building block. Marginal vitamin C deficiency is likely to affect the tissue remodelling that occurs in 'old scars' at a relatively early stage of vitamin C deficiency. The fact that the quartet was undersupplied with food energy would also affect the strength of their wounds.

81   King. *Edward Wilson: Diary of the 'Terra Nova'.* p. 240.

82   Scott. *Scott's Last Expedition.* p. 455.

83   *Ibid.*

84   *Ibid.* p. 459.

85   *Ibid.* p. 458.

86   *Ibid.* p. 459.

87   *Ibid.* p. 462.

88 Ellis. *Under Scott's Command: Lashly's Antarctic Diaries*. p. 145.
89 Seaver. *Edward Wilson of the Antarctic*. p. 293.
90 *Ibid.*
91 King. *Edward Wilson: Diary of the 'Terra Nova'*. p. 247.
92 Seaver. *Edward Wilson of the Antarctic*. p. 294.
93 Wilson. *E.A. Wilson: Memoir by his father*. p. 231.
94 *Ibid.*

Epilogue

1 Wilson, D.M. and Elder, D.B. *Cheltenham in Antarctica: The Life of Edward Wilson*. Reardon Publishing, Cheltenham, 2000. p. 107.
2 *Ibid.* p. 108.
3 Huntford, R. *Scott and Amundsen*. Hodder and Stoughton, London, 1979. p. 542.
4 Shipman, P. *Taking Wing*. Phoenix, London, 1998. pp. 119, 127 and 135.
5 Review. Report of the activities of the Game Conservancy Trust, 2006. p. 18.

Selected Bibliography

Armitage, A.B. *Cadet to Commodore*. Cassell, London, 1925.
——.*Two Years in the Antarctic*, Edward Arnold. London, 1905.
Baughman, T.H. *Pilgrims on the Ice*. University of Nebraska Press, Lincoln and London, 1999.
Blake, S. *Cheltenham: A pictorial history*. Phillimore, Cheltenham, 1996.
Brown, L. *The Story of Clinical Pulmonary Tuberculosis*. Williams and Wilkins, London, 1941.
Cadbury, D. *The Dinosaur Hunters: A True Story of Scientific Rivalry and the Discovery of the Prehistoric World*. 4th Estate, London, 2001.
Carpenter, K.J. *The History of Scurvy and Vitamin C*. Cambridge University Press, 1986.
Cherry-Garrard, A. *The Worst Journey in the World*. Picador, London, 2001.
Churchill, W. *My Early Life*. Eland, London, 2002.
Committee of Enquiry on Grouse Disease. *The Grouse in Health and Disease*. Smith, Elder, and Co., London, 1911.
Edward Wilson: Diary of the Discovery Expedition. (ed. Ann Savours) Blandford Press, London, 1966.
Edward Wilson: Dairy of the 'Terra Nova'. (ed. H.G.R. King) Blandford Press, London, 1972.
Ellis, A.R. (ed.) *Under Scott's Command: Lashly's Antarctic Diaries*. Victor Gollancz, London, 1969.
Fiennes, R. *Captain Scott*. Hodder and Stoughton, London, 2003.
Hodgkinson, R.G. (ed. A. Rook) 'Cambridge and its Contribution to Medicine', in *Proceedings of the 7th British Conference on the History of Medicine*. September 1968. Medical Education in Cambridge in the nineteenth century.

Hoflehner, J., K. Hoflehner and D. Harrowfield. *Frozen History: The legacy of Scott and Shackleton*. Josef Verlag Hoflehner, Wels, Austria, 2003.

Huntford, R. *Scott and Amundsen*. Hodder and Stoughton, London, 1979.

Keers, R.A. *Pulmonary Tuberculosis: A Journey Down the Centuries*. Ballier Tindall, London, 1978.

Lyons, H.G. *The British Antarctic Expedition, 1910. Miscellaneous Data*. Harrison and Sons, London, 1924.

Mann, T. *The Magic Mountain*. Vintage, London, 1999.

Markham, C. (ed. C. Holland) *Antarctic Obsession. The BNAE. 1901–4*. Erskine Press, Alburgh, Norfolk, 1986.

Markham, A.H. *The Life of Sir Clements Markham, KCB, FRS*. John Murray, London, 1917.

Ponting, H.G. *The Great White South*, Duckworth, London, 1932.

Ponting, H. *With Scott to the Pole*, Bloomsbury, London, 2004.

Preston, D. *A First Rate Tragedy*. Constable, London, 1995.

Robert Falcon Scott Journals. (ed. M. Jones) Oxford University Press, Oxford, 2005.

Scott, R.F. *Scott's Last Expedition*. Vol 1. John Murray, London, 1935. [Journals of R.F. Scott]

——. *Scott's Voyage of the Discovery*. John Murray, London, 1929.

Seaver, G. *'Birdie' Bowers of the Antarctic*. John Murray, London, 1947.

——. *Edward Wilson: Nature Lover*. John Murray, London, 1947.

——. *Edward Wilson of the Antarctic*. John Murray, London, 1950.

——. *The Faith of Edward Wilson of the Antarctic*. John Murray, London, 1949.

Skelton, J.V. and Wilson, D.M. *Discovery Illustrated*. Reardon Publishing, Cheltenham, 2001.

Skelton, J. (ed.) *Antarctic Journals of Reginald Skelton*. Reardon Publishing, Cheltenham, 2004.

Smith, M. *I Am Just Going Outside*. Spellmount, Staplehurst, 2002.

Soloman, S. *The Coldest March*. Yale University Press, New Haven and London, 2001.

Wheeler, S. *Cherry: A life of Apsley Cherry-Garrard*. Jonathan Cape, London, 2001.

Wilson, D.M. and Elder, D.B. *Cheltenham in Antarctica: The Life of Edward Wilson*. Reardon Publishing, Cheltenham, 2000.

Yelverton, D.E. *Antarctica Unveiled*. University Press of Colorado, Boulder, CO, 2000.

Index